Praise for

NOMADS

"A sweeping history of nomadism from prehistory to the modern age. . . . Not only readable but also vital."
——Bijan Omrani, *Literary Review*

"A fabulous piece of evocative writing, mixing personal stories with an epic sweep of history, the unique insight of location and an intimate connection to the subject. I loved it."
——Jerry Brotton, author of
A History of the World in 12 Maps

"I was riveted by the shifts to nomadic culture, *Sapiens*-like, and by the feeling of learning lightly worn and deftly transmitted. This is a major book."
——Roland Philipps, author of
A Spy Named Orphan

"A spirited defense of freedom of conscience, freedom of movement and migration, a romantic tribute to independence and to free spirit, and to being in tune with the rhythms of nature."
——Marc David Baer, author of
The Ottomans

"Anthony Sattin's *Nomads* spreads before us a sweeping panorama of nomadism that resonates through the past and echoes poignantly even in the present."
——Colin Thubron

Nomads

The Wanderers Who Shaped Our World

ANTHONY SATTIN

With illustrations by Sylvie Franquet

W. W. NORTON & COMPANY
Independent Publishers Since 1923

For information about permission to reproduce selections from this book, write to
Permissions, W. W. Norton & Company, Inc., 500 Fifth Avenue, New York, NY 10110

For information about special discounts for bulk purchases, please contact
W. W. Norton Special Sales at specialsales@wwnorton.com or 800-233-4830

Manufacturing by Lakeside Book Company

Library of Congress Cataloging-in-Publication Data

Names: Sattin, Anthony, author. | Franquet, Sylvie, illustrator.
Title: Nomads : the wanderers who shaped our world / Anthony Sattin,
with illustrations by Sylvie Franquet.
Description: First American Edition. | New York : W. W. Norton & Company, Inc., [2022] |
Includes bibliographical references and index.
Identifiers: LCCN 2022032893 | ISBN 9781324035459 (Cloth) | ISBN 9781324035466 (epub)
Subjects: LCSH: Nomads. | Civilization—History.
Classification: LCC GN387 .S29 2022 | DDC 305.9/06918—dc23/eng/20220728
LC record available at https://lccn.loc.gov/2022032893

ISBN 978-1-324-07474-8 pbk.

W. W. Norton & Company, Inc., 500 Fifth Avenue, New York, N.Y. 10110
www.wwnorton.com

W. W. Norton & Company Ltd., 15 Carlisle Street, London W1D 3BS

1 2 3 4 5 6 7 8 9 0

For Sylvie, *flâneuse*, who knows that not all those who wander are lost.

Contents

History, as nearly no one seems to know, is not merely something to be read. And it does not refer merely, or even principally, to the past. On the contrary, the great force of history comes from the fact that we carry it within us, are unconsciously controlled by it in many ways, and history is literally present in all that we do.

James Baldwin, 'The White Man's Guilt', *Ebony*, August 1965

Nomads: a subject that appeals to irrational instincts.

Bruce Chatwin to Tom Maschler, 24 February 1969

In the Zagros Mountains, Iran

A young man walks towards me with a stick slung across his shoulders and a flock at his feet. The sheep, in front, beside and behind him, are as chaotic as meltwater in the nearby stream and they carry him down the path like a crowd of rowdy children. An older man follows, weatherworn but still strong, a rifle over his left shoulder. He clicks his tongue to encourage them forward. Behind him are two women on donkeys, one older than the other, and I guess they are his wife and daughter. They look strong women, but then it is a tough life beneath the shard peaks of the Zagros Mountains. Other donkeys carry their belongings, bundled inside heavy rust-and-brown cloth that the women have woven and will soon repurpose as door-flaps when the tents are set up.

There are few trees at this altitude, but the snow has melted and there is intense beauty and excellent grazing in the valley blanketed with irises, dwarf tulips and other spring flowers. The family are smiling as they lead their sheep and grey-and-white goats along the rock-strewn track towards me, the bucks sporting majestic swept-back horns. And I am smiling with them, swept up by the excitement of the Bakhtiari tribe's annual migration from the plains into the mountains in search of summer pasture.

I had already spent several days in the care of some other migrants. Siyavash and his family had pitched their black goat-hair tents on the slope of the valley, building an enclosure for their sheep and preparing a large open-sided tent to welcome neighbours and guests. My tent was across a stream flush with meltwater and from it I had a big view of the jagged snow-covered peaks and wildflower valley. A length of fat flattened oil-pipe served as a bridge between myself and the nomads and also as a reminder that the Middle East's first oil strike, Well No. One, had been made in nearby Bakhtiari territory in 1908.

Everywhere there was beauty. If I were a photographer, I would have captured the shifting shadows and slanting sunbeams of afternoon as they tinted the snow mountains pink and cast gold across the surface of the stream. If I were a composer, I would have harmonised the rumble of water with the clunk of stones shifting across the riverbed, the buzzing of bees, the clanking of bells and the whistling and whooping of men bringing the flocks in for the night. There was beauty in all. But I am a writer and, barefoot and slightly sun-struck, I pulled out a pencil to note the pure quality of light in the blue sky, the way that colours, especially yellows, popped in the green valley and the sudden chill that descended as soon as the sun dropped behind the crest. Late that night, the nomads' tents glowed like embers across the river, the moon shone full above the mountain ridge and I fell asleep wondering how Byron had known that 'Not vainly did the early Persian make/ His altar the high places and the peak . . . there to seek the Spirit . . .' My spirits were soaring in that high place and I felt a deep welling of joy.

Over the next couple of days, Siyavash and his family introduced me to their valley and their people. They also fed me, and as we ate they talked about their lives, the land they knew, their journeys across it, the animals they raised, the children they worried about – should they send them to a state boarding school for their education? – and the many other challenges of being a herder in the Zagros Mountains in the twenty-first century. They told me about plants in the valley, the animals that passed wild above our heads and others that lived on the higher slopes. They knew all that could grow there, what to encourage, what to fear. They talked about the journey they had made from the hot lowlands into the mountains and how they would walk back again when the earth began to freeze beneath their feet, a journey their ancestors had made long before anyone began keeping records. I have heard similar stories from Bedouin and Berbers in North Africa and the Middle East, where I have spent much of my adult life, from Tuareg and Wodaabe beyond the mudhouses and libraries of Timbuktu, from swift young Maasai, flashes of orange across the red East African bush, from nomads on the edge of the Thar Desert in India, on boats in the Andaman Sea, in the uplands of Kyrgyzstan and elsewhere in Asia. Whether with Berber or Bedouin, gaucho or Moken, conversation always seemed to settle on the same issues, on continuity, on pride in belonging, on being in harmony with their surroundings, respecting all that nature offers and on the difficulties of living a nomadic life when governments wanted them to settle.

These people all reminded me of a sublime harmony that exists with the natural world. They knew their environment in a way that can only be acquired through living on equal footing with everything in that world, not in domination, through a recognition that we humans are dependent on our surroundings, something those of us who live in towns and cities too easily forget. The Bakhtiari know the significance of each tone of their herds' bleating, when they are content, or hungry, or threatened, whether a birth or death is near, just as they know how to read the clouds, and the scents carried on the winds. The more I watched and listened, the more I was reminded that we had all lived this way once – and not so very long ago, in the greater scheme of human things.

The sight of a family on the move with their animals and all their belongings excites some of us, but it fills others with terror or disgust or disdain.

> *Where have they come from?*
> *Why have they come here?*
> *When are they going?*
> *How do they survive?*
> *Who are they?*

Nomad. The word's roots run through the human story from our own time back to an extremely early Indo-European word, *nomos*. This has multiple meanings and can be translated as 'a fixed or bounded area' but also as 'pasture'. Out of this root-word grows *nomas*, meaning 'a member of a wandering pastoral tribe' and implying 'someone looking for pasture . . .' but also 'for a place where they have legal right to graze their herds', and these were both nomadic and settled, the moving settled. Later the root splits, and after towns and cities are built and more people settle, the word *nomad* comes to describe people who live without walls and beyond boundaries. *Nomad* is now used by settled people in two very different ways. For some of us the word is imbued with a sense of romantic wanderful nostalgia. But very often, it carries an implicit judgement that such people are drifters, migrants, vagrants, people on the go, on the run, of no fixed abode. They are people who are not known.

An age when ever more people travel, when so many of us are 'not known', calls for a more generous interpretation, especially as much of what we say, so many of our ideas, and such a wide range of gadgets and goods now relate to mobility and movement. Because of this, the way I use *nomad* shifts as the book progresses. At the outset of the journey, I use it to refer to hunter-gatherers and soon also to those who herd in search of pasture. By the end of the book, it includes all those who wander. Not just people who live lightly because they are obliged to, like nomads, but also those who choose to do so, the increasing numbers who describe themselves not as 'homeless' but as 'houseless', the many modern nomads who live in what some call 'wheel estate'.* An earlier version of this way of living is captured by the writer Bruce Chatwin, who described in his seminal work *The Songlines* how a British salesman spent his life flying around Africa, carrying only a suitcase. The fixed point of the salesman's life, the place that represented home for him, was a lock-up in London. In the lock-up there was a cardboard box filled with photographs and other mementoes from his family and his past. If he wanted to add some new treasure, he needed to make space by discarding an old one. For Chatwin as for me, the travelling salesman's way of life suggested a very modern form of nomadism.

It would be easy to dismiss the salesman by pointing out that he has added nothing to the world, just as he has added nothing to his box. This has been the justification for dismissing and discarding the history of most nomadic peoples – because people who live with walls and monuments, and who have written most of history, have failed to find meaning in or to recognise the value of the lighter, more mobile, less cluttered lives of those who live beyond borders.

---

* For more on the 'houseless' in the United States I recommend Jessica Bruder's *Nomadland*, the book behind the film.

But we are living at a time when the world – *our* world – shaped by the Age of Reason and the Enlightenment, powered by industrial and technological revolutions, is faltering. Social contracts are fraying and communities are breaking down. The raw materials and natural resources on which our world relies are becoming scarce, and the consequences of our actions on the planet are written large across landscapes, the climate and the fabric of our lives. Alongside new ways to recycle water and generate power, there is an urgent need for new thinking about how we live and what it means to be human. Change is needed. We need to tread with a lighter footprint, and those of us who live in cities need to find a better way of relating to the world beyond the city limits. But before we can understand who we are and what we might become, we need to know who we have been. Black Lives Matter, #MeToo and other movements are suggesting ways of looking over the walls and beyond old entrenched assumptions, constructs and prejudices to tell the histories not only of white men, but also of women and BAME and indigenous people. We also need to know the histories of those who have lived on the move, because without that, we cannot understand how human wandering has shaped who we are now.

This book traces the shifting relationships between people who move and those who are settled. I have linked some of their diverse and remarkable stories, set in some of the world's most extreme landscapes, along a chronological line that spans 12,000 years. That line starts with what we now believe was the beginning of monumental architecture, around 9500 BCE, and ends in our own time. There are other ways to make sense of the stories and there are certainly many other paths across the terrain, but this is the one I have chosen to follow and it leads from Cain and Abel to you and me. At the beginning of the narrative, all humankind lived on the move across a world in which the only barriers were the natural ones of forest, river, mountain and desert, and the ones that humans made from branches and thorns. By the end of the book, wanderers must pick their way across a world divided by borders, highways and walls, and by international agreements made by nation states.

This excavation of the wandering life is arranged into three acts.

The first returns us to early history, a time when the settled and the nomadic mostly cohabit and collaborate as they shift from hunter-gathering to farming and herding. It describes the surprising – and surprisingly early – creation of the first monuments, before following the rise of extraordinary city-states and empires along the great rivers of Mesopotamia, along the Nile and the Indus, to question why early settled people felt so threatened by the mobile world beyond their borders – a world that had once been theirs.

The second, imperial act jumps forward to a more complex form of nomadism and tracks the cyclical rise and fall of some of the great empires created by people who still lived mobile lives. In the West this period begins with the fall of the Roman Empire and has often been labelled the Dark Ages. But for Huns and Arabs, Mongols, Yuan Chinese and many other nomadic peoples, this was a time of brilliance and spectacular achievements, both in the Near East and across the immense swathe of steppeland that stretches from what is now the Great Wall in China to Hungary. Through the records and the writings of the fourteenth-century Arab historian and philosopher Ibn Khaldun and many others, we can see how much nomads contributed to the European Renaissance and how great their influence has been on our modern world.

The third act opens with the birth of the modern age, with Western scholars insisting that white men must dominate the natural world just as they were striving to dominate the human world. In this time of competition and rivalry, nomads disappear so completely from the European view, and from relevance, that the word *nomad* is not sufficiently current to be included in the English dictionary. But this is also the moment when some people sense that something significant is being lost and begin an act of recovery. Here as elsewhere in the book, the lack of nomad records forces us to look through the eyes of the settled and because of this much of the final part of the book traces the way that settled people have responded to nomads. Crucially it follows the growing recognition that there is more value in cooperation than in competition, that nomads are important to the way we settled people live, just as they are crucial to the way we understand ourselves.

★

These stories are informed by many years of research and discussion, but although this is an historical narrative it is not a scholarly volume and nor is it a definitive history of nomads. I suspect there never can be a definitive history, as we in the West understand it, of people who have lived so lightly and who have mostly only preserved their stories in oral traditions. Instead, I hope to show how nomads have long been confined to the anecdotes and afterthoughts of our writers and histories, confirming the French philosopher Gilles Deleuze's observation that 'nomads have no history; they only have a geography'.[1] This phrase seems too neat – nomads do have histories – but when I first read it, it provided an explanation for the many unanswered questions I had as to why nomads were rarely to be found in our histories. This omission is misguided and also means that we are missing their very proud and valuable history. One thing I hope this book will achieve is to foster an understanding that it is not a question of either/or, settled or nomad, because whether we have acknowledged it or not, whether we like it or not, nomads have always been at least half of the human story and have made essential contributions to the march of what many historians have traditionally called civilisation.

Although theirs seems to be the shadow side of our story, the nomad story is neither less wonderful nor less significant than ours. In the second century BCE, for instance, after the Roman Republic defeated Carthage and became masters of the Mediterranean, when China flourished under the Han emperor Wu and trade inched its way along the nascent Silk Roads between the Yellow river and Europe, Xiongnu nomad power stretched from Manchuria to Kazakhstan and included parts of Siberia, Mongolia and what is now China's Xinjiang province. At the same time, Scythian nomads and their allies controlled much of the land between the Black Sea and the Altai Mountains in Kazakhstan. Put together, these nomad territories were larger and more powerful than either the Roman or Han empires. And in contrast to the familiar claim that these mobile people were primitive and isolated, we know from burials that their leaders dressed in Chinese silk robes trimmed with cheetah fur, sat on Persian carpets, used Roman glass and had a taste for Greek gold and silver jewellery. All this raises the possibility that these nomads were the masters of a linked-up trading world that stretched from the East China Sea to the Atlantic Ocean.

This has not been the traditional Western view of what is usually referred to as the Roman or the Han world, in the same way that Western histories have tended to focus on the number of people Mongol *khans* killed, not the advances and advantages that came from the *pax Mongoliana*.

Another overlooked aspect of the nomad story is found in the shifting relationship between humankind and the natural world. The terms of those relations were transformed by the development of cities, the growth in agriculture and more recently by industrialisation and advances in technology. These changes have left many settled people increasingly detached from their surroundings, while nomads have continued to nurture their relationship with the natural world. They have done so – they have had to do so – because they have recognised that everything is interconnected and interdependent. They know it is in their interests to care for their surroundings.

It is an irony that because nomads have kept very few records, raised very few monuments or dedicatory stones and left scarce evidence of their passage through the world, much of the material I have relied on to tell these stories was written by people who are not nomadic. This poses problems because while authors from Herodotus and Sima Qian to William of Rubruck and Henry David Thoreau may have valued keeping historical records, they were not always impartial or objective. Intentionally or not, many of their observations are slanted. The nomads who feature in Western histories – the Hun leader Attila, the Mongol emperors Genghis Khan and Timur, the wave of ancient Scythians moving out of reach of rampaging Persians, and modern Syrians escaping civil war – are most often presented as barbarians living in opposition to all that civilised city-dwellers value. These prejudices run deep, as a Sumerian princess discovered some 3,500 years ago when she was considering marrying a nomad. 'Their hands are destructive,' her friends tell her. 'They never stop roaming about . . . Their ideas are confused; they cause only disturbance.' And then becoming personal, those same friends warn the princess that 'He is clothed in sack-leather . . . lives in a tent, exposed to wind and rain, and cannot properly recite prayers. He lives in the mountains and ignores the places of gods, digs up truffles in the foothills, does not know how to bend the knee, and eats raw flesh. He has no house during his life, and when he dies he will not be carried to a burial-place.'[2] But one thing that becomes clear as my story progresses is that 'barbarian' has regularly been used as a way to dismiss someone with different habits, customs or beliefs. It is a term that reveals a competitive view of humankind's development, a superiority in the observer, and it is most often used to describe a neighbour.

The vast majority of records on nomads, from ancient China and Rome to early modern Europe and nineteenth-century North America, present problems for anyone wanting to create a fuller picture, and that has had an impact on the telling of this story. The first is a lack of detail about the role that women played in nomad culture. We know, for instance, that Scythian women had great influence – much greater than their contemporaries in the Roman and Chinese empires. This is clear from the fact that there was a Scythian queen, the grandeur with which Scythians buried some of their women, the central role the wife of Genghis Khan played in building and running the Mongol Empire, and by the way the Mughal emperor Babur relied on his grandmother's brilliance as a strategist and wise counsel. But few of their voices reach us today and that is very much our loss. The other issue to note is that most reports and descriptions of nomads relate to tension and conflict. It is as if war was the only time that settled chroniclers thought it worth mentioning these 'other' people.

These misrepresentations reflect neither the reality of nomad life nor the totality of the relationship between nomads and those who were settled, which has been both complementary and inter-dependent for most of the past ten thousand years.

Re-evaluating our wandering 'other half', hearing their stories, discovering the role they have played in ours, all this allows us to see what we settled people have learned from people who move. It shows how much we have gained from cooperation. It also lets us glimpse – in the way they live lightly, more freely, in the way they have learned to adapt and to be nimble and flexible in their thoughts and actions, and in the balance they have maintained with the natural world – another way of living, the way that the 'other' branch of humankind has chosen to go since the days when we all hunted as a single pack in the generous gardens of the deep past.

PART I

The Balancing Act

It will not last. All is change, all is ephemeral.

John Stewart

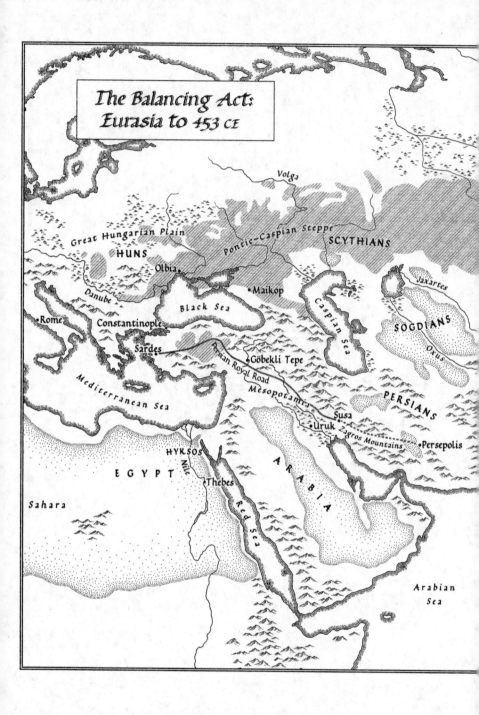

The Balancing Act:
Eurasia to 453 CE

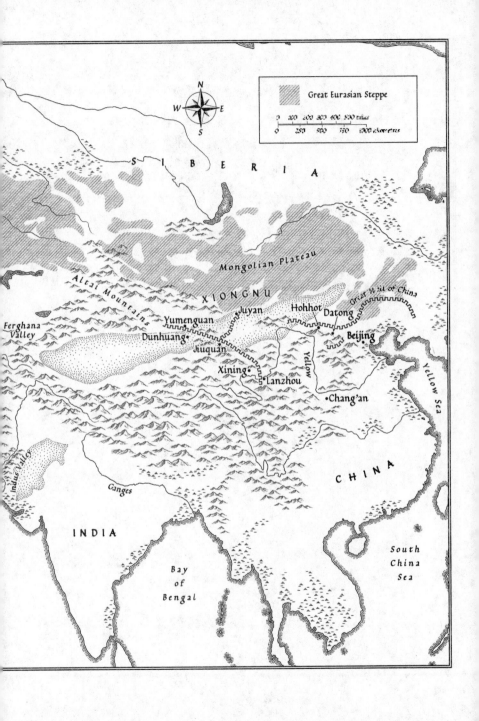

Paradise, 10,000 BCE

Global population: perhaps 5 million[1]

Nomad population: most of that number

Once upon a time we were all hunters and gatherers. The first to stop hunting and gathering did so no more than 12,000 years ago, which is but a dot on the human timeline. This was when food was abundant and there were few of us to eat it. The Bible's Old Testament and the Quran's Sura 2, *al-Baqarah*, the Cow, present this as time spent in a garden, a time of great happiness and perfect innocence in the Garden of Eden.

There are many translations of the word *Eden*, but all of them point in the same direction, from the Sumerian *edin*, meaning a *plain* or *steppe*, to the Aramaic word for *well-watered* and the Hebrew for *pleasure*. Taken together, they suggest that Eden was a well-watered steppe where food was plentiful, threats were few and humans did not need to labour. A place of pleasure. But the location of this pleasure garden remains disputed. Genesis places it 'eastward, in Eden'. In it was 'every tree that is pleasant to the sight, and good for food; the tree of life also in the midst of the garden, and the tree of the knowledge of good and evil'.[2] The water that irrigates the garden was 'divided to make four streams' or rivers. The Genesis narrator names two of these streams as the Tigris and the Euphrates, so the garden of Eden might have been somewhere on the Mesopotamian plain, now southern Iraq. The Roman historian Josephus decided that the other two rivers were the Ganges and the Nile, which expanded the range of geographical possibility. Perhaps Eden was up into the Armenian highlands, on the Iranian plateau or in the Shangri-La uplands of Pakistan.

The idea that we have lost a garden that we must strive to recover speaks to our own time of vanishing flora and fauna, climate emergency and ecological disaster. But it is an age-old anxiety and echoes of it can be heard around the world and across the ages, from the mythical Hindu garden of Nandankanan to the ancient Greek Garden of the Hesperides and the Persian *pairi-daeza*. This Persian word has a literal translation of 'around wall or brick', by which is meant a walled garden, an enclosed park, and from that comes the Greek *paradeisos*, and our paradise, another garden we long for. No doubt there is an even more ancient version. But whatever the origins of the word – and irrespective of whether any of us ever tasted forbidden fruit in a garden called Eden – this ancient story tells us that at some point we were surrounded by 'every tree that is good for food', that we were hunters or gatherers who lived off the bounty of nature, which provided all we needed to survive. The idea of Eden and paradise is seductive because it promises ease, innocence and abundance, and perhaps the earthly version was not so terrible.

Some anthropologists have called early hunter-gatherers 'the original affluent society'. The facts are still much disputed, but do seem compelling. American anthropologist Marshall Sahlins calculated that most hunter-gatherers devoted around twenty hours a week to feeding themselves, which meant that for 'half the time the people seem not to know what to do with themselves'. Perhaps they used this time to laugh, love, sing and dance. Critics have pointed to the drawbacks of seasonal food shortages, disease and conflict. But even allowing for these, and for time to prepare and cook food, even to clean up afterwards, the average hunter-gatherer spent and spends significantly less time providing for their bed and board than the average twenty-first-century urban worker. What's more, unlike those who survive the urban rush-hour, the air-conditioned work environment and 24/7 hypermarkets, hunter-gatherers get to live and work on land they understand, which they find rich in memories, spirit and meaning.

However pleasing life had been in the early hunter-gatherer 'Eden', it was hit by a perfect storm of circumstances that were made more dramatic by human curiosity and temptation. In the Genesis story, Adam and Eve are told to graze on whatever takes their fancy, but on no account to touch the fruit of two sacred trees, the Tree of Life and the Tree of the Knowledge of Good and Evil. When, somewhat inevitably, they give in to temptation, they are expelled, never to return.

It is a good story, but it also happens to reflect a moment in history when populations grew, the climate might have changed, and hunter-gathering became less attractive or less viable than farming. Those are some of the elements that shaped the story of a place called Potbelly Hill.

Potbelly Hill

The soft contours of Potbelly Hill bulge out of the limestone hills that roll over Turkey's southern border with Syria. It is a hard old land where farmers fight to make a living out of herds that scratch around the rocky slopes for grazing. It is also a land rich with a long and extraordinary history.

Five miles west of Potbelly Hill lies the city of Urfa. Sanliurfa, Urfa the Glorious as it has been known since 1984. Tradition links Urfa to Ur of the Chaldees and therefore to the birthplace of the patriarch Abraham, the Father of Multitudes. There may be nothing to prove the Abraham connection, but beneath Urfa's looming Crusader citadel, there is a large pool, Balikli Gol, Abraham's pool, where I have watched devout pilgrims and excited tourists feed carp that are said to have been divinely created. More certain are the results of a 1990s excavation in the grounds of the park, for among the pieces that were uncovered from the site was the oldest known life-size carving of a human. The freestanding figure is carved out of white limestone with black obsidian eyes, a necklace carved around his neck and his hands holding his erect penis. Someone carved this statue around 10,000 BCE. If Urfa Man had been found somewhere other than in the centre of what some claim as Abraham's birthplace, a large-scale excavation would have followed, but it received surprisingly little attention for a discovery of such significance. The archaeological focus moved to a tributary of the Euphrates river where the Turkish government was building a dam that would leave Nevali Cori, a Neolithic settlement from the 8000s BCE, underwater. Among the team of German archaeologists who arrived to salvage what they could before the flood, was Klaus Schmidt, then in his early thirties and having just completed a doctorate in early stone tools. The Germans found houses and a cult centre, votive figures and some of the earliest traces of domesticated wheat. When the dam began operating in 1991, the site disappeared beneath the water and the archaeological team disbanded. But Schmidt stayed on.

There are countless stories of great archaeological discoveries being made by animals falling down holes or running into a cave. The Roman-era catacombs of Alexandria were said to have been uncovered in the nineteenth century when a donkey suddenly disappeared down a large pothole. The Chauvet Caves in France were discovered when teenagers went in after their errant dog. According to one British newspaper, a similar story played out in this part of Turkey when an 'old Kurdish shepherd . . . following his flock over the arid hillsides'[3] noticed some big stone slabs. The truth, as so often happens, was a little more complicated, but no less wonderful.

Göbekli Tepe, as Potbelly Hill is called in Turkish, sits at the head of a gully and was an ideal vantage point for picking off trapped prey. In an area of softly rolling hills, it has a double cone tip, which was covered with grasses and early summer flowers when I first visited. One of these cones was topped by a single mulberry tree and beneath it two stone-covered graves. Not such a bad place to be buried, but our distant ancestors saw something else here. Exactly what they saw we cannot know, but it may have been some actual or imagined ley line, something that united the visible cosmos with the essences of life, its primal forces with the unknowable mysteries of death. Because of that perception, it was here that some early people made their mark and here that Schmidt came to look.

Archaeologists from the University of Chicago had visited the site in 1963 and they had recognised it as Neolithic,* with Byzantine or later Islamic burials. But they saw no reason for further research and the hill remained the domain of Ibrahim Yildiz and his son Mehmet, Kurdish shepherds whose flocks grazed while they sat beneath the mulberry tree to escape the sun. In 1994, Klaus Schmidt met an old man in one of the nearby villages who told him he had seen flints at Göbekli Tepe. But Schmidt knew that the geology here was limestone and basalt.

What Schmidt recognised, which earlier visitors had not, was that the twin cones of Potbelly Hill had been created by humans. He knew from his doctorate and fieldwork that the flints, which others had dismissed as rubble, were tools which had been used by very ancient hands to shape the softer bedrock stone. Perhaps they had been used to work the massive blocks that he now saw underfoot. At this point Schmidt knew he had two choices: 'Go away and tell nobody. Or spend the rest of my life working here.' He went back to Urfa, bought an old house and applied for permits and funds.

Göbekli Tepe is now one of the world's most important and exciting archaeological sites and it is not a household name only because no golden treasure has been found. But the discoveries made by Schmidt and his colleagues are more valuable than bling. The slabs of stone that he had seen on the surface of the cone turned out to be the tops of T-shaped pillars. These pillars are finely cut, beautifully decorated and arranged in circles of a dozen or so, with two taller pillars in the centre of the circles. The larger blocks weigh sixteen tons and some are 5.5 metres high. Many pillars are decorated with humans and animals. Unlike the herds of bovines or deer that roam across many early cave paintings and rock carvings, these are fully represented images of recognisable and threatening boar, foxes, scorpions, jackal and other creatures. Many of them, like the humans and like Urfa Man, are shown with erect penises. This may be one

---

* In this part of the world, Neolithic is dated roughly 10,000–4,500 BCE.

of the first places on earth, it may even be *the* first place where our ancestors set out to reshape the landscape to represent something out of their imagination. As we alter vast areas of our planet, we now take this for granted. But 12,000 years ago this was a revolutionary act. It is the beginning of monumental architecture, the beginning of constructed art, and it marks the beginning of the current, human phase of our history.

Schmidt and I discussed his work in June 2014 when he came to London to raise sponsorship for his digs in Turkey. He was mild-mannered and round-faced. Balding with a bushy fringe around the temples, metal-rimmed glasses, an arrowhead nose and brown beard flecked with grey, he was the very image of the quiet academic, and although he was wearing a jacket for the occasion he looked unkempt in that London drawing room and in the company of what he hoped would be his backers, city traders and businessmen in suits and ties. But when he spoke, the setting, his manner and everything else became irrelevant.

Göbekli Tepe, he assured us, was a sacred site, a religious compound. As he and the team dug deeper into the hillside, they uncovered more carved pillars and stone circles beside the first, and he was confident there would be many more. Schmidt believed that whoever occupied the hill had also known how to ferment grain – 'They made something like beer,' he said with a smile, as part of some sacred act. But now came the main surprises.

The first was the age. 'We have definitively dated Göbekli Tepe to the tenth millennium BC.' By around 9500 BCE, therefore, humans were quarrying large blocks of stone, moving and shaping them and using them to create sacred compounds. This was 7,000 years before the 'monumental age' of pyramids and Stonehenge. There is no understanding of who these people were, how they did this, where they came from nor what happened to them. But the professor was adamant that the dating would stand and so far it has.

The second surprise that sunny lunchtime was more significant. Schmidt had found no evidence to suggest that the people who built Göbekli Tepe had lived there. Later excavation may prove otherwise, but these earliest phases of occupation show no houses, no roofs or hearths, none of the detritus one would expect to find in a place of continual habitation. What they had found, and this was equally revealing, was a variety of animal bones – leopards, wild boar, Mesopotamian fallow deer, cranes, vultures and aurochs, the huge, now extinct predecessor of our domestic cattle. All this suggests that the people who built here, at least in the initial stages, were roaming hunters, people who stopped long enough to brew and to prepare meat. 'They had big feasts,' Schmidt said, smiling again, 'with grilled meat and maybe something like beer. But they didn't live there.' This is why one professor at Stanford University said that Schmidt's findings at Göbekli Tepe 'change everything' – because the people who built at least the first stratum of the sacred site were not settled. They were hunters and gatherers, wanderers, unsettled, and this has important implications.

Work at Göbekli Tepe has continued since Schmidt's untimely death, just a few weeks after our talk in 2014, and new discoveries and interpretations have raised questions about some of his theories. Ground-penetrating radar has shown that there are around one hundred and seventy stone pillars at the site. It is also now probable that the site was in use for several hundred years, and then it was abandoned. The monuments survived for several reasons, among them the fact that the pillars were buried by waste and debris thrown up by continual use and development at the site. Their survival was also helped by the lack of any other significant later settlements in the area, so there was no one who might have wanted to quarry and reuse the cut pillars.

The mystery of who built the site, and why they built it is still being pieced together, but the essential elements of their story remain as Schmidt understood them. Construction at Göbekli Tepe was begun by people who moved in small groups, families or a tribe who quarried the stone nearby and moved it at most 500 metres. This might not seem very far, but the blocks weigh many tons and it would have taken hundreds of people to move each one of them. That required both a large, willing workforce and a huge amount of organisation. It is impossible to know who had the idea to do such a thing, but we know that this is the beginning of architecture and of cultivation, and it is connected to some spiritual or cult practice.

There is nothing revolutionary in the fact that there is art on the columns at Göbekli Tepe. *Homo erectus* was creating zigzag patterns on shells in what is now Indonesia 500,000 years ago. Recent finds in Blombos Cave, South Africa, show that *Homo sapiens* was doing similar work with red ochre 100,000 years ago. Neanderthals were blowing red ochre out of their mouths and onto their hands, outstretched over the wall of Maltravieso Cave, Spain, more than 66,000 years ago. There is not even anything revolutionary in the technique of Göbekli Tepe's art, in the figures of men, of the birds that flew in their skies and the animals that inhabited their world and prowled through their dreams.

What is revolutionary is the scale of the place, the effort required to achieve it and above all the fact that bands of hunter-gatherers would have needed to cooperate with each other to create, move and decorate the pillars. Some would have worked in the quarries, cutting stone with flints, shaping and incising the rock. Others would prepare the site for installation. And yet more would provide food for them all – this would explain the wild animal remains excavated from the hill's lowest levels. This effort was sustained over many years, probably centuries, and it resulted in an accumulation of pillars arranged in circles. Some of them have been buried – and in that way creating the conical hillscape – while others were still being built. More extraordinary than the monumentality of what might have been the first ever large-scale human construction is what the site tells us about how we came to settle.

At the time when Göbekli Tepe was being built, the landscape around it, east of the river out of Eden, was more generous than it is now. Imagine it as a steppeland of wild grasses, wheat and barley, punctuated by copses of oak, almond and pistachio trees; the latter two are now intensely farmed in the area. The steppe was home to gazelle and aurochs, to migrating geese, to many other birds and animals that could be eaten and to a few that threatened humans, as bone deposits uncovered at the site have shown. An abundant land, it was, as Professor Schmidt said more than once, 'like a paradise'. This abundance made it unnecessary for humans to wander far to feed themselves. Without the need to roam, they could settle while they developed this sacred site. Göbekli Tepe was where they lived and died. Settlement brought a whole new way of being.

While they lived, they watched the sun rise and set, the moon wax and wane, stars drift across the night sky, seasons shift, animals migrate, birds flock and murmurate and, as humans had already been doing for millennia, they spent time around their fires wondering about their place in the greater scheme. How did they relate to the stars? How and why did birds move between the earth and sky? Where did heat and light come from? And thunder and rain? They will have wondered about the meaning of death too – and that great unknown of what happens to us after death provides the most likely explanation for the monuments. In constructing Göbekli Tepe, these hunter-gatherers were expressing what they understood of their relationship with the seen and unseen forces that they knew surrounded them yet could not be controlled, the forces that controlled the mysteries of life and death. This relationship is most graphically illustrated on a carved pillar where a vulture is shown carrying away a human head.

Göbekli Tepe's stone-built circles were the centre of a cult, perhaps *the* hunter-gatherer cult, a site of such immense significance that it justified the effort required to build it. 'They came to feast, perhaps to drink, for a ritual or shamanic purpose, and then they went.' Klaus Schmidt thought he would find human remains beneath the limestone floors of the pillared circles, but did not live long enough to find out and none have been uncovered since his passing. Instead, elsewhere at the site, human skulls have been found, some inscribed with patterns, others scraped clean.

Whatever happened at Göbekli Tepe – and it will be years before an explanation for the skulls and other mysteries is found – it marks a pivotal moment in human development. It may also provide evidence to prove that what has been called the Neolithic Revolution was more of an evolutionary process and for this reason: the hunter-gatherers at Göbekli Tepe needed to support themselves while they were building their cult centre, and although most of the remains found on the hill came from wild animals, there is evidence from neighbouring sites that corn, cattle, sheep and pigs were domesticated around here. Perhaps over time they exhausted all that could be hunted and gathered, or perhaps the climate changed, or there was a blight of some sort. Whatever happened, it left them with no choice but to domesticate and cultivate. Perhaps the cult became all about cultivating food. Whatever the full story, it is clear that both the evolution of agriculture and a revolution of culture took place at Göbekli Tepe some 11,000 or 12,000 years ago and the agents of change were people who lived on the move.

The Highway of History

There is a consequence to this discovery and it relates to an idea best expressed by the historian Felipe Fernández-Armesto. History, he has stated on several occasions, is 'a path picked among ruins'.[4]

This is a slick image and its combination of paths and ruins conjures up something like a highway. Step right this way, ladies and gentlemen, please just follow the line and you will be transported gloriously, reassuringly and seamlessly from the pyramids and tombs of ancient Egypt to the temples and theatres of Greece, from the glory of imperial Rome, to Byzantium, towards the consummate beauty of the Renaissance and onwards to today. As the centuries have rolled by, side-trips have been allowed off the highway to Xian, Angkor Wat, Machu Picchu, Chichén Itzá and many other places. But please stick to the main path and you will find, somewhat inevitably, that it will lead you to the triumph of the Christian West.

Most of the great Western museums were originally designed to follow this historical highway. Many of them are still laid out in a way that encourages us to leave their buildings with a sense that the cities we are stepping into – Paris, London, New York, Berlin and the rest – are an expression of all that is best about the great cultures of the past. If these happen to be the cities we live in, so much the better because we can step out into the streets, our streets, with a sense of our significance in the world.

But this view of history, however seductive, however flattering to those who live in the West, is a hangover from colonialism and it continues to favour people who built monuments and especially those who built *and* left written records. 'Highway history' rests on the assumption that architecture – the measure by which so many civilisations have been judged – was only imagined when humans settled. The Sumerians settled and built ziggurats. Egyptians settled and built pyramids, and so on down to the glories of Renaissance Europe, the grandeur of neoclassicism and the architectural marvels of our own time. Göbekli Tepe turns this on its head. The earliest hauntingly beautiful stone structures on earth (no doubt others, even earlier, will eventually be found) were created by people who did not live around them, or even perhaps in any one place, by people whose lives were nomadic.*

If 'highway history' celebrates the achievements of those who built monuments and settled in capital cities from Memphis to Babylon, from Athens to Rome, Berlin to New York, London, Tokyo and Beijing, it also discriminates against those who have trodden lightly in the world, who have left few records or ruins. Such people, many of them nomadic, are unlikely to be valued by the highway history crowd. They may even be completely overlooked if 'all' they have left us in a physical way is a cairn or a painted image in a cave, a garden, a grove or a forest that they helped preserve intact for a few thousand years. There are of course reasons for the omission, not least being the challenge of writing the history

---

* I never had the opportunity to discuss this further with Professor Schmidt, nor to walk around the ancient site with him, as he had suggested, because from London the sixty-year-old continued on to Germany, where he went swimming and suffered a fatal heart attack.

of people who have not left monuments or manuscripts. But many nomads have at least left, or preserved, their own stories. Some of their stories relate to events that happened, others are complete fantasies, while many sit somewhere between the two. As all humans did before the invention of writing, nomads tell stories to keep alive their histories, myths and their sense of self. These stories try to make sense of the world and their place in it, perhaps while sitting around a fire, as the night fills with the sounds of wild animals and the sky sugars with stars.

The obvious risk to an oral tradition is that when cultures vanish, their stories might go with them and this seems to have happened at Göbekli Tepe. We know so much about the settled ancient Egyptians because they built monuments *and* kept records to commemorate – literally to remember together – everything from the height of the annual Nile flood, the glorious achievements of pharaohs and the petty thefts of tomb robbers. But Persia's wandering sixth-century BCE Achaemenid kings committed very little either to tablet or parchment concerning an empire that was the largest the world had known. This lack of written record has often seemed negligent to literate people, which is one reason why we tend to 'rate' ancient Egypt as more interesting and significant than ancient Persia. Taken to its extreme, as it was by some nineteenth-century European colonisers, it became possible to claim that people in sub-Saharan Africa had no history and achieved nothing worth noting because they had built nothing that could compare to the Pyramids or the Parthenon. That, in turn, encouraged a false sense of superiority in the north and especially in the West, superiority that was a key driver towards colonialism. It ignored the fact that for most of the time *Homo sapiens* has been around, most of us were unable to read or write, but we were able to commit to memory long poems, huge amounts of information and extensive, multi-layered narratives. Even the lodestones of Western literature such as the *Iliad* and the *Odyssey* were consigned to memory centuries before they were written down, just as the Quran was said to have been memorised by the Prophet Muhammad, then an illiterate Arab merchant sitting in a cave, and only written down after his death . . .

So if we are to escape from seeing history as a path through ruins, we must follow a string of stories, we must be prepared to shift from myth to legend to verifiable facts, and we must travel from deepest history into our own time. We must make a journey. We know about the necessity of making journeys because each of us begins life by making the small and extremely dangerous journey from the womb to the light and ends by shifting from this world of light into eternal dark. Between those moments, we move in sun- and moonlight across a planet that is itself constantly in motion.

Out of this background of movement, it seems fitting that our foundation stories relate the experiences of people who have wandered and engaged with the natural world, as Gilgamesh did when he travelled to the Cedar Forest and then to the underworld and back, and Noah as he set sail across the floods in the hope of finding dry land, or Odysseus crisscrossing the Mediterranean on his long journey home from the Trojan War. The Buddha spent the last forty-five years of his life travelling and teaching, Moses and the Israelites trekked across the desert for forty years to reach their promised land, the Prophet Muhammad travelled to Jerusalem on a magical horse, Aborigines walk and sing up their *songlines*, Rama and his companions journey through Hindu myths, while Thor drives his goat-drawn chariot to Jotunheim to find the giant. Gudrid Thorbjarnardóttir, Gudrid the Far-Travelled, sailed to America in the tenth century. Four hundred years later, Chaucer's nine and twenty spring pilgrims made their way on foot and horseback to seek blessing from the blissful martyr of Canterbury, and William Langland, writing in England while Timur was moving across Eurasia, opened his most famous story *Piers Plowman* with the farmer dressing as a shepherd to go 'wide in the world' because it is out there and not at home on the farm that there are 'wonders to hear'.[5] The American Arapaho people's legend of the lame warrior begins in the days before horses, with young men walking into the western mountains to hunt wild animals. Many Cherokee stories open with the hero setting out on a journey. The lovesick poet Majnun goes into the desert of Arabia to recite verses about his forbidden love for Laila. Tolkien's hobbit Bilbo Baggins rushes out on his long and unusual journey 'without anything that he usually took when he went out'.[6] The journey is the rule not the exception. As you will

Roughly a fifth of the Ariaal men in each group possessed a variant gene, the DRD4-7R. Among the Ariaal living as nomads, those who carried the 7R genetic variant tended to be better fed and stronger than tribesmen who did not have it. They are the alpha nomads. But among settled Ariaal, the 7R carriers were less well-nourished and less dominant than their fellow tribespeople.

'Some of the variety of personalities we see in people', anthropologist Dan Eisenberg, one of the lead researchers of the study, explained, 'is evolutionarily helpful or detrimental, depending on the context.'[7] So where the 7R variant might help nomads towards better health and happiness in one set of circumstances, it can lead towards malnourishment and misery in others. What is happening here?

DRD4 controls the release of dopamine, a chemical that our brains produce to encourage us to learn by rewarding us with a sense of pleasure. Because of this feel-good factor, dopamine has played a crucial role in evolution by driving us to seek benefits and rewards. When we exercise or eat something delicious, when we are moved by our surroundings, take the scariest fairground ride, indulge in social interactions or a sex fest, our brains release dopamine. This in turn affects everything from our heart rate and kidney function to the way we process pain and our ability to sleep. Because dopamine helps us feel good about what we have done, our dopamine highs encourage us to repeat the experience to release more dopamine and maintain that high. The word 'addict' is often applied here, but all the drug does is to drive the receptors that make us want more. We can resist; it is up to us. That, in part, explains why some of us love to love, or are overwhelmed with lust, why others (or sometimes the same characters) become obsessive about exercise and play and taking risks. Dopamine can also help us become alpha nomads. But even if that is not on your wish list, there are good reasons why you should be interested because the same variant gene that helps nomadic Ariaal become the best-fed, most powerful members of their tribe also has an impact on our ability to learn.

One in twenty of us, and one in five of our children, are said to suffer from attention deficit hyperactivity disorder (ADHD).[8] ADHD makes it hard for us to focus, to pay attention and control behaviour, especially to control hyperactivity. For schoolchildren, this can be a huge problem because schools need order and most respond badly when children wander off because they feel like it, or speak out of turn, or sing because the mood takes them while a teacher is talking. This is part of the reason why ADHD is seen as a disorder. But Dr Eisenberg has another way of looking at it. For him, it is not a disease. It is 'something with adaptive components'. In a nomadic setting, someone with this variant of the gene may be better at protecting herds against rustlers or finding food and water. 'The same tendencies might not be as beneficial in settled pursuits such as focusing in school, farming or selling goods.'[9] Which is to say that the 7R variant is more likely to be helpful to Ariaal boys than to American schoolchildren, more likely to help those who move and to be more of a problem for those who live a settled life.

For this reason, DRD4-7R has been called the 'nomadic gene' and although Dr Eisenberg finds the label unhelpful and unscientific, it does explain why some Ariaal are well-fed, successful nomads and some are not. It might also explain why so many rock and pop stars have had a difficult time at school, why their minds wandered away from their studies: as David Bowie acknowledged, 'I was a person with a very short attention span, would move from one thing to another, quite rapidly . . .'[10] The nomadic gene might also provide an explanation for some behaviour in older people, why some of us find it hard to sit still and stay happy within four walls. If that is you, it may be something you can explain in relation to genetics. It is also something you can blame on evolution because 12,000 years ago, before a group of us got together and started constructing monuments at Göbekli Tepe, we all lived a wandering life where this genetic variant, and the diverse set of thoughts and responses it seems to encourage, was useful, perhaps even essential for survival.

Most of us have settled since then and in the past century most of us have done so in towns and cities. This dramatic shift in lifestyle out of the natural world and inside walls has turned some of us into miscreant kids, unreliable partners, drug addicts, thrill seekers, gamblers and risk takers, and it has left others struggling to resist the lure of wandering through nomadland, longing for the open road, the promise of a new city, a fresh landscape or the next partner.

If, as Dr Eisenberg's study has shown, the nomadic urge is part of our genetic legacy, if as many as 390 million of us might carry the variant nomadic gene, then this has consequences for the way we act now, for the way we look at the past and at the role that nomads play in the stories that follow.

An Evolutionary Tale

In the years before civil war reduced much of it to rubble, the Syrian city of Aleppo vied with its southern rival Damascus for the title of the world's oldest continuously inhabited city. Much as I enjoyed the sophistication of the northerners, their beautiful souk, relaxed pleasures, the looming citadel and the many layers that spoke of the city's age, I always thought Damascus was the more likely challenger. For one thing it sits beneath a mountain and beside a river, both essential for early settlers. For another, it has a compelling story which, though not exactly a foundation myth, does relate back to the earliest of times and, like the foundation myth of Rome and many other places, it involves two brothers. One of these brothers was a nomad.

Damascus is one of few cities where the highest quarters are the cheapest. Turn your back on the ancient stone walls, cross the Barada river and pass the area known as al-Salihiya, where the elegant tomb of the twelfth-century Sufi master Ibn Arabi lies beyond a lively fresh-food market. Continue past imposing townhouses and twentieth-century apartment buildings, continue until the cityscape closes down and roads become so narrow that only the slimmest vans can pass between the housing blocks, and so steep that most people still prefer to ride than walk. Continue beyond the end of the road and the last houses, the newest and poorest in the city. Beyond them the red earth of the Jebel al-Arbaïn, the Hill of the Forty, is dotted with white rocks and an occasional patch of scrub. A path of steps cut into the steep slope leads to a small compound of whitewashed buildings − you can't miss it, it's the only one here and you might not be alone on the path. When you reach the gate, you will be invited to enter the courtyard and from there you enter the mouth of a cave, the Cave of Blood.

The tradition for this place probably goes back millennia. The fourteenth-century Moroccan traveller Ibn Battuta tells us that Abraham, Moses, Jesus, Job and Lot all prayed in the cave. Why here? Because this is where tradition places the world's first fratricide, where Cain killed Abel. Enter the cave and look up and you will see, as Ibn Battuta saw almost eight hundred years ago, 'the blood of Abel, the son of Adam (on him be peace), God having caused a red trace of it to remain on the stones. This is the place in which his brother killed him, and dragged his body to the cave.'[11]

In case you are not familiar with the story − and even if you are − the bearded guardian will relate it to you, adding specific details to suit the location and his mood, and perhaps also what he perceives of your mood and your generosity. 'And Abel was a keeper of sheep, but Cain was a tiller of the ground.' After he has finished, he will invite you to pray for the soul of the murdered nomadic brother, there, in the cave still stained with his red blood, and after that you may be invited to assist in the financial salvation of the guardian himself. Mashallah!

Let us call it the Neolithic Evolution, for revolutions are by nature quick and we know that agriculture was a slow development. When construction began at Göbekli Tepe, in the mid-9000s BCE, the people who worked on it were hunters and gatherers who had time to cut, move and raise huge slabs of stone. It may be that as the project developed, some people devoted themselves to hunting, others to gathering, to food production, quarrying, decorating stone and so on. Eventually some of them settled and cultivated crops and raised animals. Then, around 8000 BCE the sacred hill was abandoned. It is impossible at present to say why, but it must have been something significant, either a sign – perhaps a comet or some other celestial apparition – or a fact that could not be ignored, a lack of food or water or an abundance of illness. For whatever reason, the place that had consumed so much time and energy, that had required such ingenuity and had changed the range of human experience, suddenly lost its attraction and the people moved on.

When it was abandoned, Göbekli Tepe had been in use for at least 1,500 years, which is the same span of time as from you and me back to the abdication of the last Roman emperor. In that time, the Neolithic or Agricultural Evolution had changed the way humans lived. Perhaps evolution had something to do with why it was abandoned. The Göbekli Tepe rites were probably only celebrated once or twice a year at the outset. But in its later stages it was permanently occupied and sufficiently sophisticated for 150-litre vats of beer to be brewed for large-scale feasts. But the biggest change that the Göbekli Tepe period witnessed was the beginning of farming.

The first strain of Einkorn wheat was domesticated on the Black Mountain, which you can see, on a clear day, from the mulberry tree at the top of Göbekli Tepe. Wheat was followed by peas and olives, and sheep and goats, all domesticated in this area and all while the sacred site was still attended. In the thousand years after its abandonment, people in China domesticated rice and millet, pigs and silkworms, while in the Indus Valley they began to farm sesame and eggplant, and domesticated the camel. By 6000 BCE farmers in the Nile Valley learned how to nurture the sycamore fig and chufa, and to tame the donkey and the cat.

The spread of agriculture was driven by a number of factors that included a change in climate, a warming that made gathering wild foods more difficult. There was also less food to be gathered. The fat years of hunter-gathering, which led to the creation of Göbekli Tepe and other Neolithic centres, saw a rise in the number of people. More people required more food and this led to more hunting and, inevitably, to a collapse in the supply of animals to hunt. The same cycle had already decimated wild animal populations on the American continents and in Australia, among other places. We think of species extinction as an issue we have created in our own time, but big sabre-toothed cats and massive ground sloths, which had accounted for as many as half of the world's large beasts, had already been hunted to extinction by the time Göbekli Tepe's animal-decorated pillars were raised. Perhaps the sacred site was a statement of contrition carved in stone.

Seen in this light, agriculture might not have been a giant step for mankind. Instead it might have been desperate crisis management, the only option for hunter-gatherers whose success had decimated their food supply. And if that was the case, Göbekli Tepe may have been abandoned because there was no longer sufficient food to sustain the community who were needed to maintain the site. Schmidt had talked of the people on the hillside and the surrounding area living in a kind of paradise. That was in the beginning. By around 8000 BCE, they may have stripped that paradise clean, and if that is what happened, then their departure was another version of the Fall, a repeat of the expulsion from the *pairi-daeza* of Eden, the start of another long journey.

Refugees from Göbekli Tepe faced the same challenge as the children of Adam and Eve and subsequently people in all parts of the world: what sort of agriculture could they engage in? Trial and error, good crops and bad, showed them what would grow in the soil and with the available rains or irrigation water. Farmers made the most of their resources and kept back as much of their harvests as they could, holding grain and seed as stock or capital, which was when the trouble started. 'In process of time', it is recorded in the Book of Genesis (4:3–5), 'it came to pass, that Cain brought of the fruit of the ground an offering unto the Lord.' That would have been fine, but 'Abel, he also brought of the firstlings of his flock and of the fat thereof. And the Lord had respect unto Abel and to his offering: But unto Cain and to his offering he had not respect.'

I have always found this judgement harsh. Why was Cain's offering not accepted? Why stoke the rivalry between the brothers? There are many interpretations, one of which points to Cain's religious and moral doubts. But the judgement could also be an example of the God of the wandering tribe showing preference for nomadic pastoralists over tillers of the soil. Whatever the reasoning behind the preference for Abel's offering, the Genesis author is clear that

Cain killed Abel, a murder that highlights one of the consequences of the Neolithic Evolution, the conflicting interests of herders and tillers, of nomads and the settled. What comes out of this, to return to Genesis, is that God tells Cain the earth will not easily or willingly give up 'her strength' to him and he becomes an outcast, travelling east of Eden, where he founds the first city and names it after his son Enoch.

'Everyone believes his own customs to be far and away the best,' observed the fifth-century BCE Greek historian Herodotus.[12] Until the Neolithic Evolution, until humans had to leave the garden and start farming, until Cain and Abel and a judgement on whether the fruit of the ground or the fat firstlings of a flock was a more suitable offering, there was only one set of customs, one way to survive and that was by hunting and gathering.

It is easy to imagine that all of a sudden, from one season to the next, the people of Göbekli Tepe and hunter-gatherers around the world, hundreds of thousands of them in the Near East, chose to stop moving and stay at home to till the land, but this was not what happened. The old ways did not stop with the domestication of wheat. For one thing, long before the construction of Göbekli Tepe, some communities were already partly settled, living out of caves and basic shelters, roaming in search of meat. On the other hand, long after the domestication of wheat and goats, hunter-gatherers still roamed across what is now Anatolia, the Nile Valley and elsewhere. But agriculture, the settled life that it required and the surplus of food that it made possible, brought about a radical change in the way humans lived.

Life for hunter-gatherers was what we would regard as remote. There were rarely more than ten people per square mile because there was rarely enough food to feed more. In a dense modern city such as Manila in the Philippines, as many as 200,000 people are now living in that same space. What stops them from starving or having to fight their neighbours for food is the ability to produce an excess which can be stored and kept until it is needed. This is one of humanity's great achievements, one of our main claims to progress. Making sure that people can eat is not just a duty for politicians, it remains essential to their survival. Failure to provide has led to the downfall of rulers and regimes from ancient Rome to the Ancien Régime in France. In our own time, the most obvious way to gauge the health of the economy is the ease with which we can put food on our tables. The so-called Arab Spring of 2011, which brought down several long-entrenched regimes, was sparked by a sudden rise in food prices and the suicide of Mohamed Bouazizi, a Tunisian fruit and vegetable trader. But while surplus levels might have remained volatile, they made settled communal living possible.

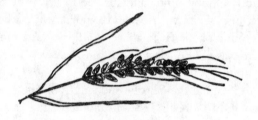

Çatalhöyük

The author of Genesis described what happened between the loss of Eden and the founding of the first city in four hundred words, but the process was long and complicated as is clear from Çatalhöyük. Chatal-Hoyuk, as it is pronounced, was not a city in the way we understand the word now. It was a proto-city, a development positioned somewhere between Göbekli Tepe, with its sole cultural and sacred use, and Cain's city of Enoch.

About five hundred years after Göbekli Tepe was abandoned, around 7500 BCE, settlers made a home on a mound above the Anatolian plain, close to the Çarşamba river and about a hundred miles from the Mediterranean. The mud-brick houses they built had no entrances at ground level and no streets or passages between them. They formed a huddle of mud boxes whose flat roofs served as paths and where roof flaps allowed entry to the homes below.

Climb down the ladder and you step into a large open space divided by platforms of varying heights. Immediately under the ladder there is an oven, like a tandoor or pizza oven, for cooking and heating. The mud walls and floors are plastered and whitewashed. In some places, bulls' horns have been set into the walls, part of a ceremony whose meaning is lost but whose significance will have related to the power of the natural world and the need these people felt to atone for the shedding of an animal's blood, a reminder that they recognised their place in the delicate balance of the natural and spirit worlds.

In some houses, walls are painted in shades of ochre with scenes of humans, animals and landscapes. Looking across a gulf of 10,000 years, we may never be able to see the house as it appeared to the family who lived there, but it was obviously more than just a place to shelter from the weather and be safe from animals, although that was important. Restored and rebuilt over the centuries, with ancestors buried beneath the earth floor and neighbours on hand to share food, labour and perhaps trade, this was a home, or homes, for up to 8,000 people. But as with Göbekli Tepe, one day (in this case around 7000 BCE) the people of Çatalhöyük packed up and moved on.

Why was the proto-city abandoned? Perhaps the Çarşamba river shifted its course, making the settlement unviable. Perhaps the growing population put pressure on the site and its surroundings – how far did they now have to travel to hunt game, gather wild fruits and nuts, or even find wood to keep their home fires burning? Maybe there was a pandemic, or a warming or cooling of the climate. We look for a reason that makes sense to us, but maybe the people left because the distant volcano rumbled, the sun was eclipsed, the moon burned red or migrating birds did not return, because there was a warning sign or symbol that convinced those thousands of people that they needed to leave their homes and abandon the bones of their ancestors and thousands of female, male and animal votive figures.

Whatever the reason for their departure, they moved off into a very different world from the one that existed when Çatalhöyük was founded. The evolution set in motion by the warming climate, which had led to the creation of Göbekli Tepe and the subsequent domestication of crops and animals, changed the region as it would eventually reconfigure the world. It changed humans as well. After Eden, alongside hunters and gatherers, latter-day Cains tilled fields of wheat and corn, peas and beans, while Abels herded sheep and goats, the patriarch Abraham among them, pushing his flock along the fertile corridor between Urfa and what would become the Holy Land in the same way that the Bakhtiari family I had seen move their animals up the Zagros Mountains, travelling light, with only what was necessary for survival.

Çatalhöyük's refugees are likely to have loaded significantly more than survival packs as they moved to another site where they could settle and put down roots, where their gods could be worshipped and appeased, their families flourish. One of those places is mentioned in Genesis as the city Cain created, Enoch. Here too there was a development; the new city had strong walls.

The Walls of Uruk

Ancient Greeks called it Μεσοποταμία, Mesopotamia, the land between two rivers, a name that recurs in Aramaic, Hebrew, Syrian, Farsi and Arabic. The rivers are two of the 'streams' out of Eden, the Tigris and Euphrates, their valleys and floodplains stretching from southern Turkey to Kuwait and to the Bakhtiari winter grazing lands in south-west Iran. Mountainous in the north, marsh in the south, Mesopotamia is immensely fertile between the rivers and increasingly desertified east and west of them. Settlers were attracted to the river, and nomads to the desert fringes. This is where early agriculture flourished and, not unconnected, where the city and most of its early characteristics were set. This is also where the deep past and recorded history meet, where myths and legends match fact and physical evidence, and where the world's first cities, the fixed counterpoints to nomadism, were built.

The first city was probably a place called Eridu, which, according to early sources, was founded by a king called Alulim, who ruled for 28,800 years. His son and successor, Alaingar, ruled for not less than 36,000 years, but eventually 'Eridu fell'.[13] While Eridu's whereabouts remains a matter of conjecture, the remains of Uruk★ have been found on the banks of the Euphrates, halfway between Baghdad and the Persian Gulf. It was there that the city as we understand it took shape during the 4000s BCE and lives that we would recognise as being city-led were first lived.

Like Göbekli Tepe 5,000 years earlier, Uruk began as a shrine where hunters and herders came to worship two deities – the god Anu, whose titles included Sky Father, Lord of the Constellations and He 'who contains the entire universe', and Anu's granddaughter, the goddess Inanna. Like Anu, Inanna had many titles and many aspects, but her origins are connected to fertility, to the rising of rivers and the sap, to the riches of the harvest and the fat of the flock. Married to the shepherd god Tammiz, she remained individual, independent, dominant. Associated with the Venus star and the lion, known as the Queen of Heaven, Inanna embodied primal female power. She was beautiful, fertile and predatory, with a voracious sexual appetite. 'You loved the shepherd, the grazier, the herdsman,' a Sumerian poet wrote, 'and turned him into a wolf.'[14]

At some point someone built a house near the shrines, perhaps for a priest, and then settlement followed, which grew, expanded and overlapped until there was a mass of houses, a temple complex and a palace compound, and the whole place was separated from the rest of the world by high walls.

★ Uruk may be the Enoch referred to in Genesis – say the names fast enough and you can see why they might be one and the same.

Life inside walls was very different from life tilling the fields or herding in the hills. When people lived close together behind walls, their habits, rituals and outlook changed. No more nomadic camp life, nor the animistic urges of those who remained at large in the wide open world and therefore also at the mercy of the forces of nature. More significant, and of central importance to our story, there was a change in activity, in what the people of the city did with their time. Hunter-gatherers and herders lived in a world whose constant changes and evolving situations required them to be able to perform multiple tasks and to be flexible in their decision-making. The city scorned these jacks of all trades. Instead it needed and encouraged its inhabitants to become static and to be predictable in their behaviour. The city encouraged specialisation and citizens became butchers, potters, soldiers, priests and priestesses or a king. Each role had its own specific status in an ever-more-rigid hierarchy. As the occupations of the majority of inhabitants became more specialised, they also began to be only of use in the urban world, for what would a bureaucrat, a financial manager, an accountant, a roofer or plasterer do in the natural world? And so it has been ever since.

Other divisions appeared as Uruk developed, the most pernicious being between those who had enough and those who had more. Mud-brick houses within the walls of Uruk all had shrines dedicated to their household gods and storage spaces for grain, oil and other non-perishable commodities. Some people turned out to have more skill or luck than others. They reaped better harvests, drove harder bargains, were sharper in trade, and one way or another, by fair means or foul, they ended up with surplus food, clothing, jewellery or other possessions. Wealth and stock differences had existed in mobile communities, but they were less significant and less divisive: there could be no hoarding when everyone needed to pack and transport their belongings. But staying put encourages accumulation, as anyone with an attic or basement will know, and no one accumulated more than the king. As we often do with our own rulers, the people of Uruk wondered at the wealth and power their ruler had accumulated, at the privileges he took for himself and at the abuses that followed. Then their wonder turned to despair and they looked to the gods and to nomads for a solution.

We know this because one of the oldest complete narratives from the distant past describes the king of Uruk as 'a wild bull lording it, head held aloft'.[15] The young men of Uruk were harried, the young women unable to return home without the king claiming droit du seigneur. 'By day and night,' the old story-tellers relate in this first tale of inner-city problems, 'his tyranny grows harsher.'

Offspring of Silence

The story of the King of Uruk was known in the city of Nineveh near modern Baghdad, along the Mediterranean coast and even up the Nile. But with the passing of the ancient world and the ability to read cuneiform, the story was lost. The clay tablets on which it had been recorded lay hidden beneath the Mesopotamian soil until 1840, when Nineveh was excavated. The fragments were sent to the British Museum in London, but they were not translated until November 1872 when George Smith, a thirty-two-year-old London printer and cuneiform expert, came upon them. According to one of the museum's staff, when Smith translated a section of the story, he suddenly 'jumped up and rushed about the room in a great state of excitement, and, to the astonishment of those present, began to undress himself'. When he was calm enough to speak, Smith said, 'I am the first man to read that after two thousand years of oblivion.' 'That' was a tablet with lines from the story of the King of Uruk, of Gilgamesh.

In the Nineveh text, the seat of Gilgamesh's power is called 'Uruk-the-Sheepfold', which harked back to a time when people built corrals, stockades, bomas, thornbush barriers, ditches and heaped stones to protect themselves and their stock from predatory animals and unwelcome humans. But by the time the epic story was written down, the epithet no longer fitted for the city had replaced its wooden sheep fences with brick walls: 'Climb Uruk's wall,' Gilgamesh urges the boatman who brings him home from his journey to the underworld.

> Walk back and forth! Survey its foundations, examine its brickwork!
> Were its bricks not fired in an oven? Did the Seven Sages not lay its
> foundations? A square mile is city, a square mile date-grove, a square
> mile is clay-pit, half a square mile the temple of Ishtar: three square
> miles and a half is Uruk's expanse!★[16]

This mighty wall, the scribes tell us, was 'like a strand of wool', rimmed with copper.

The great wall of Uruk changed everything. It did more than keep out people from the rival cities of Ur, Nippur and Nineveh, perhaps even the Egyptians. It separated people in the city – and at its height there were some 80,000 of them – from the 'others'. It separated the regulated, man-made, urban environment from the unbridled forces of nature. It also kept the fast-evolving community of forward-thinking, specialised, sedentary people away from the old primal world of diverse-thinking, animistic hunter-gatherers and nomads. Uruk's walls were a physical manifestation of anti-nomadism.

The walls also served to keep people inside the city, where they suffered at the hands of their overbearing king. He is described as:

★ This grandiose claim inscribed on ancient clay tablets was corroborated when archaeologists traced a wall in Iraq that runs for seven miles on a dried-up stream of the Euphrates around the ruined mound of Uruk.

Surpassing all other kings, heroic in stature,
brave scion of Uruk, wild bull on the rampage!
Going at the fore he was the vanguard,
going at the rear, one his comrades could trust!

And yet they could not trust him because he was also 'a violent flood-wave', his passions unleashed and unchecked. He raped daughters, bullied men, insulted elders and became so cruel that the good people of Uruk prayed in despair to their gods. *Save us from our king.* The gods responded by creating a foil, a wildling who would stand up to the dictator.

Enkidu is described as an 'offspring of silence'. Fashioned from clay by the goddess Aruru, he embodied the primal force of the natural world. He was also everything the wall was designed to exclude:

All his body is matted with hair,
he bears long tresses like those of a woman:
the hair on his head grows thickly as barley,
he knows not a people, not even a country.
Coated in hair like the god of the animals,
with the gazelles he grazes on grasses,
joining the throng with the game at the water-hole,
his heart delighting with the beasts in the water.[17]

Gilgamesh chooses not to confront this force of nature himself. Instead, he sends a woman, Shamhat, who is described by the tablets as a 'harlot' although she may also have been a priestess of Inanna/ Ishtar. Whatever her role or experience, nothing would have prepared her for what was to come. After waiting two days by the watering hole, Shamhat saw the herd come to drink and with it came Enkidu:

Shamhat unfastened the cloth of her loins,
she bared her sex and he took in her charms.
She did not recoil, she took in his scent:
she spread her clothing and he lay upon her.[18]

Enkidu's initiation into knowledge has parallels with Adam and Eve's story, but is more explicit. 'For six days and seven nights,' the ancient tablets tell us, 'Enkidu was erect, as he coupled with Shamhat.' But he had to pay a price for tasting this forbidden fruit and when 'the gazelles saw Enkidu, they started to run, the beasts of the field shied away from his presence'. The wild man tried to run after them, but he had become weak. Like Adam and Eve, he was now an exile from the natural world.

When Shamhat directs him towards the city, flattering him that one so handsome should surely be living in the sacred enclosure, Enkidu expresses neither doubt nor regret about leaving the primeval forest. Instead he looks ahead to the high walls and the raving king of the unseen city. 'I will vaunt myself in Uruk,' he tells the beautiful prostitute/priestess.

First Shamhat takes him to a shepherds' camp, a halfway house where he samples the two most popular and enduring products of farming, bread and beer. After seven goblets of beer, Enkidu is happy, singing and sufficiently malleable for the shepherds to prepare him for Uruk-the-Sheepfold; they shear him. 'The barber groomed his body so hairy,' the story goes, 'anointed with oil he turned into a man.'

As a man, he needed to dress.

Once dressed, he 'became like a warrior'.[19]

A warrior needs a weapon.

The transformation, the domestication of Enkidu from a wild one as mighty 'as a rock from the sky' to a man too slow to run with wild animals, was complete and he was ready for the city.

It is a wedding day when Enkidu arrives beneath the high walls of Uruk and people have gathered in the square for the festivities, some of them to see Gilgamesh claim his self-given privilege of bedding the bride before the groom. But when the king goes towards the wedding house, Enkidu is there, blocking the door with his foot. Neither of them backs down and a fight ensues.

> They seized each other at the door of the wedding house,
> In the street they joined combat, in the Square of the Land.
> The door-jambs shook, the wall did shudder.[20]

The vivid familiarity of this encounter carved on a clay tablet thousands of years ago is remarkable, but so too is what happens next. Gilgamesh kneels, recognising that he has met his match. As anger drains away, Enkidu asks why, with all his powers and privileges, he would rob these ordinary people of the great pleasure of their wedding night? The king's reply is not recorded. Instead, 'They kissed each other and formed a friendship.'

Later, Gilgamesh suggests that the two friends go on an adventure to cut down the forest of cedars and to kill the bull of heaven. Enkidu warns him that 'This is a journey which must not be made' but it is made. The sacred cedars are cut down (they were essential for temple doors), the bull of heaven is killed and, to make matters worse, Gilgamesh then rejects the amorous advances of the goddess Ishtar. She and other gods demand vengeance for the king's pride and the price they exact is the life of Enkidu. When his companion dies, Gilgamesh is distraught and refuses to allow him to be buried 'until a maggot dropped from his nostril'.

The epic projects two archetypes: Enkidu who runs with the animals and belongs to the mobile natural world and Gilgamesh the settler king of the city-state. Like so many foundational myths, it is Cain and Abel revisited, but also revised. The taming of the wild one will have cheered the long-ago listeners, many of whom would have been settled, but they might also have grieved at the triumph of Uruk.

Uruk – a real, historical city that is now reduced to a mound of mud – gave us much of importance beyond the story of its early king. This was where writing was invented, where the first mountain-like ziggurat was built, where the cylinder seal was first used, where the sexagesimal numeric system was created that we continue to use to measure time (seconds and minutes), angles and geographical coordinates. There seems also to have been an historical king called Gilgamesh who ruled Uruk before 2500 BCE at a time when the natural world was being subdued, the rivers controlled so that the land could be cultivated, where forests were cut down and wild animals and wild people were either tamed, killed or banished. Part of his grief would have stemmed from a realisation that he and his people were changing the world, that nothing would ever be the same. Gilgamesh the king, and those who listened to the story, would have understood the immense difficulty, even then, of reconciling the urge towards cities and settlement with the loss of contact with the natural world. They would have recognised that the city's success at taming their world would bring about environmental breakdown. But there was one change humans brought about that seemed to have only positive outcomes and it involved horses.

Horses

'Geography lies at the basis of history,' as the eighteenth-century philosopher Immanuel Kant recognised and, in doing so, anticipated by a couple of centuries Gilles Deleuze's observation that nomads only have a geography, not history. Kant's comment was refined by Johann Herder, one of his contemporaries, into 'history is geography set in motion'. This is a neat summary of the inextricable link between the two and it points to why the steppes feature large and often in this story: the nomads who came off them, who had been shaped by them, went on to shape our world in more profound ways than nomads elsewhere.

Landscape and climate influence who we are and how we act and for that reason you cannot comprehend the United States and Canada without knowing about the Great Plains, the vast grassy flatlands between the Mississippi river and the Rocky Mountains, and that they were once grazed by fat herds of buffalo and bison, which were hunted by Sioux, Cheyenne, Comanche and other native, nomadic tribes. Similarly, in South America, pumas once hunted Pampas deer and bighorn sheep across the lowland Pampas that stretch from Brazil through Uruguay and down to southern Argentina, where gauchos later herded cattle. China's great North Plain runs from the Yan Mountains to the Tongbai and Dabie mountains and has been the centre of Han culture since the earliest days. But most significant for my story of nomads is the Great Eurasian Steppe.

'A wide boundless plain encircled by a chain of low hills'[21] is how Anton Chekhov describes the steppes. 'Huddling together and peeping out from behind one another, these hills melted together into rising ground, which stretched right to the very horizon and disappeared into the lilac distance; one drives on and on and cannot discern where it begins or where it ends.' For once, this is not writer's hyperbole: Eurasia accounts for over a third of the planet's landmass and its overwhelming vastness, one of the steppes' most dominant features, really does run 'on and on'. From the meadows of Hungary almost to the granite gates of Chang'an, the early Chinese capital, this grassy corridor reaches across 9,000 kilometres to link the Mediterranean with the Yellow Sea, east with west.

The grass-belt falls neatly into western and eastern parts, separated by the Altai Mountains, a not-insurmountable buckle of highlands, and also a spiritual heartland for many nomad tribes. The lower-level Western Steppe is spared the extremities of Siberian winters and blistering summers, especially between the Danube and the Volga where the grasslands are cut through by a series of rivers. The east is harsher, hotter, colder, drier and has always been a more challenging place for nomads to survive: in the winter of 2010, for instance, 9,000 nomad families in Mongolia lost all of their livestock to the cold and another 30,000 lost half of their herds.[22]

And yet, as the historian Barry Cunliffe points out, the steppe corridor is one of the world's great conduits and if you saddle up on the Great Hungarian Plain before meadow saffron heralds the arrival of spring you could reach Mongolia before the great winter freeze, assuming your papers are in order. Apart from crossing rivers, woods and marshes, and making your way through the uplands of the Altai Mountains, for most of the journey you would be riding 'on and on' over steppe grasses, milkwort and wild hemp. Lapwings, wheatears and partridges would break cover in front of you, rooks, hawks and eagles would scout your movements, while grass crickets, locusts and hoppers scoot out of your way. The old hills would run away to the left, while the misty plain stretches ahead and a deep, transparent sky arcs above. Today, this vastness remains one of our planet's most daunting geographical features. How might it have looked thousands of years ago to people who were obliged to travel on foot and without either wheels or motors, people who shared their land with wild horses?

Horses flourished on the steppes because they had the constitution to cope with the harsh winters, their hoofs being strong enough to scratch through ice and snow to reach frozen grasses. Steppe people were hunting wild horses more than 10,000 years ago, when people elsewhere were tracking aurochs, boars and goats. The jump from hunting to herding was not a difficult one. In a typical herd, a single stallion leads mares and colts, so if you kill the stallion, you could corral the mares and then hobble the docile young, ensuring a supply of milk and meat to help you through the winter. Horses were herded on the westernmost Pontic–Caspian steppe at least 6,000 years ago and soon became so essential for nomadic survival that they were interred alongside cattle and sheep in human burials. Then something fundamental changed in the relationship between humans and horse: we learned to ride.

If you have tried to ride bareback on an unwilling horse or have watched a rodeo, you will know that an untamed mount will buck and storm until it has thrown the rider or exhausted itself. Was it a rodeo-style dare from a young man on the steppe that led to humans riding horses? Or a smart move from a tribal leader who calculated that he could herd twice as many sheep on horseback as he could on foot? We shall never know, just as we may never know when that horse was first ridden. Certainly by the fourth millennium

BCE: remains found in a northern Kazakh* burial site from that period contained ten tons of animal bones, 99.9 per cent of which were equine. Many of the jaws and teeth show the sort of wear you would see on a horse fitted with a bit, which suggests steppe people were riding horses around 5,000 years ago, at a time when the first pharaoh was unifying the upper and lower lands of Egypt, when Gilgamesh built the incomparable walls of Uruk, Aborigines were engraving rocks around what is now Sydney, settlements began to appear in Central America and the Cycladic civilisation emerged in Greece.

More than the domestication of crops, the ability to ride was a revolution. The equine revolution. The horse has been the most efficient and enduring means of transport humans have ever used and the ability to ride a horse transformed life on earth, perhaps nowhere more so than on the steppe, where it made nomadic pastoralism possible. A herder on foot can walk maybe twenty miles a day. Bareback, as the first riders were, they could cover twice that distance or more, although distance was just one aspect of this revolution.

As with horse riding, the origins of the wheel and the wagon are hotly debated. The evidence, which is scarce, includes a four-wheeled structure scratched onto the side of a pot found in southern Poland, of around 3500 BCE; two clay models of carts, one from Hungary, the other Turkey, both dated around 3400 BCE; a clay tablet found in the Temple of Inanna in Uruk, of around the same date, which shows a similar sort of wagon. The oldest remains of a full-size wagon were interred on the Pontic–Caspian steppe around 3000 BCE as part of an elaborate grave structure. From this and other burials in the region – thousands of them have now been found – we know that the first wagons had a rectangular wooden frame roughly a metre wide and two and a half metres long. With a simple box-seat up front, it would have looked similar to the sort of wagon driven by nineteenth-century settlers in the American West. Wheels were fashioned from strips of wood that were rounded and dowelled together and with a centrepiece for the axle. When

* Botai, near the Ishim river.

pulled by an ox, rattling across the steppe would have been slow and painful, especially at first. But it allowed the elderly and young to be moved, along with more goods than a single animal could carry. Later, someone had the bright idea of streamlining the wagon and harnessing a horse, and the chariot was born. While the ox-and-cart made nomadic pastoralism possible on a large scale, the chariot had equally far-reaching consequences as it changed the nature of warfare. The horse-bit also brought changes, making it possible to complete that summer journey from the Great Hungarian Plain to Mongolia and on into China. There is no evidence that anyone ever rode the entire steppe corridor in those early centuries, but nomads were now on the move across the continent and it would only be a matter of time before horse-riders connected these two very different parts of the world. Around 5,000 years ago, long before there was something called the Silk Road, nomads roamed across the Steppe Route, driving herds, riding horses, linking west and east, mountain and desert, and the two great poles of settled civilisation, China and Europe.

Who were these masters of the vast empire of grass?

Children of the Sky God

The identity of the early steppe nomads is only partly understood, but some of their impact is easier to identify, in part because it has been immense: not least their language, now spoken by half of the world's population. It was this language that provided a clue to uncovering their identity, although the process was long and tortuous and little progress was made before 2 February 1786. On that day William Jones, a forty-year-old judge from London, raised his impressive eyebrows and addressed the 'Asiatick Society of Bengal' about 'what discoveries in History, Science, and Art . . . we might justly expect from our enquiries into the literature of Asia'.

Beyond his legal duties, Jones was the sort of passionate linguist who found pleasure in translating *The Thousand and One Nights* from English back into Arabic. On this February evening in Kolkata, he spoke about his adventures in Sanskrit. Several minutes into his speech, he announced that 'whatever be its antiquity, [Sanskrit] is of a wonderful structure; more perfect than the Greek, more copious than the Latin, and more exquisitely refined than either'. Then he delivered news of his explosive discovery: there was a stronger similarity between these languages 'than could possibly have been produced by accident; so strong indeed, that no philologer could examine them all three, without believing them to have sprung from some common source, which perhaps no longer exists'.[23] The idea that Greek, Latin and Sanskrit came from the same lost mother tongue was revolutionary and Jones went on to add Gothic, Celtic and old Persian to the same linguistic family.

If there was no great stir in the Grand Jury Room that evening, it was probably because Jones was the only Englishman who could translate Sanskrit; no one was equipped to challenge his assertion. But even now his comments divide linguists, archaeologists and historians and for good reason: if, as is now widely accepted, these languages came from a common source, what was it? How did it evolve? And who were these people who spoke it?

A step towards answering these questions was soon taken by another brilliant linguist and polymath, Thomas Young, who has been described as 'the last man who knew everything'. He now saw that 'the Indian, the West Asiatic, and almost all the European languages' also belonged in this lost language group. Writing in 1813, Young explained that all these languages were 'united by a greater number of resemblances than cannot well be altogether accidental'.[24] It was Young who called the mother of these languages 'Indo-European'. It came out of the steppes and in its various forms is today spoken by more than 3 billion people.

Two centuries of study by scholars across a range of disciplines has led to the discovery that certain words are common to the whole family of Proto-Indo-European (PIE) languages. Because these words are so widespread, they throw light on what was of importance to early steppe nomads. These include words for horse, cow, pig, sheep and dog as well as the word *reg*, ruling, from which we have *raj*, *regal*, *rex*. The Indo-European word *fee*, which we understand as payment for work, originally meant flock, herd, farm animals, occasionally also money. Other common words include bow, arrow and sword, mother, father, brother and several relating to in-laws, which confirms the importance of family relationships, herding, and fighting or at least defence among Indo-European speakers. One particularly significant figure emerges from the linguistic fog to unify the diverse speakers of this ancient language and in the *Rig Veda* he is the lofty *Dyaus Pitr*, the Sky Father – 'God bright by day' – whose name and attributes echo down to us from Greek Zeus and Roman Jupiter to the Christian 'Father who art in Heaven'.

Each new piece of research raises more questions as to who these children of the sky god were and where they lived. Given the global spread of Indo-European languages, the idea that the 'children' originated in one place and emerged from one culture – Anatolia perhaps, or Ukraine, southern Russia, western Kazakhstan – remains contentious. But a convergence of linguistic and physical evidence now places the original Proto-Indo-Europeans on the Pontic–Caspian steppe, north of the Black and Caspian seas, and enclosed by the Dnieper and Ural rivers. They lived there after the domestication of the horse and many of them were nomadic.

Nomads as we know live lighter and leave fewer traces than settled people, but that does not mean they leave nothing. Hundreds of huge circular mounds have been found around the Caucasus, in Siberia, in Kazakhstan and further east. Some of these mounds are over 30 metres high and 500 metres around their perimeter. They are known as *kurgan*, a Slavic word for barrow or tumulus, and they contain burials. People were buried in kurgans for thousands of years and in a variety of circumstances, so although there are many differences between them, there are also some common characteristics. A wall or moat usually surrounds the mound, and a ceremonial path leads to the tomb entrance. On the outer slopes of many kurgans, horses were buried after being ritually sacrificed to accompany the deceased to the other place. Several people were often buried in a single kurgan but there was usually a main burial, at the centre of the mound, often placed inside a wagon or a wood-clad chamber and surrounded by clothes, weapons, pots and huge funerary cauldrons.

One of the most famous kurgans belonging to a wealthy herder is ten metres high and dates to the late third millennium BCE, before Egyptians were building pyramids. Like Tutankhamun's tomb, the Maikop mound was undisturbed until it was discovered in 1897 by two Russian archaeologists, Nikolay Veselovsky and Nicholas Roerich.* A single human corpse had been laid in each of the tomb's three rooms. One of them was a woman of status, surrounded by clay and copper pots and jars, with gold-wire earrings and gold and carnelian beads scattered near her corpse. The central burial was even more impressive, with the deceased sitting upright in a longer room that had wood-lined walls and a floor patterned with river stones. The burial had been covered by a canopy decorated with 125 gold plaques and supported by gold and silver poles. Near the corpse, which was painted red with cinnabar, lay a cache of treasure including two gold diadems, copper axes and swords, and seventeen gold and silver vessels of great beauty and exquisite workmanship.

One of the most striking things about this burial, interred 4,000 or 5,000 years ago thirty miles from the Black Sea, in what is now the Russian Republic of Adygea, is the origin of the objects in the kurgan. The gold and silver had come from the Near East, lazurite beads from Central Asia and turquoise and carnelian mined south of the Caucasus Mountains or maybe in Iran. The copper weapons with curved blades held in place by silver pins were similar to those made in Troy. These beautiful objects suggest that perhaps as early as 3500 BCE nomads and herding communities on the steppes were trading in commodities from India and Afghanistan. As always, it

---

* Roerich later gave up archaeology and worked as an artist and stage designer. In Paris, he collaborated with Igor Stravinsky, composer of *The Rite of Spring*, premiered by the Ballets Russes in 1913; Stravinsky was inspired by Roerich's descriptions of pagan rituals.

would have been a two-way trade, with the nomads selling their own produce, their weavings, leatherwork and horses. There were also cultural exchanges, for we know that their Indo-European language spread as far as the north of Scotland, east across Central Asia and south through the Near East into North Africa and down to South Asia, to what is now India and Pakistan. Along with their words, children of the sky god, masters of the steppe empire, sent their nomadic ideas and customs, and the sense of mobility and reach that horses had made possible.

In Quest of Fame

We can come closer to some of these early Indo-European nomads in the Indus Valley in modern-day Pakistan. Imagine an ancient city that has been abandoned, its wells dry, the drains that once kept the city famously clean now clogged with debris. The workshops where beads, terracotta bowls and strikingly modern figurines were fashioned, the bronze foundries where statues of dancing girls were cast, the Ravi river docks where merchant sailing boats tied up – all now silent and still. The wind throws dust over the brick walls of abandoned houses. In the 2000s BCE, when horses and alcohol were being welcomed in Britain, when the Minoans were building Knossos as the centre of Mediterranean trade and power, the Indus Valley was one of the world's great hinges. Rice had been domesticated and barley grew high, elephants were tamed and zebu cattle were generous with their milk, and out of these and other riches it became a centre of craft and trade. Then the world became warmer, the rains failed, wells dried up, crops withered, cattle died and people moved on, those who were able to, to other, wetter places. The ones who remained huddled in shadows thrown by houses, by the huge granary that was now empty or beneath the sacred fig whose deity had abandoned them.

That is one vision of what may have happened to Harappa, Mohenjo-daro and other early Indus Valley cities. The difficulties presented by the lack of evidence have been compounded by ideology and politics, but it seems that these cities went into decline from around 1900 BCE and within two hundred years most had been abandoned. It has long been suggested that they incubated disease and were torn apart by infighting, but what if something else happened? What if they were conquered before they were abandoned and the Indus Valley collapse was brought about by human intervention, in particular by nomadic invasion? Ancient texts offer clues in the way that Homer's *Iliad* throws light on the fate of Troy. One text in particular, a hymn to the god Indra from Hinduism's oldest sacred text, the *Rig Veda*, points to the fate of the Indus Valley cities:

> No one has seen that might of thine, productive of bounty
> every day renewed, O Indra.
> This one great power of thine our eyes have witnessed,
> wherewith thou slowest Varasikha's children,
> When by the force of thy descending thunder, at the
> mere sound, their boldest was demolished.
> In aid of Abhyavartin Cayamana, Indra destroyed the seed of Varasikha.
> At Hariyupiya he smote the vanguard of the Vrcivans,
> the rear fled frightened!
> Three thousand, mailed, in quest of fame, together, on the
> Yavyavati, O much-sought Indra, Vrcivan's sons, falling before
> the arrow, like bursting vessels went to their destruction.[25]

The *Vedas* (hymns) were composed in the Punjab about 1500 BCE in Sanskrit, an Indo-European language. Although not written down until around 300 BCE, they are among the oldest-surviving compositions in any Indo-European language. This particular Veda tells us that 3,000 'mailed' warriors, hoping for fame, faced 'the seed of Varasikha', the Vrcivans or Harappans. They fought along the Drishavati or Zhob river of Baluchistan. Whatever the exact location, the text suggests that the Indus Valley was invaded by Indo-European-speaking people, that the invaders found fame and glory and that the defenders fell 'like bursting vessels'.

There is no archaeological evidence to support this story; no mass of arrowheads or other tell-tale signs have been found. As one commentator has noted, this lack of evidence might be due to the Vedic people's insistence that they did not build cities because they 'did not seek power, but rapture'.[26] But it is more likely that instead of the Veda's suggestion of an epochal military showdown, Indo-European nomads and migrants arrived in the Indus Valley in small bands, over time. Most of them would have left their central Asian homeland and come with wooden-wheeled ox-carts, slowly, inexorably driving their herds. But others, scouts and young warriors, would have been mounted on chariots or horseback, bronze swords by their sides, supple bows and full quivers slung over their shoulders, eyes on the prize of winning fame on the Yavyavati.

The *Vedas* also tell us about the lives of the people who spoke this language, what they valued and what they hoped for from their gods. They tell us that they consumed a mind-shifting concoction called *Soma*, a stimulant extracted from a still-unidentified plant. 'We have drunk Soma and become immortal,' the Vedas relate, 'we have attained the light, the Gods discovered.' 'These glorious drops that give me freedom have I drunk.' Inspired by the potion, Vedic poets conjured a world where might was right, god-sanctioned and endless, where to thrive, a man must value the cow and even more so the horse – the poets call Soma 'the Stallion's seed prolific'. With it, when the gods were with you and all was well, your carts would roll easily across the plains and your chariot would speed you into battle to vanquish enemies, rustle their cattle, provide for your own and to win fortune and a fame that would live long after your body was rotting in the tomb. This above all: you stormed into battle certain that your exploits would be remembered, your name still spoken.

Some of what we know about these people comes from a series of burials discovered in Sinauli, about 40 miles due north of Delhi on the Yamuna river. Among the burials were three chariots, said to be the first of their kind found in the region, and several coffins decorated with copper-plated figures of men with crowns – similar to the huge brass effigies that were laid over the tombs of Crusader knights. Swords, daggers, shields and helmets have also been found. 'We are now certain', the excavation director reported, 'that when in 2000 BC the Mesopotamians were using chariots, swords and helmets in wars, we also had similar things.'[27]

The nationalist narrative suggests that 'we', the people of India, had chariots and bronze swords much earlier than previously known. But the story is probably more complicated. What the Indian excavators seem to have uncovered by the Yamuna river was the burial of Indo-European fighters. These men had perhaps not been in the region long enough to have adopted local habits and so they were buried according to their old customs, in the ways of their old steppe homeland.

The horse, with which one could count one's blessings through the harsh winter and one's wealth at all times.

The chariot, swift as the wind.

The composite bow, an intricate construction of maple wood, antelope horn, deer gut and leather, held together with a fish-based glue.

The *comitatus*, the word meaning *escort* but implying a more elaborate and passionate band of men – 'we few, we happy few, we band of brothers',[28] as Shakespeare put it – tied tighter than the deer gut on their bows, a group who vowed to live together and if need be to die for one another.

A love of stories, especially epic histories and sagas that tell of the glorious adventures of men and the fickle whims of gods.

All this and more was carried by nomads moving off the steppes; 'now invading, now receding', as the second-century BCE Syrian writer Lucian described them, 'now contending for pasturage or booty'.[29] We know now that they spread from the twin Pillars of Hercules across Eurasia to the Middle Kingdom and the Pacific

Ocean and that they brought far-reaching and long-lasting change to the ancient world. Nowhere is their arrival and influence clearer than in that most insular of nations, Egypt.

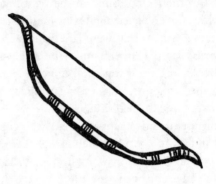

The Lord of Wanderers

Johann Herder's maxim – that history is 'geography set in motion' – applies perfectly to Egypt. Historical glory, and the rise and fall of empires, has always been linked to its geography. Beneath its veneer of timelessness, Egypt has undergone many transformations since the time, at least 6,000 years ago, when what is now the Sahara Desert was a vast savannah and its people gathered wild food, tracked bovids and a range of other animals, and painted scenes of themselves swimming at Gilf Kebir. After the climate warmed and the rains failed, the forests and wild grasses shrank, Egyptians found themselves defined by their geography. By 3500 BCE, they were hemmed in by desert to the south, east and west, cut off by the Mediterranean in the north and so completely dependent on the river that Herodotus did not exaggerate when he called their desert-bound land the gift of the Nile.

Sacred sites connected to the movement of the sun and moon, the shifting of stars and seasons, had long been maintained along the Nile. These shrines were also dedicated to the mighty thought-threading river and to the unfathomable mystery of the way it rose to flood the land at the height of summer. As the savannah turned to desert and rainfall became a thing of legend, hunters and gatherers had no choice but to settle around these sacred sites. Settling left them dependent on the river and on their ability to raise wheat, barley and spelt, flax, henna and lotus. Most years, when the Nile rose its average of seven or eight metres, Egypt was a land of plenty. But there were years when it did not and then the valley was a vale of tears. A margin of two metres in flood levels was the difference between drought and disastrous flood, between feast and famine, laughter and tears.

Because of this absolute dependence on the river, the population recognised the need for organisation: everyone must be ready to plough and sow as soon as the dung beetles pushed up through the drying skim of black silt. The need for organisation spawned bureaucracy and a pyramid system with the pharaoh at the pinnacle, priests, scribes, bean counters and tax collectors lower down, while the majority of Egyptians laboured in fields or on boats. No wonder a scribe, around 2400 BCE, counselled his son to pay attention at school and 'put writing in your heart that you may protect yourself from hard labour of any kind . . . The scribe is released from manual tasks.'

Fear of famine was as constant as the love of gold in ancient Egypt, and famine, it was known, was caused either by a failure of the river or a failure in organisation. So it comes as no surprise that ancient Egyptians obsessed about order in society, nor that one of their most popular and enduring myths concerns the struggle between order and chaos, good and bad, fertile and barren. It is the story of two brothers, one settled, the other mobile.

There are many versions of the myth of Osiris and his brother Seth and most of them start with the arrival of a good king, Osiris, who teaches the people of the Nile how to organise themselves to make the most of the flood and ensure a harvest that will sustain the population, how to worship gods and, through all of this, how to maintain that most essential of values, order. It is Osiris who teaches them how to settle and be Egyptian. Under his rule, harvests are good, the population increases, cities grow and what we know as Egypt emerges. To paraphrase an ancient hymn, thanks to Osiris every belly is full, every backbone is straight and every tooth can be seen because people are so happy they are laughing.

Seth, meanwhile, lords it over the desert. He is king of the hard-lands and of the nomads who live there. As well as being god of the wilderness, Seth was also a protector of the gods and dead pharaohs. He alone of all the gods was immune to the sleep-drug administered by the most feared of all demons, Apophis, the three-headed serpent whose task was to stop the deceased from reaching paradise.

The more the people cherish Osiris, the more the valley flourishes, and the more jealous Seth becomes. It is Cain and Abel relocated to the Nile, but with a very different outcome. Seth invites Osiris, their sisters and friends to a feast at which the god of wanderers unveils a beautiful casket made from exquisite materials and explains that it is a gift for whoever can fit inside it. Many try, but only Osiris fits the box exactly and as soon as he is inside, Seth orders it locked, filled with molten lead and thrown into the Nile. Osiris, the settler king, lord of farmers, is burned, suffocated. Dead.

As the story remained popular over several thousand years, there are many versions of what happens next, but all of them have Isis, Osiris's wife and Seth's sister, finding the casket and retrieving the corpse. When Seth hears that the body has been found, he hunts it down and cuts it into fourteen parts, which he scatters along the length of the Egyptian Nile. Isis, grieving but still devoted, collects thirteen parts, which she arranges in place and wraps tight in linen – creating the first mummy. The missing part, his penis, she fashions out of Nile mud and summoning her considerable magical powers she turns herself into a bird and hovers over it . . .

The child conceived from this union is a son called Horus. When he grows, Horus becomes the avenging king and fights his uncle Seth over many years. Eventually he succeeds in restoring order. The late (Graeco-Roman era) version of the struggle between Seth and Horus, carved onto the outer walls of the Temple of Horus at Edfu in upper Egypt, shows how the uncle turns himself into a hippo-potamus, but as his magical powers seep away he becomes smaller and smaller until he is of a size where Horus can draw his knife to kill him. The need for the forces of both chaos and order is beau-tifully expressed by a statue of the Pharaoh Ramses III (twelfth century BCE) in the Egyptian Museum, Cairo. A thousand years older than the Temple of Horus at Edfu, the statue was carved from a single piece of pink-flecked granite and shows the life-size pharaoh flanked by Horus and Seth, both touching the pharaoh's crown to show they support him.

The parallels between the struggles of nomads and settled people, of those who live on rich lands and poor, of the 'first fratricides' of Osiris and Seth and Cain and Abel are striking, but there are key differences in the way that Seth and Cain are regarded. Cain became an outcast, while ancient Egyptians worshipped nomadic Seth for thousands of years. Their devotion suggests a more diverse, complex and nuanced response than the simple Roman- and Christian-era duality of good an jd evil. It shows that earlier Egyptians recognised the need for diversity, for both the creative forces of the unsettled and the order brought by the tillers of the land, just as a thousand years earlier Mesopotamians recognised that they needed both the forceful king Gilgamesh and the wild man Enkidu to keep him in check. The tiller and the herdsman, the settled and the nomadic. The great and enduring challenge for Egyptians was how to maintain the balance between the two.

Nomads on the Nile

The north was Egypt's most porous border. Its wide Nile delta and Mediterranean plain were easily reached from Libya in the west and through what is now Palestinian Gaza in the east. Nomads had long passed this way, a fact reflected in the Old Testament story of the patriarch Jacob sending his sons 'down into Egypt'. By the early second millennium BCE, Egyptians had built a string of forts along the eastern border, both to monitor movement and to support Egyptians heading into the Sinai Desert to mine turquoise, but the borderlands were open – there was no wall or ditch – and nomads and traders moved and migrated easily along the coast and into the Nile Valley. Among them, around the 1900s BCE, was a group of nomad herders called the Hyksos.

The identity of these people, as with so many early nomads, is still uncertain. The name Hyksos is a Greekified version of the ancient Egyptian *heqa khasut*, 'rulers of foreign lands'. But many of their leaders had Semitic names, so perhaps they were from the Fertile Crescent and they may have originally come from the steppes and settled in Mesopotamia or Palestine until other tribes pushed them west into the land of the pharaohs. At one point they were called the 'shepherd kings', which supports the idea that they were nomads.

It was long assumed that the Hyksos invaded Egypt and conquered the northern part of the country in 1638 BCE, but new bio-archaeological research[30] suggests that, as with Indo-Europeans along the Indus Valley, the arrival of the Hyksos was more of a long, slow migration than a sudden invasion as they drove their horse-drawn chariots and herded their flocks across the fertile delta, traded into the valley and eventually settled. By the early 1600s BCE, when the Indus Valley civilisation was coming to its end, people in England were exporting tin to Europe and the Olmecs were extending their power in Central America, a weak central government along the Nile allowed the Hyksos to establish themselves as a power in the north, ushering in a unique century and a half of foreign rule.

Foreign occupation was traumatic. Manetho, an Egyptian priest writing more than a thousand years later, recorded that 'having overpowered the rulers of the land, they burned our cities ruth-lessly, razed to the ground the temples of the gods, and treated all the natives with cruel hostility, massacring some and leading into slavery the wives and children of others.' Fifty years after the Hyksos were pushed back beyond the eastern border, when Egyptians had reasserted pharaonic rule over the whole valley, the mighty Egyptian queen Hatshepsut, in the nearest thing we have to her last testament, inscribed on the wall of her funerary temple in Luxor that 'I have restored that which had been ruined. I raised up that which had gone to pieces formerly, since the Asiatics were in the midst of . . . the Northland, and vagabonds were in the midst of them, over-throwing that which had been made.'[31] Perhaps that was how it felt to Egyptians of the south, in the aftermath of the expulsion of the foreigners. But the Hyksos influence provided Egypt with the means to create the empire of Ramses, Tutankhamun and the rest, which continues to dazzle us.

The usually reliable Egyptian bureaucracy is curiously vague about the identity of the first Hyksos ruler in Egypt. It may have been Yakbim Sekhaenre, around 1800 BCE, or Semqen, 150 years later. Whenever the Hyksos takeover happened, what is important is that until that time Egyptians had enjoyed 1,500 years of dynastic rule, most of which had been stable. Stability allowed a strong economy to develop, along with a clear identity, robust traditions and an efficient bureaucracy. To the people of Mesopotamia, where the soil was fertile but the rivers less generous than the Nile, this seemed an enviable life. But stability brought its own problems. It bred complacency, conservatism and cultural exclusion, as a result of which Egyptians lost touch with what was happening elsewhere in the world. Not for nothing did the prophet Isaiah note that the strength of the Egyptians was to sit still.

The Hyksos century was certainly a period of chaos by Egyptian standards and as Queen Hatshepsut recognised, things do seem to have 'gone to pieces', with two and sometimes three kings ruling at the same time – a Hyksos in the delta, an Egyptian along the main valley and a Nubian in the south near Aswan. Any foreign occupation of the sacred valley, the mirror of heaven, the abode of gods, was obviously intolerable, but at least the Hyksos rule seems to have been light-handed, with the foreigners mostly paying rever-ence to Egyptian deities and enjoying Egyptian customs to the point of adopting many of them, including the worship of Seth, the god of the wasteland and wanderers, whose popularity understandably soared during this period of rule by nomads.

But cultural transfer works both ways and while the Hyksos were adopting Egyptian gods, Egyptians were learning from the nomadic intruders. Not least, they were learning how to use their weapons. Egyptians had always used a bow made from a single branch to shoot their arrows. The Hyksos introduced them to the composite bow, with its Indo-European origins, which gave them much greater accuracy and range. An equally significant adoption was the horse-drawn chariot. The first recorded time the Egyptian army used the chariot was when the princes of Thebes sailed their warships north to push the Hyksos out of the delta. These chariots were such a novelty that the Egyptian language had no word to describe them. So when a man named Paheri came to honour his grandfather, the veteran commander Ahmose, by carving an account of his involvement in the glorious victory over the Hyksos on the wall of Ahmose's tomb, the scribe was obliged to use an image of a chariot where the word would have been.*

The outcome of the reign of the Hyksos was more beneficial for Egyptians than foreigners. The Hyksos were pushed out of Egypt and back into the ever-more-crowded Fertile Crescent, where they were eventually overwhelmed by another wave of nomadic people riding down off the steppes. But in Egypt, the hundred-year interregnum of the Hyksos was followed by the most glorious period of that nation's long history. Refreshed by overcoming the challenges posed by the nomads, bolstered by the improvements to weapons that the foreigners had introduced, enlivened by interaction – some peaceful, some very bloody – with Hittites, Amorites and other nearby kingdoms, Pharaoh Ahmose and his successors of Egypt's New Kingdom created an empire whose borders were pushed north into what is now Syria and south far into Nubia/Sudan. For three hundred years from around 1500 BCE, when the early Mycenaean culture was just taking hold in Greece, and Indo-European nomads were migrating to the Indian subcontinent, Egypt glittered with gold. The Theban god Amun became the great god of Egypt while his cult centre at Karnak (Luxor) developed into one of the world's largest and most sublime religious complexes. Pharaohs such as Hatshepsut, Seti I and

---

* The tomb of Ahmose, son of Ebana, can be visited at El Kab, south of Luxor.

Ramses II raised spectacular temples. Monotheism was tried and rejected. One measure of the wealth of the Egyptian Empire can be seen in the burial of the young pharaoh, Tutankhamun. When he died, tragically young, he was interred in glittering splendour, as well as with six chariots and more than a dozen composite bows.

I cannot tell you that none of these things would have happened without the nomadic intervention. But innovation had disappeared from the Nile long before the Hyksos rode their chariots into the valley. Egyptians had long feared the chaos and destruction nomads would bring, but we now know that what emerged from this cohabitation and collaboration between the mobile and the settled was a period of glorious achievements. While the pharaohs of the New Kingdom set about restoring their country, the outlook of ancient Greeks was being transformed by the arrival of Indo-Europeans.

Greeks

There were no scribes to tell us how nomads overwhelmed the old Greek world, no witness statements detailing the arrival of men on sweating stallions and chariots, armed with long swords and curved composite bows, inspired by their desire for a glory that would live long in memory. But the story is there to be discovered both in the words of the great Greek poet Homer and among the evidence beneath the ground. We know that the story has shaped what we think of as Greek culture, the world of Achilles and Odysseus, and of the golden age heroes. More surprisingly, it is a story that is nomadic in origin.

We know that nomadic Indo-European fighters reached the Aegean Sea before 1500 BCE because that is the rough date of the shaft graves that were uncovered in the Peloponnese in 1876 by a German adventurer. Heinrich Schliemann had many remarkable qualities, not least his ability to make money; before arriving in Greece, he made a fortune selling weapons parts to the Russian government during the Crimean War and was wealthy enough to retire by his mid-thirties. He was a gifted linguist and could converse in a dozen languages. But foremost, by the time he reached Greece in his early fifties, was his sense of drama and desire for a reputation.

Schliemann was also impatient and, like any eager speculator, was in a hurry for a return on his investment in archaeology; he wanted ancient treasure and he found it. When he uncovered rich and extraordinarily beautiful funerary objects that had been buried for 3,500 years, he was quick to celebrate. He was also quick to make assumptions. Not content with finding burials from Greece's heroic age, some of them objects of wonder, including a golden funerary mask, Schliemann decided to attach to his discoveries the names of famous long-dead people. Agamemnon's name still resonated from the Trojan War thanks to Homer's poetic magic in the *Iliad*, in which he is called the 'lord of men', a king who survived the war and returned to his palace in Mycenae, Trojan concubines in tow, only to be murdered in his bath by his cheating wife Clytemnestra. Now, Schliemann claimed without any supporting evidence, here was the great king's face to look upon, the historical epic made real. Look upon this gold mask, he announced with nothing more to support his claim than a hunch, and you are looking at the vivid face of Agamemnon, on whom Schliemann claimed it had been modelled.

Just four months after his arrival in Mycenae (in archaeological time, this is but a moment), Schliemann sent a telegram to the King of Greece to announce the discovery of Agamemnon's tomb and enough treasure 'to fill a large museum which will be the most marvellous in the world'. Schliemann said he was working for the love of science and wanted no share of the gold diadems, the hundreds of gold leaves, golden figures of animals and golden masks. This was surprising given that the Mycenae tombs delivered one of the richest archaeological hauls of all time, only eclipsed half a century later by the discovery of Tutankhamun's tomb. But for all his self-promotion, Schliemann's greatest achievement was one that he himself did not recognise and it had nothing to do with Agamemnon.

Five years before the discovery of the Mycenae shaft graves and 'Agamemnon's gold', Schliemann had been even more successful at a place called Hisarlik, a 30-metre-high mound on a grassy plain in north-west Turkish Anatolia. This promising site overlooks the Scamander river and the Dardanelles, the narrow waterway that connects the Sea of Marmara with the Aegean. In two years of digging, Schliemann and his team uncovered the ruins of the city that Homer had called 'strong-founded' and 'gate-towering'. This was Troy, an economic and military centre in the region, controlling the Dardanelles and the passage between Asia and Europe. The city turned out to be enormous, home to as many as 10,000 people, its ruins covering fifteen acres. At their core, the high point, was a walled citadel of palace and temple and it was there that Schliemann found treasure and again, without any convincing corroboration, he gave it a label. Look, here is the treasure of Priam, the defeated king of Troy.

At the heart of the world of Agamemnon and Priam, of the heroes and villains of the Trojan War, there lay an existential tension between two very different ways of life, two competing outlooks, a clash of culture between the people of Troy and those of Greece. The *Iliad* and the *Odyssey* were distilled from oral traditions and time-polished myths. So although they speak of the conduct of a real war in which many lives were lost and of the long return journey of Odysseus to his home in Ithaka, they refer to a time and a world far from the Scamander plain. As Adam Nicolson describes so beautifully in *The Mighty Dead*, these Greeks were not the people of Plato and Aristotle, the Parthenon and Phidias, of democracy and the *polis*. These were earlier Greeks who carried with them memories of the steppes north of the Black Sea, and their manners and motives still echoed those of the nomadic Indo-European warriors who had invaded Greece, as they had invaded the Indus Valley, fusing their ambitions and values with those of the archaic native people.

Two moments stand out in the epics, and in Nicolson's account –

at least they do if you are in search of nomads – and both involve Odysseus. The first is when Achilles confronts King Agamemnon. Achilles, beloved by Zeus, is the child of a union between a man and a goddess. He is a wild spirit, brilliant and fierce but also mercurial and untamed, while Agamemnon is a king of men. The pair echo the Sumerian king Gilgamesh and his wild companion Enkidu. During the Trojan War, Achilles acquires a concubine, a bright-eyed princess called Briseis, with whom the hero forms a deep attachment, but Agamemnon has her brought to his tent. Achilles retaliates by withdrawing from the fighting. When it becomes clear that the Trojans will overwhelm the Greeks without Achilles in the field, Agamemnon sends silver-tongued Odysseus to negotiate the champion's return.

Agamemnon will return the girl, Odysseus tells him – 'untouch'd she stay'd' – and when Troy falls Achilles will have other rewards: his ships will return home heavy with gold and brass, 'Besides, full twenty nymphs of Trojan race/ with copious love shall crown his warm embrace.'[32] And there was more: after the war 'shall he live as my son' and marry one of Agamemnon's daughters, 'each well worthy of a royal bed' and each with a dowry that would include seven ample cities, one of them being Cardamyle. To the city-based king it must have seemed an irresistible offer. But what would all this wealth, all these possessions mean to a hero shaped by the nomadic steppe-world?

Achilles replies that the Greeks went to war for honour, because the Trojan prince Paris had kidnapped the beautiful Helen. But Agamemnon had done exactly the same thing and kidnapped beautiful Briseis, yet none of the Greeks had opposed him or objected. 'Slave as she was,' Achilles explains, 'my soul adored the dame.' More than injustice, Achilles rages with the sting of lost honour: what use was wealth when one's reputation was tarnished? For these reasons, he finds Agamemnon's offer an insult. 'His gifts', he tells Odysseus, 'are hateful.' Not the riches of the kingdom, 'the golden tides of wealth', not even control of the Egyptian Empire would persuade him to stay and fight because – and here's the point – 'life is not to be bought with heaps of gold'.

Achilles then explains why he *will* stay and fight. Not for vast herds, which are easily captured, nor 'steeds unrivall'd on the dusty plain'. He will stay for the honour of it, for glory. He has weighed up the options – leave and enjoy 'years on years, and long-extended days' or stay and fight for 'deathless renown' and 'immortal praise'. Life or fame, comfort or glory. This choice echoes down from the *Rig Veda* hymns and beyond them, from the nomad world on the steppes where life was often short for a man with a horse and the skills to brandish a weapon. That life and inevitable death were made worthwhile by the certainty that a hero would be remembered by comrades, his exploits repeated around campfires long after he had fallen. This shared admiration of bravery in battle and joy in storytelling were characteristic of nomadic life. There was an identity to be found in that remembrance, passed down from life on the steppes, which mirrored the way that Homer's stories of wild men and their noble endeavours were passed down through generations until they were captured in characters, on paper, fixed between book bindings and brought within walls.

The second stand-out Homeric moment that relates to nomads and the steppe-world occurs halfway through the *Odyssey*. The journey home from Troy has been long and full of challenges and diversions for Odysseus and his companions. Many had died visiting the Cyclops, the home of the ruler of the winds, the Laestrygonians who destroyed all but one of the Greek ships, and then the survivors came to the land of the beautiful, dangerous goddess Circe. Here, again, there are echoes of other places, earlier stories, for when Circe uses magic to turn some of Odysseus's companions into pigs, the hero avoids a similar fate – and becomes the goddess's lover – when he eats a herb called moly, perhaps not so different in effect to soma. He stays a year and when he leaves Circe tells him that his route back to Ithaka will take him through the dark underworld of Hades. A journey, a quest, an old man who will tell him his fate. Just as the Gilgamesh author gave us a hero who went in search of the man who survived the flood, who will tell him that he must recon-cile himself with death, so Homer sends Odysseus to the underworld to hear his fate from a Theban prophet named Tiresias.

Tiresias is blind, but he has a vision of what is to come, of Odysseus's further wanderings, the loss of more companions to a watery grave, his eventual return to Ithaka where he will find his palace full of suitors, his faithful wife Penelope keeping them at bay. But blind Tiresias tells him that even after he has killed the suitors – 'princes on princes roll'd' – he would still not be able to rest at home. Instead of sitting by his hearth or lying in the bed he had carved long ago from an olive tree, Odysseus will have one last journey to make, a return to the source, to where his people came from, a place far from the sea, to people

> Who ne'er knew salt, or heard the billows roar,
> Or saw gay vessel stem the watery plain,
> A painted wonder flying on the main!

On this journey Odysseus should carry an oar, strapped to his back, and continue across this land until he meets a shepherd. At that place, Tiresias explains, he should plant the oar as a homecoming for the seafarer and also as an altar 'to calm the god that holds the watery realm'. Then there would be sacrifices:

> A threefold offering to his altar bring,
> A bull, a ram, a boar; and hail the ocean king.

Nothing could be stranger than sacrificing these first-domesticated land animals to the sea god Poseidon and so far from the sea. But do this, he is assured, and you will live a quiet life and die a peaceful death:

> This is thy life to come, and this is fate.

Except that this is not his fate. Odysseus does return to Ithaka, where he kills the many suitors in his palace, and reunites with the patient Penelope in their olive-tree bed. The book ends with a visit to his father in an orchard, a garden in what the most enthusiastic of poets still called a rugged land. There, in a *pairi-daeza*, an Eden both literal and symbolic, among the figs and vines that father and son had planted long ago, Odysseus's long and winding journey comes to an end, not looking back towards the nomadic steppe-world, but forward to a settled future in which Indo-European beliefs and customs would be absorbed into the Mediterranean world, the nomadic and settled reconciled and combined to shape what we recognise as ancient Greek culture and the basis for the modern Western world.

Homer resolves the conflict he had seen between the mobile and settled by having Odysseus and his Greek companions turn their backs on their nomad origins. Their coming rivals, the Persians, would do otherwise. They embraced the nomadic and changed the world in the process.

Persians and Others

Ancient Persians left few written records and scarce traces of their greatness, like so many other nomadic cultures. So to understand them, I turned to the pine- and oak-clad slopes of Olympia in the fifth century BCE and looked for witnesses among the Greeks. For most of the ancient year, these wooded uplands ten miles inland from the wine-dark sea were visited only by pilgrims heading to the sanctuary of mighty Zeus. Even after a grand temple, and a statue carved by the master Phidias no less, were completed, Olympia was only really packed when the games were held and a hundred oxen were sacrificed to the Sky Father.

During the Olympic Games, people came from all over the Greek *poli* to watch naked noblemen box, run, throw discus and javelin and race mule-carts for glory and olive-leaf crowns. But among the crowd there were some who were drawn neither by religion nor sport.

They were there to gauge the latest cultural trends and to catch the new work of poets and playwrights, painters and sculptors. In the mid-fifth century BCE, one of these creatives unveiled a radically different form of writing for which he coined a new term – history.

Herodotus was born in Halicarnassus, now Bodrum in Turkey, at a time (c.484 BCE) when the port-city paid tribute to the Persians. As a young man he may have sailed to Egypt and crossed Mesopotamia to Babylon. He may have lived in the *magna Grecia* colonies of southern Italy. He may also, as the ancient suggests, have attended the Olympic Games and entered the great temple of Zeus, where, according to the author Lucian, 'he seized the moment when the gathering was at its fullest, and every city had sent the flower of its citizens; then he appeared in the temple hall, bent not on sight-seeing, but on bidding for an Olympic victory of his own.' His new work 'bewitched his hearers',[33] as it does today, and is probably the earliest surviving work of non-fiction.

As one of Herodotus's nineteenth-century translators has noted, there are so few verifiable facts about the man that 'to compile them into a biography is like building a house of cards, which the first breath of criticism will blow to the ground'.[34] But while there is no evidence to prove that Herodotus ever attended the games, we do at least have the work Lucian claims was read there. The *Histories* is an enquiry into the great events that had recently threatened his world. It starts with the Trojan War and ends with the protracted conflict between Greece and Persia. Herodotus was driven to write, he tells us, to explain what had happened and why, so 'that human achievement may be spared the ravages of time'.[35] It is a rare source of information about life in ancient Persia.

The Persian plateau is a hard land surrounded by mountains, with a desert at its centre. For at least five centuries before Herodotus, the Massagetae, Medes and Sarmatians, the Sidri and Borgi, Bactrians and Gedrasians, Carmanians, Tapurians and other nomadic tribes had roamed across this terrain. They were all Indo-Europeans, living in tents and out of wagons, easy in the saddle, deadly with sword and bow, riding off the steppes and along the east and west shores of the Caspian Sea in search of water and grazing for their herds. For centuries these climate-change migrants remained divided and distinct.

Warlike and often warring, they showed allegiance or animosity towards one another according to the ebb and flow of power and the abundance or dearth of grazing. Then one of them, the Medes, left their heartland south of the Caspian Sea and, forcing the other tribes into submission, occupied so much of what is now Iran that they overextended themselves, and were in turn defeated by another of their nomadic neighbours.

The tribe that overwhelmed the Medes had its heartland in the southern part of the plateau, a region to which they gave their name, Fars or Pars, from which we have the name Persia. Under their leader Cyrus the Great, the Persians built on their conquest of the Medes. Hoping for alliance but prepared to do battle, they had established their rule from Macedonia to the Indus Valley, from what is now Oman up to the Black Sea. By 539 BCE, in the age when the Buddha was said to have found enlightenment, when the first Singhalese king ruled Sri Lanka and China was divided among many princes and kings, the Persians were masters of 40 per cent of the world's population and Cyrus was living up to his titles as the Great King, King of Kings, King of the Four Corners of the World.

With empire came greater power, privilege and wealth; after the Persians defeated the Lydians and their legendary 'golden' king Croesus, they moved, in Cyrus's view, from the thistle to the feast.[36] Surely the ruler of such an empire would live in a magnificent palace, in a magnificent city. He would surely also leave a magnificent and slightly exaggerated account of his achievements; this was what rulers of other empires had done. But Cyrus and his Persians were nomads, and his empire was notable not just for its size but for being an alliance of nomadic tribes and city states, an alliance made possible by the nomadic respect for diversity. 'The Persians are greatly inclined to adopt foreign customs,' Herodotus tells us, and as they conquer so they are changed. But despite their willingness to adopt ideas and conventions from elsewhere, they remained nomadic, in part because their land was so poor that only persistence and ingenuity – which included digging a vast network of *qanat*, subterranean water channels – made agriculture possible. Even then, most of Persia was still only suitable for the *nomas*, the moving settled and their herds. The nomads I met in the Iranian mountains all mentioned links back to ancient Persia, with the Bakhtiari claiming direct descent from the third-century Sasanian kings. As they moved up and down the Zagros Mountains in search of grazing for their sheep and goats, they were living a life that is, in its essential elements, very similar to that of ancient Persians: a life shaped by the landscape.

It was to the landscape that one of Cyrus's successors, Darius I, looked when he decided to leave a record of his more numerous achievements, his many titles and his genealogy – 'eight of my dynasty were kings before me'. This record used the three main languages of the empire, Old Persian, Elamite and Babylonian, and was written in cuneiform, the common script (the Persians never did develop their own alphabet). But instead of consigning his message to parchment, papyrus or clay tablet – Darius had the nomad's suspicion that they could be lost or destroyed – his declaration was a carved inscription a hundred metres up the flank of a limestone mountain fifteen metres high and twenty-five wide. The mountain he chose, at Bisotun (also spelled Behistun), has a flank that drops in a straight line from the heights down to the edge of a river valley and is significant for two reasons. For one, it overlooks the Persian Royal Road, the great highway of empire which ran from the royal city of Susa in the east, near the Persian Gulf, through Mesopotamia to Babylon and on to the Aegean Sea near what is now Izmir in Turkey. 'It has staging posts', Herodotus enthuses, 'built by the King [Darius] along its entire length, and excellent hostels, and the whole road is both well tenanted and secure.'[37] This was one of ancient Persia's great achievements and an ideal project for people who were nomadic and committed to movement. Its 1,677 miles of road literally held the huge empire together. And there was an ancient pony express, as Herodotus explains it, for 'the Persians have found a way of sending messages so efficient that there exists nothing mortal possessed of greater speed. There are horses and riders posted along the entire stretch of a given route . . . Neither snow nor rain, neither the heat of day nor the pitch of night, will prevent him from completing his assigned journey in the fastest possible time.'[38] Placing his inscription above the Royal Road ensured that Darius's claim to power was seen and widely shared.

But the fact that the inscription was cut into the side of a mountain was also significant. As Herodotus recognised, mountains had special significance for the Persians, as for many other nomadic people. Herodotus wrote that the Persians did not build temples because unlike the Greeks and Egyptians their gods had no human form. Instead he understood that Persians prayed to the Sky Father, which is to say that they worshipped the sky and the elements, water, air, fire and earth, as Indo-Europeans had done. Because of this, they did not look for the divine in stone temples, but on mountaintops, the wild sanctuary of gods. 'It is a tradition among the Persians', Herodotus wrote, 'that sacrifices to Zeus, whom they identify with the all-embracing dome of the heavens [the Sky Father], be made only on the peaks of the very highest mountains.'[39] Recognising the importance of mountains to ancient Persians helps to unlock the mystery of the most famous of all ancient Persian monuments, Persepolis.

Persians had built on the lower slopes of Kuh-e-Mehr, the Mountain of Mercy,* long before Darius came to power. But in the fourth year of his thirty-two-year reign, Darius commissioned what would become the great sacred, ceremonial and diplomatic centre of his empire, as well as its treasury. The Greeks called it Persepolis, 'the city of the Pars'. (The Persian name has not survived.) But in spite of its many functions, Persepolis was not a capital city as we understand it, in part because Persians were not settled city people. Their nomadic traditions and the harshness of their land did not encourage them to settle. Instead, Persepolis was a place of ritual, and one in particular: each spring at the time of the Persian New Year festival of Nowruz, the shahenshah (king of kings) went there to affirm his relationship both with the gods on the mountain and with all the many peoples gathered to pay tribute. Persepolis might borrow heavily from Egyptian, Babylonian and other Mesopotamian architectural traditions, but in its relationship to the mountain sanctuary of the gods, it affirmed a very Persian identity and belief.

When Persepolis was finally completed by Darius's grandson Antaxerxes I, it was one of the most sublime structures humans had

---

* Also known as the Mountain of Mithra, the Indo-European 'lord of wild pastures' (Kriwaczek, *In Search of Zarathustra*, p. 119).

ever built. Against the lower slope of the mountain, Darius's architects had created an enormous platform, 300 metres on one side, 450 metres on the other. It was and still is reached via a magnificent double staircase of 111 wide steps, 111 also being the number of stages along the Royal Road. Each step brings you closer to the twin cedarwood doors of the Gate of All Nations. The gate was more than a portal, for it enclosed an immense hall where stone-carved winged-bull columns and orange-, green- and blue-tiled walls sat beneath a sixty-foot ceiling. This opened onto a succession of ever-grander spaces, more sumptuous halls, the enormous royal treasury, an open square that could accommodate tens of thousands of people . . . and then came one of Darius's finest creations. The Apadana or audience hall is raised above the palace so that visitors climbed a pair of double-reversed stairways and ascended towards the imperial presence, beneath the divine mountain summit. Where the 111 steps that led from the plain up to the Gate of All Nations were left bare, their massive limestone blocks smoothed and polished, the Apadana staircase is carved with images of representatives of the Sogdians and Arians, Lydians, Cappadocians, Arabs, Ethiopians, Libyans, Bactrians, Scythians, Egyptians and the Shahenshah's many other diverse subjects. Each of these characters is shown being led by a Mede or Persian usher, and watched over by the great king's bodyguard, the Immortals.

Before beginning at Persepolis, Darius had completed another imperial complex at Susa using Lebanese cedar, Bactrian gold, lapis lazuli and carnelian from Sogdiana, turquoise from Chorasmia, Egyptian silver and ebony, and ivory from Ethiopia and Sind.[40] All this and more was used to embellish Persepolis, which Diodorus Siculus, a Greek historian writing around 50 BCE, described as 'the richest city under the sun and the private houses had been furnished with every sort of wealth . . . Scattered about the royal terrace were residences of kings and members of the royal family as well as quarters for the great nobles, all luxuriously furnished, and buildings suitably made for guarding the royal treasure.'[41] It was more than just the richest place under the sun. By bringing craftsmen and materials from across this largest of all empires, Darius united the great cultural endeavours of the past and present and merged them into a glorious Persian future. Persepolis was a physical representation of the many diverse elements that made up the empire, 'a tent in stone'[42] as one observer has noted, and as such it was a fitting monument to nomad power. So it served for two hundred years, until Alexander the Great arrived on his great Hellenising march eastwards.

When Alexander defeated the main Persian army in Mesopotamia in October 331 BCE, he brought an end to the Achaemenid dynasty, leaving the last Shahenshah, Darius III, to be murdered by one of his own. Following this victory, Alexander moved quickly along the Royal Road – although he came from the settled world, part of his genius had been to adopt the best of nomadic qualities, among them being speed and ease of movement. At Babylon and then Susa, two other imperial 'capitals', he was welcomed with great ceremony, as Cyrus and Darius had been before him. The imperial Persian army made a last, desperate stand at what was known as the Persian Gates, up in the Zagros Mountains, but Alexander fought his way onto the plateau and into the Persian heartland. By the following January, he was at Persepolis.

Alexander removed vast quantities of gold and silver from Persepolis, a hoard of treasure that required thousands of camels and mules, and took weeks to carry away to Babylon, from where it would finance both his fledgling Hellenistic empire and his ongoing campaign in the East. Looting was to be expected, but what happened next was not. With the treasure removed, Persepolis was put to the torch, the flames licking the huge cedarwood doors and columns, the wood lintels and roofs burning with such intense heat that even the limestone split. We cannot know why Alexander allowed Persepolis to burn. Some historians suggest it was revenge for the Persians burning Athens a hundred and fifty years earlier, in 480 BCE. But I am more convinced by other motives, including one advanced by Bruce Chatwin.

When Chatwin looked at Persepolis in 1971, he saw it as an expression of power from a ruler with a shaky claim to the imperial throne. Chatwin arrived on the Merv Dasht plain in the company of Qashqai nomads:

> We were walking to Persepolis in the rain. The Qashqais were soaked and happy, and the animals were soaked; and when the rain let up, they shook the water from their coats and moved on, as though they

were dancing. We passed an orchard with a mud wall around it. There was a smell of orange blossom, after rain.

A boy was walking beside me. He and a girl exchanged a fleeting glance. She was riding behind her mother on a camel, but the camel was moving faster . . . and so we went on to Persepolis.

Passing Persepolis I looked at the fluted columns, the porticoes, lions, bulls, griffins; the sleek metallic finish of the stone, and the line on line of megalomanic inscription: 'I . . . I . . . I . . . The King . . . The King . . . burned . . . slew . . . settled . . .'

My sympathies were with Alexander the Great for burning it.

Again I tried to get the Qashqai boy to look. Again he shrugged. Persepolis might have been made of matchsticks for all he knew or cared – and so we went on up to the mountains.[43]

Chatwin also saw the irony of the modern city of tents, ordered by the Shah of Iran as part of the celebrations of 2,500 years of Persian culture, which were to be held later that summer. This tented camp, part of the last Persianesque nomadic hurrah before the Shah was toppled by the Islamic Revolution, had been created not by Iranians but by the House of Jansen, a Parisian interior design company. Inside the tents, staff from Maxim's of Paris served champagne, caviar and exquisite imported delicacies to a crowd of global celebrities, political leaders and royalty, all come to celebrate the Shah, while many Iranians struggled with poverty. 'I . . . I . . . I . . .' Chatwin thought as he passed the ancient platform, 'The King . . . The King . . .'

To Chatwin, Persepolis spoke of self-aggrandisement and legitimisation, but I think the most striking aspect of the ruins – especially in relation to remains of other ancient cities – is how unlike a city they are. And unlike a temple. Herodotus explained this away by noting that 'the setting up of statues, temples and altars is something very alien to them [the Persians] – so much so, in fact, that they regard the entire practice as idiocy.'[44] But if no specific temple has been identified on the platform of Persepolis, no evidence of sacrifice, of gullies for blood to run, that might be because building the platform was in itself a sacred act and the entire place was sacred space. The platform was a stage for the king to perform his own renewal each spring, confirming that he was chosen by gods, and affirming his sovereignty over the twenty-seven subject nations or tribes, each of whom sent representatives bearing gold, horses, linen and other tributes.

As well as being a stage, as Chatwin recognised, Persepolis was a statement of power, for it reaffirmed the empire in its fusion of art and architectural styles and symbols drawn from Egypt to the Caspian Sea and across to the Fertile Crescent. Persepolis was a celebration in stone of the diversity of Persian imperial culture and that would have ensured its destruction, even as the imperial cities of Babylon and Susa were spared, because Alexander would have recognised its significance just as he would have understood the sanctity of the Persepolis platform – before beginning his campaign in the East, he had sacrificed to Zeus at Dion, a similar platform-sanctuary on the lower slopes of Mount Olympus. In an age when meaning was most eloquently and persuasively expressed in symbol, by destroying Persepolis Alexander announced the passing of the Achaemenids and their old world order.

But while the master of the new world could destroy symbols, he could not destroy the nomadic world. Its values and its people lived on and they were creating an empire not so very far away from Persepolis.

We Have No Cities

At the same time as the Medes and Fars were spreading across the Iranian plateau, around the ninth century BCE, when the great Zhou dynasty was ruling China and the Etruscans were emerging in Italy, another tribe from the steppes first appeared in the Near East. The Scythians built no imperial centres, had no *polis* and preferred to live lightly on the move. But that does not mean they had no empire.

Across the settled regions, it was rumoured that their children could ride horses before they could walk and knew how to draw a bow and shoot an arrow as instinctively as Roman or Chin children knew how to pull wheeled toys or spin tops. As the second-century BCE Chinese historian Sima Qian wrote, 'The little boys start out by learning to ride sheep and shoot birds and rats with a bow and arrow, and when they get old, they shoot foxes and hares which are used for food.'[45] By adulthood they were killers on horseback, stringing scalps on their belts or bridles as proof of their prowess. Where people were valued according to the number of people they killed, whether men or women, whether they rode east or west, there would be bloodshed and misery. They were every citizen's nightmare and yet we do not even know what they called themselves.

Their name Scythian is an Indo-European word connected to shepherds, but it is a catch-all, in the way that Persian or Greek or Indian encompasses a range of once distinct peoples. In this case it describes an alliance of tribes who lived beyond the Black and Caspian seas and included the Sarmatians and Massagetae, Royal Scythians, Sakas and many others. What they and their contemporaries further east, including the Xiongnu, had in common was a steppe homeland that was alive with spirits, across which they roamed with slow, heavy-wheeled carts, driving horses, cattle and sheep in search of pasture. Which is to say they were nomads. These migratory tribes had many other things in common: they tattooed their bodies, wore leather clothes, fashioned exquisite gold jewellery to decorate themselves and their horses, and carried swords, spears and composite bows. If burials are a measure, then Scythian women enjoyed both status and influence. They were animists who worshipped the sky god, whose beliefs roamed across the field of the sky and who considered fire, earth, air and water as sacred. They fermented alcohol from mare's milk and got drunk on it and on wine – 'drunk as a Scythian' was a common jest in ancient Athens, where to have a taste for undiluted wine was described as 'doing a Scythian' – although it is not clear whether they enjoyed getting drunk for the fun of it or as part of a sacred ritual. They also used hemp/cannabis, which they burned on a brazier in a small tent, filling the place with smoke and howling with delight as they got high. But this too was probably ritualistic.[46] Their shamans were transvestites whose drug habits allowed them to cross to the other side of consciousness, from where they delivered oracles in a falsetto shout. Very little in their wild way of living or in their wilder world related to the Greeks or Persians to their west, or the Han Chinese in the east, all of whom considered them barbarians. But what if they were no more barbaric than anyone else of that time?

Scythians first appear in the histories in 612 BCE, when they joined the Medes and Babylonians to sack the great city of Nineveh and bring down the Assyrian Empire. But what drew these steppe people south into Mesopotamia was not just the age-old warrior-baits, the promise of glory and the lure of loot. The weather was changing, and the drying out of the steppe forced nomads and their herds to spill into the surrounding lands, each group pushing those in front of them onwards in search of pasture. These local shifts happened at the same time as a larger seismic shift across Eurasia. Between 800 and 200 BCE, Persia, Greece, Rome, Mauryan India and Han China all emerged as imperial powers. It is widely agreed that the migration of nomads provided a catalyst for the rise, and in some cases the sudden fall, of these empires. But what about the vast landmass between Rome, Greece, Persia, India and China? It seems very likely that this expanse of the central Eurasia steppes, between the Danube river and Caspian Sea in the west and the Great Wall of China in the east, was itself some kind of diverse alliance, an empire for lack of any other title. We could call it the Scythian Empire.

One problem with calling the vast nomadlands an empire lies in our understanding of what constitutes an empire. The common assumption is that they – and lesser kingdoms, such as the newly formed Judah and Israel – revolved around capital cities and a central administration. Pataliputra, Chang'an (Xi'an), Athens and Rome all had walls and armies to protect them from what lay beyond their self-defined limits, anticipating the blunt statement from a twenty-first-century American president that 'if you don't have Borders, you don't have a Country'.[47] But while settled people believed borders and walls were essential for protecting their kingdoms, and cities were equally essential to focus power and administration, nomads knew – as we know in our own time – that they are not good for mobility. A lack of mobility, of easy cross-border movement, is as bad for nomads as it is for traders, pilgrims and all other migrants.

This span of six hundred years, beginning around 800 BCE, also saw the shaping of texts and ideas that remain essential in our own time. They emerged in part as a response to the need to regulate the behaviour of the peoples of empire, of the wall-protectors and of those who lived within. The Edicts of Ashoka carved on pillars and rock walls across south Asia, the Torah/Old Testament translated into Greek in Alexandria, the diverse and lasting works of Socrates and Plato, Aristotle, Confucius and Gautama Buddha were all created during this six-hundred-year period. Among this extraordinary outpouring, the clearest expression of how life *should* be conducted within walls and borders was put down by ancient Greeks, which seems appropriate as they also gave us words to describe the urban experience, many of them derived from the word *polis* (the *city* but also the city-state), such as politics, polity, polite and police. These were rarely used in relation to nomads, whose world was often presented – by those who lived within walls and borders – as existing in opposition to the *polis*.

In one fundamental way at least, the nomadic world did occupy the opposite pole. However much it developed, nomadic culture remained almost entirely oral. There were obvious reasons for this mistrust of writing – texts needed to be transported, libraries were vulnerable, and words themselves risked being misunderstood or reinterpreted. Better put ideas into stories that could be told and retold across the empire and the ages.

Plato, born in Athens at a time when the city was politically volatile, expressed the values and requirements of the *polis* most clearly. Athens emerged from the mid-fifth-century BCE Persian War as the leader of the Greek alliance, but its prominence frustrated some of its partners, notably Sparta. This resentment had sparked the Peloponnesian War, which was already underway when Plato was born in 424 BCE and was still flickering on thirteen years later when the democratic rulers of Athens were overthrown. The war only ended when Plato was twenty and with Athenian defeat. Another war against Sparta broke out nine years later and that, too, dragged on. Against this background of continual conflict, political disturbance and social disorder – and also as a response to the execution of Plato's teacher Socrates – Plato shaped his thoughts about the ideal society and the entity that sat at the heart of that society, an ideal city.

In his *Laws*, Plato imagines a conversation between an Athenian and some people from Crete who want to found a colony. The Athenian is quite specific as to how the new *polis* should be structured. For the perfect functioning of society, economy and politics, a city should be home to 5,040 people. With that many citizens, each family would have enough farmland to support themselves. Plato saw primogeniture as the best solution to the complexities of inheritance, with the elder son inheriting the parents' land. Other sons could be 'given' to families without a male heir. If there were too many landless males, they could be sent to found a new colony, presumably of 5,040.

Plato located his ideal city-state at the precise distance of 80 *stades*, about 9 miles, from the sea and for this reason: 'if the State was to be on the sea-coast, and to have fine harbours, and to be deficient in many products, instead of producing everything – in that case it would need a mighty saviour and divine lawgivers, if, with such a character, it was to avoid having a variety of luxurious and depraved habits.'[48] Access to the sea, said the philosopher, made 'men's souls knavish and tricky' and their city 'faithless and loveless'.[49] Luxury and depravity were the twin worms that brought decay to the city. As Plato lived in Athens, a city known for its sophistications, which was also less than half his recommended distance from the water, he was perhaps thinking about the city of his birth.

Plato also recognised the need for diversity, for Abel alongside Cain, and there was a role for nomads in his cities. Although their physical circumstances were diametrically opposed to those who lived within the *polis*, Plato's ideal city was not necessarily closed to them. Far from it. The philosopher knew from his own experiences that Greeks were always fighting with each other and therefore they needed outsiders to provide balance. But – and this is the crux of his laws – all aspects of city life must be controlled. Central control, regulation and law sit at the heart of his plan for a well-ordered society, with men on top, women and the natural world kept in their place. This and much else he considered to be things that Greeks (mostly) had and barbarian shepherds and goat-herders up on the mountains (mostly) did not. If, as Socrates and Plato argued so strongly, humans could only live a full and fulfilling life inside a city, then those who lived outside must be living lesser lives (unless, of course, they were gods who, as we know, lived on Mount Olympus).

Nomads, *barberoi*, were by implication 'lesser people' living unfulfilled lives beyond the city. Their environment was remote, difficult to access and extreme in landscape and climate. They were rarely literate and, in Plato's view, lacked both arts and industry, the two great achievements to have flourished within the city's walls. And yet, just as would happen during the Industrial Revolution and in our own time, while these achievements pleased the mind, there was a nagging fear that the cost for these advances included the sacrifice of an older and purer way of life, a life lived in the beauty of the natural world. For this reason, as with William Blake at the start of the nineteenth century and Bruce Chatwin in the twentieth, neither Socrates nor Plato could resist looking wistfully beyond the city walls towards the lost wilderness, to *arcadia* and our earlier, purer, innocent state of being.

Arcadia was a real province in the Greek Peloponnese, a lush unwalled region where people lived more in harmony with nature. At the same time it was a mythical place that harked back to a lost Golden Age. While both places were home to nomads, pastoralists moving their herds according to the cycle of seasons, mythical Arcadia was home to Pan, the half-goat god of shepherds and of the wild mountains and from whom the Greeks derived the word panic. But what if that other world was not so lawless, was not the realm of panic and pandemonium? What if there was an arcadian empire, not on mainland Greece but further east, on the steppes, a realm of Pan that was as large and powerful as that of the settled Persians or Greeks, of the Romans or Chinese? Plato would have ridiculed the idea. An empire of nomads, of *barberoi*. To him, the words were irreconcilable. But Herodotus, who composed the *Histories* around the time of Plato's birth, saw things differently.

Scythia

The first Scythians to appear in Herodotus's *Histories* would have confirmed his audience's worst fears, for the tale he tells, set in the 580s BCE, opens with a band of nomads 'caught up in some tribal blood-feud . . . skulking into Median territory'.[50] The king of the Medes offers them asylum and to repay the king's hospitality, the Scythians go hunting. Each day they return with game for the king's table. After a while, the king is so impressed by their prowess that he decides to send some Median youths with the Scythians, to learn their language and acquire some of their skills in the saddle and with the bow. Then one day the nomads return with no meat. Seeing they have brought nothing for his table, the king mocks their hunting skills. The following day the humiliated Scythians kill and butcher one of the Median youths, send the choice cuts to the king's table and ride on to Lydia before anyone realises what they are eating. Blood-feuders, child-butchers, skilled hunters; this is how Herodotus introduces us to nomads.

The most surprising aspect of this archetypal story is that it comes from someone who had first-hand experience of nomads. Herodotus had collected some of his material on the Scythian doorstep, near the Dnieper river on the eastern shore of the Black Sea, where he had heard the Scythians' own version of their origins. They said they were descended from the mighty thunderer Zeus and the goddess of the Dnieper, but the Father of History was sceptical: 'I do not myself believe them,' he wrote, 'not when they make such a claim.'[51] From others on the Black Sea, he heard they were descended from Heracles and a creature who was woman from the buttocks up, snake below. It was from Heracles, these Greeks told Herodotus, that the hero's son Scythes received a bow and a belt with a golden cup hanging from the buckle. Yet another story, which Herodotus thought 'the most plausible to me', described the Scythians as nomads who had migrated from further east in Asia. Perhaps because of their own nomadic origins, Persians recognised the Scythians as a threat. Even though they seemed to want nothing more than to trade with the Persians, Cyrus, founder of the Persian Empire, King of Kings, Ruler of the Four Corners of the World and King of the Universe, could not leave them alone.

Cyrus had already conquered the Medes, had moved west across the Near East, and fought his way north to the Hellespont and east to the Indus and India. He had proved himself mighty in battle and savage in opposition, and had created the largest empire the world had seen. Cyrus had both Mede and Fars blood in him – both were nomadic tribes that had migrated from the Indo-European steppes – and he believed prosperity flowed from open trade and the free movement of people, from diversity and what we would call multi-culturalism, perhaps even universalism. His empire's borders were open and goods moved relatively easily between the Mediterranean and Mesopotamia, Persia and India. People migrated as well. It was Cyrus who allowed the people of Judah to return to Jerusalem to rebuild Solomon's temple, ending a half-century of weeping by the rivers of Babylon. Given his backstory, Cyrus's first approach to the Scythians should have been a friendly one. Instead, it was an invasion.

The Scythians he encountered were led by a woman, Queen Tomyris. The King of Kings sent the nomad queen an offer of marriage. Herodotus records that she 'knew full well that it was her kingdom rather than herself that was being wooed'.[52] When she rejected his offer, Cyrus ordered a bridge of boats to be built across the Jaxartes river (Syr Darya), intending to move an army across. While the bridge was under construction, Queen Tomyris urged the Persian king to abandon his campaign. 'Look after your own people,' she urged him, 'and I shall look after mine.' But she knew her words were wasted. 'Peace is the last thing you want – and so you are bound not to follow my advice.'[53]

Among Cyrus's entourage was Croesus, the King of Lydia. His name has since become a byword for unimaginable wealth, but at the time of Cyrus's northern expedition, that proverbial wealth had disappeared, Lydia had been absorbed into the Persian Empire and Croesus was part of the imperial entourage. Hearing the Scythian queen's message, Croesus suggested that Cyrus lay a trap for the Scythians by preparing a banquet of the finest food and wine and then withdrawing the main Persian army, leaving just a few non-combatants to serve the feast. When the Scythians saw what was happening, they killed the Persian servants, feasted and drank too much – drunk as Scythians again – and fell asleep. This proved Croesus's point that nomads were stupid: why else would they refuse to live a settled life? With their enemies asleep, the Persians returned, killed many and took others captive, including the Scythian commander, Queen Tomyris's son Spargapises.

When Tomyris heard that her son had been taken, she was incandescent with rage. The message she sent, according to Herodotus, opened by insulting Cyrus and ended with a threat: if anything happened to her son, 'ravening blood-drinker though you may be, yet I will glut your taste for blood'.[54] Inevitably, something did happen. Spargapises woke from his wine-induced sleep, discovered that he had been taken captive and demanded to be released from the chains. As soon as this was done, he took a sword and killed himself. No half measures with nomads, Herodotus suggests.

When the queen heard that her son was dead, she went to war. Herodotus tells us that the battle was 'the most terrible that has ever been fought between two rival barbarian peoples'. The tactics, 'thanks to my own researches, are a matter, not of opinion, but of record'.[55] First, bronze-tipped arrows darkened the sky. Then spears were lowered and sharp daggers drawn. The Scythians, wearing gold helmets, wielding bronze double-headed axes and drawing their deadly bows, slew the greater part of the Persian army. Cyrus, who had won the Persians their empire and ruled as King of Kings for twenty-nine years, was among the casualties.

When the fighting was done, with the field a mass of blood, bone and twisted armour, Queen Tomyris appeared. She was carrying a large wineskin filled with human blood. When the body of Cyrus was found his head was severed and brought to the queen. Herodotus quotes her as saying, 'I threatened then that I would glut your thirst for blood. Now – have your fill', and she plunged the head into the blood-filled wineskin.*

So to Herodotus's first view of these migratory Asian herders as child-butchers and skilled hunters, we must add that they were regicides. Unlike the Spartans, who died gloriously at Thermopylae, the Scythians were also capable of defeating the massed armies of the greatest empire the world had known. Yet we still know very little about them and most of what we do know relates to warfare.

More would be revealed during the reign of Darius, who seized power eight years after the death of Cyrus's son Cambyses. Darius expanded the Persian Empire to its greatest extent and built his great monument at Persepolis. On the walls at Persepolis, a Scythian is shown alongside other tribes and nations who bent the knee to the great king. A Mede usher takes the Scythian by the hand towards the royal audience hall. This would seem to confirm the statement Darius had had carved onto the mountainside at Bisotun, overlooking the Persian Royal Road (and found in more portable form around the empire, including in Aswan, Egypt, where fragments were recently uncovered): 'With an army I went off to Scythia, after the Scythians who wear the pointed cap. The Scythians went from me. When I arrived at the river, I crossed it then with all my army. Afterwards, I smote the Scythians exceedingly.' End of story. Except it is not.

Something about this Scythian carved on the wall at Persepolis makes him stand out from the crowd paying homage to the King

---

* This scene inspired the seventeenth-century Flemish painter Peter Paul Rubens among others.

of Kings and I stared at it for some time trying to work out what it was. It is not that he wears a tall pointed cap with earflaps, nor that he has long hair, a thick beard, a tunic and the trousers of a horse-rider. It is that unlike all other 'foreigners' paying homage at Persepolis, the Scythian is allowed to enter the royal presence bearing arms. A sword hangs from his belt and he has slung a quiver of arrows across his shoulders. This could be a tacit acknowledgement that, in spite of Darius's pronouncement on the mountainside at Bisotun, the great king had not conquered the Scythians. At the very least, it is recognition of Scythian might.

Herodotus was born thirty years after Darius's invasion of Scythia, but he is our best guide to this as to so much of the period. He relates how Darius had a bridge constructed over the Hellespont, which he crossed with an army of 700,000 seasoned fighters. His arrival into Europe was impressive, but it was also slow and that gave the Scythians time to confer with the Taurians, Boudinians, Sauromatians, Neurians and many other allies, all of whom agreed that they should avoid fighting a pitched battle with the vast Persian army, which they were bound to lose. Their plan was to stay out of Persian range. Herodotus, in a passage of great significance to understanding migratory people, almost an abiding definition, explains how they arranged themselves so that no invader could ever overtake them, unless they wished to be caught:

> Rather than build cities or walls, they all carry their homes around with them on wagons, practise their archery from horseback and depend for their living on cattle rather than the fruits of the plough. How, then, could they fail to defy every effort made to conquer them or pin them down?[56]

Soon after Darius's army reached Scythia, his scouts spotted two enemy divisions. When the Scythians withdrew, the Persians gave chase, and continued to give chase through Scythia, through the lands of the Melanchlaeni and those of the Agathyrsians. Eventually a frustrated Darius sent a swift herald on horseback after the Scythian king Idanthyrsus. Either stand and fight, Darius commanded, or send the traditional tribute of earth and water, 'my due as your master'.[57]

Idanthyrsus replied that he had 'never before fled any man because I was afraid of him – and I am certainly not fleeing you now. In fact, I am doing nothing at the moment that I was not in the habit of doing in times of peace.'

Picture the scene as the messenger returned to his master, the great Persian emperor seated in pomp on his throne, his feet on a footstool above a magnificent carpet. Around him, a throng of advisers, white-robed, omen-reading *magi* and bronze-clad Immortals. Perhaps he stroked his generous, pointed beard as he heard word from the Scythians. Perhaps he looked to the skies in the belief that the god Ahura Mazda was there to advise him, but no sign is known to have appeared.

Somewhere ahead of him was a horde of Scythian fighters in leather trousers, heavy jackets and peaked caps, swords hanging from their belts, quivers of arrows over their shoulders. It should have been a straightforward conquest, a clash of armies, another glorious victory for the Persians. But all was forestalled by this clash of very different cultures and of assumptions, because although the Persians, like the Scythians, were essentially nomadic, they had acquired some of the trappings of a settled empire.

Why, Darius wished to know, would the nomads not face the Persians in battle?

To this the Scythian leader replied, 'We have no cities – nothing that we need worry you might capture. We have no crops – nothing that we need worry you might destroy.'[58]

The Scythians understood the Persians, but Darius seems not to have understood the nature of Scythian life. Or at least he seems not to have considered that he might be facing a rival confederation of tribes that was, by any other name, a nomad empire.

The Scythians now had the upper hand because although the Persians were nomadic at heart – Darius had had blue, the colour of the Persian pastoralist, woven into his ceremonial robe out of respect for his nomadic heritage – the Achaemenid idea of conquest was to defeat an army and capture a city. Without a capital to sack, Darius needed to find a way of drawing the Scythians into battle. The only way to do that would be to desecrate the one thing the Scythians would fight for, the tombs of their ancestors.

Idanthyrsus had warned Darius about this. 'Attack those graves', Herodotus records him as saying, 'and you will soon discover whether we are fighters or not.'[59] Darius may not have known what was contained in the tombs, or perhaps he was not prepared to anger the Scythian gods. But Herodotus knew about them for he tells us that a Scythian king was buried in grand state, a room being excavated for him which was panelled with wood and in which was placed 'a choice selection of all his other possessions and some golden cups'. The king's cup-bearer, groom, cook, steward, messenger, one of his concubines and some horses were strangled and laid nearby and the whole burial was then covered with a huge barrow.

Archaeologists have, over the past three hundred years, corrected some of that description, added new facts and more details. Huge kurgan barrow graves have been found across what might have been the Scythian alliance, from the Caspian Sea to Mongolia, and all are arranged in a very similar way to those described in the *Histories* and not unlike the burial mound of Philip of Macedon, Alexander the Great's father, in Vergina, northern Greece. The royal Scythian mounds were circular and varied in complexity, one of the most impressive of which was found at Arzhan, east of the Altai Mountains, in the early 1970s. Built of stone and larchwood in the late ninth century BCE and over 120 metres across the centre, its seventy chambers contained the remains of 15 humans and 160 horses. Later tombs, such as the sixth- to fourth-century BCE tombs at Kuban, on the Black Sea, contained more; one had 360 horses included in the burial, suggesting the symbolic nature of these extraordinary tombs.

Whether out of respect for the ancestors or for Scythian deities, Darius did not desecrate the grave-mounds. Instead, his vast Persian army chased the Scythians through what is now Ukraine and southern Russia until they discovered what Napoleon and Hitler were to learn: long marches across this vast land wear down even the best-trained armies and stretch supply lines dangerously thin. Eventually, frustrated by being on the move without a major military confrontation and fearing his growing vulnerability, Darius abandoned the chase and ordered a line of forts to be built on the west bank of the River Don. These would serve as a frontier and should have allowed him to annex western Scythia where Ionians, Scythians and

easy to imagine the father of history shrouded by lamp smoke, surrounded by a swirl of people, hearing the clink of the town's curious dolphin-shaped bronze coins, smelling the sea in front of him, a very foreign world to his back. He has come to this meeting place between east and west to listen to Greek traders, who are there for the horses, leather, wool, carpets, metals – especially bronze – and perhaps also for the Scythian shamans, whose rituals informed Greek Orphic mysteries. Herodotus has come to trade in stories and, like a twenty-first-century news reporter, he busies himself sifting and sorting details from conversations, and noting his own impressions of the place and the people he meets. Then he produces lists: there are tribes he has never met and perhaps not even heard of until now, such as the Androphagi, whose name translates as 'man eaters', and there are landscapes beyond the sea and the great river that he has never seen. But because he went to Olbia all those millennia ago, we can reach back through time and across the steppes to glimpse ancient nomads in the east.

Some of what this early historian tells us is clearly fantastic and in places even he is aware of that. The Iyrcae, he records, were a tribe who hunted by climbing trees, waiting for wild animals to approach, while their horses and hunting dogs lay below, flat on their bellies, ready to give chase. But some of what he writes is not so improbable. What he calls Scythian country is level and rich in deep-soiled grasses, but beyond that there are mountains, presumably the Altai, which divide the east and western steppes between the Gobi Desert and Siberia and today straddle China, Russia, Kazakhstan and Mongolia. Herodotus heard tell that the people of these mountains 'are all of them bald from birth'.[61] They were also said to have snub noses, long chins, wear leather trousers and heavy coats, as we know Scythians did, and speak a language unlike others. 'Each man lives under a tree,' Herodotus recorded, and 'when winter comes, he wraps white, waterproof felt around it.' Clearly these were nomads, living in *gers* or yurts. Beyond their lands was, as far as the critical Greek listener in the fifth century BCE was concerned, beyond knowing. He said the mountains were impassable, although the bald nomads had told him that the people who lived there had feet like goats. Beyond them, stranger still, were people who slept half the year. 'This', Herodotus tells us, 'I find impossible to accept.'

Had he visited Olbia a few hundred years later, after Alexander the Great had destroyed Persepolis, fought his way past the Scythians and into Afghanistan, when China was beginning to see the benefits of peace and prosperity and while Rome was aggressively expanding its power and influence around the Mediterranean, he would have discovered that his world was connected with that of the Grand Historian of ancient China. Perhaps he would have met people from beyond the Altai Mountains and heard stories from people who had been there. Perhaps he would have met Xiongnu nomads, or traders from the Han Empire, or even Gan Ying, the Chinese emperor's envoy, who reported that the Romans 'always wanted to send envoys to Han [China], but Anxi [Parthia], wishing to control the trade in multi-coloured Chinese silks, blocked the route to prevent [the Romans] getting through'.[62]

And if that had happened, then Herodotus would have discovered for himself that people east of the Altai Mountains did not have goat-feet and nor did they sleep six months at a time. Instead, he would have found a world of constant movement and understood the similarities between the Scythians, whom he did meet, and the Xiongnu, who may, at some point, have been part of the confederation of tribes that formed a great nomadic alliance. He would also have discovered how the settled peoples of China and of the Mediterranean had similar negative responses to these migratory people who lived between them.

Long before the rise of the Han dynasty (from the second century BCE), people south of the Yellow river complained about migrants threatening their borders and their way of life. We know this thanks to the work of Sima Qian (Ssu-ma Ch'ien), the Grand Historian of China, in the first century BCE. Nomads, he recorded, were 'a source of constant worry and harm to China'.[63] They had also been a source of harm to him personally.

Little is known about Sima Qian's life beyond what he tells us himself – he shares this and much else with Herodotus. His great work, the *Shih Chi (Shiji)* or *Records of the Grand Historian*, completed around the end of the 80s BCE, can be read as a companion to

Herodotus's *Histories*, for like the Greek, Sima recorded the things he saw and heard as faithfully as was possible at that time. But the two works have different scopes: Herodotus sets out to explain the circumstances and events of the war between the Persians and Greeks; Sima's ambition is to write a history of China from its early beginnings to his own time. Sima would be my guide to Chinese nomads as Herodotus had been to Greeks, Persians and Scythians.

Sima owed both his position and his project to his father, who was Grand Historian and Court Astrologer before him. His official duties mostly involved divination, and recording the decisions of the emperor and his council. Had he restricted himself to his duties, he might have fared better, but then there was trouble with nomads.

In 99 BCE, a force of Xiongnu attacked northern China. There was nothing surprising about this – nomads had been harassing the border for centuries. But this time Wu, the Han emperor, decided to strike back and sent an army under General Li Ling. The expedition was rich in optimism but poorly planned. Without sufficient supplies or backup, Li marched his 5,000 men for a month in search of nomad raiders. When they neared the Altai Mountains, far beyond the borders of Han China, the general sent a messenger back to the emperor with a grossly exaggerated description of his expedition and of the successful engagements he had fought against the nomads. Soon after sending the report, the Han came face to face with the main Xiongnu force – 110,000 of them according to one report – and the clash was as bloody as the outcome was inevitable. The nomads suffered losses, but only 400 of the 5,000 Han soldiers made it back across the Chinese border.

When news reached the palace in Chang'an, Sima wrote that the emperor 'could find no flavour in his food and no delight in the deliberations of his court'. When it was subsequently learned that instead of death in battle, or suicide in defeat, the general had surrendered and was now a prisoner of the nomads, the emperor, who was volatile at the best of times, erupted.

It was at this point that Sima stepped out of line and spoke up for the disgraced general. In his biography, Sima explains that he and General Li had never been very close. 'Our likes and dislikes lay in different directions; we never so much as drank a cup of wine together or shared the joys of intimate friendship.'[64] So when he spoke up and called the general one of the finest men in the empire, he did so out of conviction, not sentiment. But his comments were not taken the way he hoped and he was arrested for trying to deceive the emperor. He was tried, found guilty and sentenced to be castrated.

Sima seems to have had a knack for alienating people and this, along with the severity of the charge, might explain why no one at court spoke up in his defence. Nor did he have any family connections who could intervene, or a personal fortune to pay a bribe. When a report reached the court that General Li was now leading a force of nomad cavalry against his countrymen, it was clear there was no way around the sentence.

In cases of castration – as in hopeless military situations – a man was expected to commit suicide rather than submit and live with the shame. But Sima was not a common man and he did submit to the punishment. He then retired to what he calls the 'silkworm chamber', a warm, draught-free place where castration victims were left to recuperate or die. He emerged 'mutilated in body and living in vile disgrace' but with his writing talents and determination intact. Once free, he retreated from public life and resumed his *Records*, justifying his decision to live because 'I have things in my heart which I have not been able to express fully' and because it would be a greater shame 'to think that after I am gone my writings will not be known . . .'[65] Among them was the earliest detailed description of Xiongnu nomads.

This conflict between the settled and nomadic was not new. A century earlier, towards the end of the 200s BCE, Chinese soldiers had driven a force of nomads away from the border and chased them onto the Mongolian plateau. The earlier poets of *The Book of Odes* described it this way:

> *We smote the barbarians of the north.*
> *We struck the Xianyun* [Xiongnu]
> *And drove them to the great plain.*
> *We sent forth our chariots in majestic array*
> *And walled the northern region.*

The wall mentioned here was the first version of what became the Great Wall of China. Its construction and the increased Chinese activity had unexpected consequences to the west. Until this point, the Xiongnu had been a loose confederation of migrating tribes. But faced with growing Han pressure, they emerged with a more defined structure, a clear leadership succession and with different groups designated to the cardinal points of the compass and identified by different colours.

What I find striking is how many similarities there are between Sima's nomads, who originated in the Altai Mountains, and Herodotus's Scythians. 'They wander from place to place following the grass to herd their animals. The majority of their animals are horses, cattle, sheep . . . They have no walled cities where they stay and cultivate the fields, but each does have his own land.'[66] They honoured and made offerings to the unseen forces that shaped their lives, to heaven and earth, to the ghosts and spirits of their ancestors. They respected the elements of the natural world. They cast bronze among other metals. They spoke many languages, including something similar to Scythian Indo-European. And as with the Scythians, we do not know what they called themselves – it certainly would not have been Xiongnu, a Chinese word that translates as 'illegitimate offspring of slaves'.[67]

The Xiongnu were ruled by a hereditary king, a *shan-yu*, and Sima tells a story of a leader called Tuman. Although succession usually went to the elder son, Tuman wanted his favourite younger son to succeed him. To get around this problem, he sent his elder son, Modu, as a hostage to a rival nomad tribe in the north-west. Tuman then attacked his rivals, expecting that Modu would be killed in the fracas. Instead, the son escaped with one of the enemy tribe's best horses and his father rewarded this bravery by giving Modu command of 10,000 Xiongnu cavalry.

Modu trained them hard, treated them well and expected of them what a Scythian lord would expect of the *comitatus*, his band of brothers: unquestioning obedience, unswerving loyalty and the certainty of a common death. Modu put his men to the test by ordering them to shoot their arrows wherever he shot his; those who did not would be put to death. Modu aimed his first arrow at his favourite horse and some of his band followed suit; those who did not were killed. Next he aimed at his favourite wife and then at his father's favourite horse and again those who did not follow him were executed. Next, he aimed at his father and then rival family members and some unconvinced officials. When it was over, the coup was complete: the *comitatus* stood above all other bonds, any competition within the tribe had been eliminated and Modu was the new *shan-yu*.

Whatever the veracity of that particular story – and as with the Scythians, we have no account of this from the people involved – it is known that a leader called Modu did unite the tribes, harness nomadic power and, in spite of the Great Wall, expand Xiongnu trade and influence. He was helped by a string of high-level defections from Chinese royalty, generals and foot soldiers.

As with the Scythians at the other end of the steppes, Sima tells us that Xiongnu children were raised in the saddle to become formidable warriors. What he does not reveal is the more sophisticated social and political structure of the Xiongnu. The *Records* presents them as a single tribe, an ethnic group, but archaeology and recent genetics have revealed something very different: they were a complex grouping of different ethnicities who spoke a variety of languages and covered a huge swathe of Central Asia. Many were migratory pastoralists, others were farmers and some few even lived behind walls. All were bound by a sophisticated social and political system, which recognised the *shan-yu* as leader. This, it seems, was not a tribe, but an alliance of states in the process of becoming an empire.

The mounted Xiongnu became more than a match for the armies of the newly formed Han dynasty, as was clear in 200 BCE when the first Han emperor, Gaozu, led a huge force north to secure his borders. He engaged the Xiongnu at a place called Baideng, on the Inner Mongolia border, and was utterly defeated. He also almost lost his life when he and his escort became separated from the main body of his army. Modu would have taken him prisoner, perhaps even executed him, but in keeping with nomad tradition, he listened to his queen's suggestion that the emperor would be of more value if he was spared and allowed to return to Chang'an.

In the subsequent peace treaty, Emperor Gaozu recognised the Xiongnu as more than a bunch of barbarous thieving herders. They would now be treated as the equals of the Han and the *shan-yu* would receive annual gifts of silk, grain, wine, gold and iron. With the first shipment, Gaozu also sent his eldest daughter to marry the *shan-yu*. In return, Modu agreed not to attack China. Over the next sixty years, the Han tribute continued to grow and ever-greater quantities of silk and grain were shipped west until as much as 7 per cent of China's output was handed over as 'gifts' to the nomads. By then, the balance of power had tilted, as is obvious in a message from a Han official who had defected to the Xiongnu: 'Just make sure', he warned Han officials, as Abel might have threatened Cain, 'that the silks and grain stuffs you bring the Xiongnu are the right measure and quality, that's all . . . If there is any deficiency or the quality is not good, then when the autumn harvest comes we will take our horses and trample all over your crops!'[68]

With each gift, each exchange of pleasantries, Modu became bolder – as well he might for he was the leader of an empire that extended thousands of miles west of the Chinese wall. Five years later, Modu was sent another imperial wife along with the annual tribute from Chang'an, but this did not stop him writing directly to the emperor's mother, the Dowager Empress Lü. The letter is remarkable for its temerity, but even more so for giving voice to a man who has been seen both as nomad hero and a barbaric savage. 'I am a lonely widowed ruler,' he writes, ignoring the arrival of the second noble wife for him from Chang'an, 'born amidst the marshes and brought up on the wild steppes in the land of cattle and horses. I have often come to the border wishing to travel in China. Your majesty is also a widowed ruler living a life of solitude. The both of us are without pleasures and lack any way to amuse ourselves. It is my hope', the nomad *shan-yu* concludes, 'that we can exchange that which we have for that which we are lacking.'[69]

That last phrase was understood in Chang'an to be an offer of marriage. The prospect of the warlord from beyond the wall joined in union with the mother of the Han emperor and the effective power behind his throne, may have amused the nomad, but the empress was enraged and is reported to have wanted to send an army to punish the Xiongnu for their lack of respect. Instead, she wrote a letter that is stunning for its abasement: 'My age is advanced and my vitality weakening. The *shan-yu* must have heard exaggerated reports. I am not worthy of his lowering himself.' Then comes the plea: 'But my country has done nothing wrong, and I hope that he will spare it.'[70]

With all due respect to the empress, perhaps she had not understood. When Modu wrote of exchanging 'that which we have for that which we are lacking', it was likely to have been trade, not marriage, that he was proposing. But the Han wished to keep the nomads away from the border, and it would be difficult to maintain a buffer zone if there were trading posts. So the Xiongnu continued to raid across the border and take what they felt the Han were denying them. In the thirty-third year of his reign, in 176 BCE, Modu wrote again, this time to the emperor. 'All the people who live by drawing the bow are now united into one family,' he explained in clear reference to a Xiongnu imperial alliance, an empire, 'and the entire region of the north is at peace. Thus I wish now to lay down my weapons, rest my soldiers, and turn my horses to pasture . . .'[71] But as the Chinese statesman Chia I explained to his emperor, the nomads wanted more than peace to pasture their horses. 'It is the border markets which the Xiongnu need most badly.' Chia, rejecting the Han instinct to stay away from foreigners, thought it was a good idea. Open border markets and trading posts, he counselled the emperor, and offer them as much raw meat, wine, stews, cooked rice and barbecues as they can eat. Set up taverns that can serve a few hundred Scythians at a time and before long they will crave Chinese food more than they crave a fight.

It was a shrewd assessment, shrewdest in its recognition of the nomadic need to trade, for like almost all mobile people, the Xiongnu's stock was time-sensitive. They needed to shift the horses and cattle they had raised just as much as they needed to acquire rice and grain before winter set in and just as much as the Han needed Xiongnu goods.

The Han agreed to open markets with one condition, that there would be no trade in weapons. To get around this, Modu looked west and took control of the Gansu Corridor and Tarim Basin, where Xiongnu traders were able to exchange their own animal products, and silks, porcelain and other luxuries bought from China, for iron and weapons. If it did not exist before, then this was the beginning of what we know as the Silk Roads.

Inspired by the success of this nomadic trade, the Emperor Wu sent some of his own people to Central Asia. He had two main reasons for his decision, to break Chinese dependence on Xiongnu horses, and to make contact with the Yuezhi, a nomadic tribe who had been pushed west by the Xiongnu. The Han emperor hoped these nomads would join him to fight their common enemy. A young gentleman of the court was chosen to lead this delicate mission.

Zhang Qian left imperial Chang'an in 138 BCE with an entourage of a hundred men. It is a sign of the Han's lack of experience in planning this sort of expedition that Zhang was immediately captured by the Xiongnu. He was held for ten years, during which time he took a Xiongnu wife. When he finally managed to escape, he did not return home, but continued on his way and eventually made contact with the Yuezhi, but found them settled and unwilling to fight. Having reached what is now Afghanistan, Zhang began his journey back to China, but was recaptured by the Xiongnu and held for a further two years. When he eventually returned to Chang'an, thirteen years after his departure, Emperor Wu listened with interest to his stories from Central Asia, of the many 'great states rich in unusual products whose people cultivated the land and made their living in much the same way as the Chinese. All these states, he was told, were militarily weak and prized Han goods.'[72]

Disappointed by the failure of their military alliance against the Xiongnu, but tempted by the possibilities of trade with these 'great states', the Han emperor sent Zhang on a second mission. This time he left with 300 men, 10,000 sheep, many horses and a commodity that was sought after across second-century BCE Asia and around the Mediterranean: bolts of Chinese silk. Zhang only travelled as far as the Fergana Valley (Tajikistan), but his envoys reached the Bactrians (Afghans) and Sogdians (Uzbeks). When he finally rode back through the great stone gates of Chang'an in 116 BCE, he brought news of a world previously unknown to the Chinese. He told of lands of many wonders, of the thousands of horsemen the Parthian king sent to greet his delegation, of the 'heavenly horses' of the Fergana Valley, which, as Sima mentions in his *Records*, 'the emperor [Wu] had divined by the Book of Changes and been told that "divine horses are due to appear" from the northwest'.[73] He thought the Bactrians were poor soldiers but excellent traders. He told of a people called the Shendu (Indians) who lived in a hot, damp country along a great river (the Indus) and who rode elephants into battle, and of Persians, who were nomads. He brought alfalfa seeds, grown as horse fodder, and other exotic produce.

For his troubles, Zhang Qian was honoured by the emperor and is revered in China today in the way that Marco Polo and Christopher Columbus are in the West. But the most important thing Zhang brought back was neither a map nor exotic produce, it was the idea of the benefits of diversity and interaction, that China would benefit by trading across Central Asia and into Western markets. The Han had always believed that China *was* the civilised world, that those who lived beyond the borders were abandoned by heaven, so there had been no reason for them to stray beyond their wall. Now they were prepared to go west.

When Modu wrote to Dowager Empress Lü suggesting that the Xiongnu and Han become trading partners, the Han Empire stretched from the Korean peninsula and the Yellow Sea in the north, to the South China Sea near what is now Hanoi in Vietnam. The Roman Republic, with the conclusion of the Third Macedonian War in 168 BCE, included much of Italy, Spain, Sicily, Sardinia and Corsica as well as Illyria, the Dalmatian coast and Macedonia, where they had just brought to an end the dynasty founded by Alexander the Great's general Antigonus. The Parthians ruled ancient Mesopotamia and Persia. These and other empires and ancient kingdoms we know about through their own chronicles or those of their adversaries, as well as through the monuments they left behind. We know about Carthage, about the Kushan Empire, and Cleopatra and her Egyptians, who were absorbed into the Roman Empire in 30 BCE. But we know little about the empires of the Xiongnu and their western 'twins' the Scythians.

At the height of Modu's power, in the second century BCE, the Xiongnu controlled, directly or indirectly, all the territory from Manchuria to Kazakhstan, southern Siberia to Inner Mongolia, and to the Tarim Basin of what is now China's Xinjiang province. The Scythians, in spite of the incursions of Cyrus, Darius and Alexander, still occupied much of the land between the Black Sea and the Altai Mountains in Kazakhstan. We know that the Altai elite dressed in silk, trimmed their clothes with fur from cheetahs trapped in the Caspian forests, sat on carpets woven in Persia and looked into mirrors made in China. We know that the gold buckles and other elaborate decorations worn by Scythian and Xiongnu elites had the same designs and animal motifs. And we know that Roman glass, Persian textiles and Greek silver have been found in Xiongnu burials. All this tells us that the migratory world was trading goods between the Yellow river and the Persian Gulf long before the Han emperor had the idea of sending merchants down the Silk Roads to trade with Parthia, Persia or the Mediterranean.

Reference to the fabled Silk Roads conjures images of caravans of camels and horses skirting deserts, negotiating mountain passes and crossing steppes. But there was no single road or great highway that spanned ancient Eurasia in the way the Persian Royal Road had connected the Persian east with Mesopotamia. As the historian Peter Frankopan puts it, there was 'a network that fans out in every direction, routes along which pilgrims and warriors, nomads and merchants have travelled, goods and produce have been bought and sold, and ideas exchanged, adapted and refined'.[74] China stood at one end, the Mediterranean at the other. As their empires and power grew, so too did the demand for luxury goods. In Rome in the first century BCE, Chinese silk was so rare that only the ruling class could afford to wear it: if ordinary people had Chinese silk, it would have only been a small piece, worn perhaps as a decorative panel, like a medal. It was the same with pearls, rubies, emeralds and other eastern jewels. But demand expanded the market and encouraged traders to push along more of those conduits north and south of the Gobi Desert, until in the first century BCE, the trade was so vast that the Roman author Pliny the Elder launched a tirade against exotica and against the women who desired it:

> We have come now to see . . . journeys made to Seres [China] to obtain cloth, the abysses of the Red Sea explored for pearls, and the depths of the earth scoured for emeralds. They have even taken up the notion of piercing the ears as if it were too small a matter to

wear those gems in necklaces and tiaras unless holes were also made in the body into which to insert them . . . at the lowest computation, India and Seres and the [Arabian] peninsula together drain our empire of one hundred million sesterces every year. That is the price that our luxuries and our womankind cost us.[75]

According to some estimates, that was one half of a per cent of the GDP of the entire Roman Empire, spent on luxuries from the east.

Throughout the centuries of this trade between the Chinese and Roman empires, few Chinese were ever seen in Rome and few Romans in China. If they went, it was for a particularly significant moment as, for instance, during the reign of the Emperor Augustus, who came to power in 27 BCE. The Roman historian Florus, writing a century after the event, noted that

> even Scythians and Sarmatians sent envoys to seek the friendship of Rome. Nay, the Seres [Chinese] came likewise, and the Indians who dwelt beneath the vertical sun, bringing presents of precious stones and pearls and elephants, but thinking all of less moment than the vastness of the journey which they had undertaken, and which they said had occupied four years. In truth it needed but to look at their complexion to see that they were people of another world than ours.[76]

And in truth it needed but a closer look to recognise that these were private traders, not official missions: there are no records in Rome or China of an emperor sending officials to the Roman court and for good reason. It was considered too difficult. In 97 BCE, for instance, a Han general sent an envoy, Gan Ying, to the Mediterranean. Gan reached Mesopotamia, at that time part of the Parthian Empire. His westward travels ended at the Persian Gulf, where he was told he would need to board a boat to reach Rome and that the journey could take up to two years. The envoy decided, as most would, that it would be better to return home with the information he had gathered than to risk all on the fickle sea.

The mostly nomadic people of Central Asia knew otherwise. The Xiongnu and their western partners the Scythians understood the benefits to be had by linking the east and western worlds of Herodotus and Sima. Steppe people were the early drivers of the trade in luxury goods. The social bonds of people who lived inside walls were mostly local. But people of the steppes, whose need to migrate had led them to master horses and to invent wagons and chariots, had the habit of crossing vast distances. They knew how to organise themselves. They were comfortable with the unfamiliar. They could tolerate strange customs and found ways around indecipherable languages. To them, it was the Greeks, Romans, Chinese and even Persians, the people who had turned away from the natural world and lived behind walls, who were abandoned by heaven. Which is perhaps why heaven sent a *flagellum*, a flail, to punish them and why Romans had good reason to be anxious about what was coming from the east. By then, Pliny's complaint about the cost of 'our luxuries and our womankind' seemed absurd: Silk Roads trade was the least of the empire's problems.

449 CE

It was a two-week journey from the court at Constantinople to Serdica (Sofia). The men from the 'new Rome' of Constantinople were led by the emperor's ambassador Maximinus and escorted by two Huns, Flavius Orestes, the Hunnish king's secretary, and Edeko, the Hun ambassador to Constantinople. Between them, they carried

Emperor Theodosius II's hopes of finding a solution to the great problem from the east: Attila the Hun and his undefeated army of nomads. Theodosius hoped to keep Attila at bay with Roman gold – 7,000 pounds of it in the last shipment – at least until he finished building his walls around Constantinople.

Attila was a mighty warrior with his roots in the steppes, but he was no Achilles and he would not have said, as the Greek hero did, that 'life is not to be bought with heaps of gold'. Far from it. He had an empire to run, an army to pay and allegiances to maintain and all that required gold. Like a twenty-first-century conglomerate, he needed to achieve continuous expansion to survive; the more gold he acquired, the more power he could mobilise. This insatiable appetite was one reason why Theodosius's offer did not calm the Hun. The 7,000 pounds of gold was a fortune, but it was a fraction of the imperial income and Attila threatened war, again, if more gold was not sent. He also demanded the return of Huns who had defected to the Romans. To settle these issues, the Roman emperor had despatched high-ranking delegates and, with their departure, had set two very different plots in motion.

Ambassador Maximinus and his assistant Priscus were to discuss issues of concern to Attila, such as buffer zones and borders between the Roman and Hun empires, the location of cross-border markets that were vital to nomadic interests, the delivery of seventeen Hun defectors and the increased shipments of gold. Unknown to Maximinus or Priscus, their mission had another objective: Theodosius's eunuch minister had bribed Attila's ambassador, Edeko, to assassinate his master. Fifty pounds of gold was the blood price. In Constantinople, they watched the Romans and Huns ride north and hoped that the second scheme would be successful.

The journey had its moments, as for instance at Serdica, where the Roman envoys bought sheep and cattle, and ordered a feast to be prepared. They started by drinking, with the Romans toasting Theodosius. When the Huns saluted Attila, the Roman translator Vigilas commented that it was not proper to compare a man with a god. The Huns realised that the translator was referring to Theodosius, not Attila as god, and they became so angry that gifts of silk and pearls were brought to calm them. Their arrival at Naissus (Niš) was equally troubling and not just because the birthplace of the Emperor Constantine was now under Hun control. Six years earlier, Attila had sacked the place and killed almost all its inhabitants and it was still a scene of carnage. 'All towards the riverbank', Priscus noted, 'was full of the bones of men killed in the fighting.'[77] Early one morning they reached the Danube and their hearts sank because they had lost their bearings and thought they were seeing the sun rise in the west. This they took as a sign that 'portended unusual events'.[78] Were they fearful of their mission? Or were they anxious to be alive in an age when a nomad might be seen as a god?

For centuries, markets between the settled poles of the Chinese and Roman empires had helped maintain a kind of order in the world, even in the nomad world. Borders were open, roads were busy, and Hun and Goth traders, along with those from Scythia, Xiongnu, Persia, Parthia and elsewhere, carried merchandise and hopes for profit. Migrating nomads played a central part in this delicate balancing act, but they also increased the risk of trade disputes and outbreaks of violence in the Roman lands, given the differences in culture and outlook between the settled and migratory. As many as a third of the people in the Roman Empire lived in urban envir-onments and many of the remainder lived rooted lives. But when Rome struggled to feed its expanding population, as the empire's farmers pushed the boundaries of agricultural land into what had been grazing land, they found it expedient to cooperate with nomads.[79] Nomads thrived on the uplands, the poor lands, across steppes and desert fringes, but many of them also played a part in the empire's agriculture, both as labourers at harvest-time and because farmland benefited from sheep and goats grazing on the stubble of harvested fields. Rome also followed the Greek example and used nomad forces in some of their armed conflicts, particularly nomad cavalry as there was no great equestrian tradition among the Romans; Numidian riders in North Africa and Scythians and Sarmatians in Asia were happy to fight alongside each other.

But in the early fourth century CE, the climate changed both literally and metaphorically in ways that would transform the world. Winters became harsh and long, summers dry and hot. When rains failed across Eurasia, rivers ran low or dried up completely and the

Caspian Sea receded. As drought threatened famine, people across Eurasia moved in search of water for their crops, their animals and themselves.

For people used to living on the move, drought was a grave problem, but not impossible to overcome. Because they spent much of their lives migrating to find fresh pasture and new markets, nomads were better equipped to adjust to the changing climate than many settled people. But the distances tribes now needed to travel to find pasture or water were so great that many were forced to relocate. The Xiongnu moved into China as part of a rising tide of people washing past the Great Wall, heading east and south. But China had also been hit by drought and even the Yellow river, the 'mother of China', was running low. Famine was closing in so fast that the Jin emperor, Sima Chi, known as the 'Missing Emperor' for reasons that will become apparent, was considering moving his court out of the capital. The Xiongnu reached him first.

Under a *shan-yu* named Liu Cong, the steppe nomads over-whelmed the imperial army, captured the emperor and occupied his capital. At the New Year banquet of 313 CE, Liu Cong forced the emperor to serve him wine. When the emperor's entourage, the Jin princes and dukes, expressed outrage at this *lèse-majesté*, Liu Cong had them all poisoned. This might have been good for Liu Cong's stature, but trade dislikes uncertainty. News that a nomad had murdered the divinely chosen emperor of China travelled quickly along the roads of Eurasia, even to a lonely watchtower on the eastern end of the Gobi Desert, near the Jade Gates that marked the Chinese frontier. The winter had been harsh, the world cast in darkness. Now the emperor was dead and the Xiongnu rampant. When news reached them from the capital, the guards wondered what would they watch over now? And for whom? Unable to find a happy answer, they agreed to pack their bags, abandon their watch and leave the tower. In their hurry, they left behind the westbound mailbag and one of the letters in the bag was still lying where it had been left in 313 CE when it was discovered in 1899. The sheet of paper, folded in a brown silk envelope that was then covered in coarse cloth, was addressed to someone in Samarkand, 2,000 miles to the west. 'Sirs,' wrote the author to his trade masters, 'the last emperor, so they say, fled from Luoyang because of the famine, and fire was set to his palace and to the city, and the palace was burnt and the city [destroyed]. Luoyang (is) no more.'[80] Now the emperor was no more and no one was secure, not even the Xiongnu.

Millions moved west as well as east. Waves of migrants arrived off the Pontic–Caspian steppes into Europe with Bulgars, Avars, Pechenegs, Iasi among those who forced a crossing of the Volga, Don and Dnieper rivers. At each riverbank, the same sequence played out, with the tribe staying on the east bank until hunger, the force of numbers or a greater threat from behind pushed them across the rivers, ever westward. Many headed towards the Danube.

In the fourth century, neither the Eastern nor Western Roman Empires was equipped to resist or to accommodate the huge influx of migrants at their borders, and the stress of their arrival was felt in every aspect of life. In commerce, the flow of goods was interrupted. In religious matters, diversity, which had long been one of the strengths of the Roman empires, came under threat. In 313 CE, the year the Xiongnu killed the Jin emperor, Constantine, the Roman emperor, newly converted to Christianity, declared that 'it was proper that the Christians and all others should have liberty to follow that mode of religion which to each of them appeared best.'[81] But freedom of conscience was challenged by the huge influx of what most in the Roman Empire considered barbarians. As has happened in our own time with refugees and migrants moving north and west into Europe and the United States, there was a conservative backlash. Freedom of conscience, like freedom of movement, began to be seen as a weakness, paganism was banned, pagan temples closed and their revenues appropriated by the state. But there were other more immediately damaging consequences.

In 376 CE, 200,000 Goths were forced to cross the eastern Roman border at the River Danube. Goths had probably originally come from the Baltic region, but for the past couple of centuries they had been migrating around the Pontic–Caspian steppe, which might explain why some Roman writers confusingly refer to them as Scythians – to many of those writers, they were all barbarians. The Emperor Valens, who was campaigning against the Persians, had neither the focus nor the manpower to resist the Goth arrival, so he granted permission for them to cross the Danube and ordered that they settle in Thrace. But the sheer number of Goths led to problems similar to those we have seen during the twenty-first-century European migrant crisis. With a lack of infrastructure to accommodate them, local administrators were overwhelmed and local operators saw an opportunity to extort money in return for transport or supplies. As migrant groups became fragmented, families separated and food supplies ran short, the Goths rebelled, leading to a showdown at Adrianople, near modern-day Edirne in Turkey. The battle pitted 15,000 Goths against a Roman army of a similar size, led by the emperor himself. The Goths were victorious, the core army of the Eastern Roman Empire was crushed and Emperor Valens killed. Another emperor dead.

The tribe who forced the Goths across the Danube in 376 were Huns, nomads from the central Asian steppes. The Huns were certainly connected to and may have been a branch of the Xiongnu. Both tribes originated in the heart of Eurasia in the Altai Mountains. They used similar weapons, had similar state structures and there is even a strong etymological connection of the word Xiongnu to Hun. If there were distinctions, they would have been lost on the Goths, who were so terrified of the easterners they crossed into the Roman Empire. The Huns then followed.

There are no surviving Hunnish descriptions of the Romans, but Romans left many accounts of the Huns, the most famous being that of the fourth-century historian Ammianus. Edward Gibbon, writing fourteen hundred years later, would describe Ammianus as 'an accurate and faithful guide' and praised him for not 'indulging the prejudices and passions which usually affect the mind of a contemporary'.[82] One wonders whether Gibbon had actually read Ammianus because this is what the 'accurate' Roman had to say about Attila and his people.

> The people called Huns, barely mentioned in ancient records, live beyond the sea of Azof, on the border of the Frozen Ocean, and are a race savage beyond all parallel. At the very moment of birth the cheeks of their infant children are deeply marked by an iron, in order that the hair instead of growing at the proper season on their

faces, may be hindered by the scars; accordingly the Huns grow up without beards, and without any beauty. They all have closely knit and strong limbs and plump necks; they are of great size, and low legged, so that you might fancy them two-legged beasts.

Worse than their appearance was their way of life. Ammianus continued:

> They are all without fixed abode, without hearth, or lax, or settled mode of life, and keep roaming from place to place, like fugitives, accompanied by the wagons in which they live; in wagons their wives weave for them their hideous garments, in wagons they cohabit with their husbands, bear children, and rear them to the age of puberty. None of their offspring, when asked, can tell you where he comes from, since he was conceived in one place, born far from there, and brought up still farther away.

Ammianus's attack on the Huns even extended to the way they dressed and the food they ate, offering what might be the first mention of *steak tartare* when he described how they soften raw meat 'by placing it between their own thighs and the backs of their horses'.[83]

This vitriol might have been more justified had Ammianus lived in the following century, that age of Roman doubt, when the Huns, who only went into battle when negotiations had broken down, defeated Roman armies on several occasions. Imagine what Ammianus would have written had he witnessed how the Visigoths had burst into the inviolate capital of the world and how, in spite of prayers, bloody sacrifices and clouds of incense, on 24 August 410 their leader Alaric allowed his fighters to sack Rome with just one injunction: thou shalt not kill. When the Visigoths left the imperial city, they were laden with treasure. Treasure could be replenished, but the memory of what had happened hung malodorously around the great city, still discernible forty years later when Maximinus and Priscus were sent from Byzantium to discuss terms with Attila, whose 'barbarian' empire matched that of Rome, his dominion stretching from Central Asia across eastern Europe to what is now the Baltic Sea and Dutch border.

Priscus's beard had gone grey and his long hair was thinning, but he still had a sharp eye and his judgement remained invariably sound; he was no Ammianus. He had visited the Huns, whom he calls Scythians, at least once before and he knew how civil they could be. He remembered on his previous visit he had met a Greek man being held in the Hun camp. Priscus had expected that the man would welcome having his ransom paid, his freedom bought, but he did not. Among the Huns, the Greek explained, he was a free man and he stayed with them not because he could not leave, but because this was where he chose to live. He also preferred to fight with the Huns because their common soldiers were treated better than the *miles* (foot soldiers) in Roman legions. Even times of peace were sweeter among the nomads. As a commoner in Rome, he suffered because 'the exaction of the taxes is very severe, and unprincipled men inflict injuries on others, because the laws are practically not valid against all classes. A transgressor who belongs to the wealthy classes is not punished for his injustice, while a poor man, who does not understand business, undergoes the legal penalty.'[84]

Another thing Priscus knew from his earlier visit was that the Huns would treat the Byzantine emperor's ambassadors with respect, so he was surprised when Attila refused to allow them into his presence. Then Priscus was told of the plan for Edeko, how the Hun ambassador had been bribed by the Byzantine emperor to kill Attila – and how instead of killing his master, Edeko had revealed all. Priscus recognised that this moment of drama and volatility was also an opportunity.

The Byzantine embassy was allowed to follow the Hun leader's entourage on a journey of several days, but when Attila made a detour to take another wife, the Romans were sent on ahead to the Hun capital. They were entertained as they travelled through the Hun lands; in one village, for instance, they were sent 'food and attractive women for intercourse, which', Priscus explained, 'is a mark of honour among the Scythians. We plied the women generously from the foods placed before us, but refused intercourse with them.'[85]

Priscus's up-close account is fascinating, not so much for what it says about fifth-century diplomacy – Attila's massive army, and his knowledge of the assassination plot, ensured that the embassy returned to Constantinople without winning any concessions – but for his front-row view of the nomad leader and his followers.

Although he was descended from nomads, Attila had realised that all empires needed an administrative centre and so he had created a capital. The only permanent building in this nomad 'city' on the east bank of the Danube was a stone bathhouse built for one of Attila's wives. The pavilions of Attila's 'palace' were made of wood, 'some carved and fitted together for ornamental effect',[86] with most other buildings being of canvas or felt. This city, Priscus notes with some amazement, Attila preferred over all the cities he had conquered. No trace of it has yet been found.

Soon after arriving in the Hunnish capital, the ambassadors paid their respects to Attila's chief wife, who greeted them from a soft couch, the floor of her pavilion covered with felt rugs on which sat a group of girls embroidering linens. Later, the diplomats were invited to an imperial banquet in a large wooden hall. Attila was seated on a couch in the centre. He was a short man with a broad chest, dark skin, small eyes and flat nose, a patchy black beard and hair now flecked with grey. He was in his early forties and, all things considered, although he was no beauty, he was far from looking like the archetypal bloodthirsty barbarian. Behind him was another couch and, screened off by fine linen and beautifully embroidered fabrics, the raised bed on which he slept. Two of Attila's sons sat on chairs near him while his eldest son sat even closer, on the edge of his couch. Rows of seats lined the walls to the left and right of the couch. To be seated to the right was a great honour, as Priscus knew, but he and his party were seated towards the end of the left-hand row.

Priscus was impressed by Attila's behaviour, if not his bearing: 'the power of his pride', he writes, 'is reflected in the movements of his body.'[87] He would have heard enough about the coming ruler of the world to assume that this uber-barbarian had a lust for blood that was only outdone by his lust for treasure, but clearly the man in front of him did not match the image. 'Though a lover of war,' Priscus explains, 'he was not prone to violence. He was a very wise counsellor, merciful to those who sought it and loyal to those whom he had accepted as friends.'[88] He had modest habits as well, and although he could have lived in a great palace, he preferred to live on the move or in his wooden pavilion. He could have eaten from 'lavishly prepared dishes served on silver platters', which everyone around him enjoyed, but instead ate grilled meat off a wooden board. 'His clothing was plain and differed not at all from the rest, except that it was clean. Neither the sword that hung at his side nor the fastenings of his barbarian boots nor his horse's bridle was adorned, like those of the other Scythians, with gold or precious stones or anything of value.' The scourge of the gods turns out, in Priscus's telling, to be 'temperate'[89] and a family man: 'when his youngest son, whose name was Ernach, came up and stood by him . . . he drew him closer by the cheek and gazed at him with gentle eyes.'[90] Here, finally, is Attila, a family man, captured in the words of someone who had met him and had no reason to embellish.

Perhaps it was by refusing the glitter of gold and the temptations of settled society that Attila stayed true to the spirit of the steppe-world and his nomad origins. He had never lived on the steppes – he was probably born and raised on the Great Hungarian Plain. But he lived on the move, worshipped the Sky Father and other old gods, maintained the old steppe cults and was guided by signs and omens interpreted by his shamans. However much he observed the old ways, and however many omens were seen to confirm that the gods were with him, he was heading west not east.

The following year, Honoria, empress of the Western Roman Empire, sent her eunuch Hyacinth to propose a union between Attila and herself. She had many reasons for doing so. One of these was an impending marriage to a dull senator, forced on her by her brother, Emperor Valentinian, after Honoria had been caught in flagrante with the head of her household. To save herself from that marriage, and to save the great empire from her brother's inadequacies as a ruler, her eunuch, Hyacinth, approached Attila with an offer of union. To seal the deal, Hyacinth was carrying the empress's ring, a token not so much of love as of the seriousness of the *augusta*'s intention to work with the Hun to transform the Roman Empire.

Later, there was much debate both among Romans and Huns as to exactly what Honoria had proposed. Attila insisted he had received an offer of marriage – a union of their houses – and that he had accepted. Attila will have known that Honoria's mother, the Empress Aelia Galla Placidia, taken from Rome by the Visigoths forty years earlier, had willingly married the Visigoth leader, Ataulf, on New Year's Day 414, in Narbonne cathedral, with Ataulf dressed as a Roman general. Attila will also have known that Placidia bore Ataulf a son, named Theodosius, who would have challenged for the imperial throne had he not died within the year. Ataulf died then as well and the empress returned to Rome, married Emperor Constantius III and gave birth to two children, both of whom survived: the future emperor Valentinian, and his sister Honoria, the woman now proposing union.

There were many advantages for the Hun leader in a union with Placidia's daughter, among them an imperial-sized dowry. Attila demanded that Valentinian hand over his sister and half the Western Roman Empire and it is a measure of Valentinian's weakness that although he refused, he did not laugh down the suggestion that his sister, born to the purple, might want to marry a barbarian. In Rome, in the inauspicious year of 450, such things were possible. Instead, the emperor insisted that the proposal had never been made, that the alliance Honoria had proposed was political not conjugal. How could it be otherwise when Roman power was held by men, not women?

With the empress's ring as proof of her proposal, Attila persisted with his demands for the *augusta*'s hand in marriage and her dowry. When he was refused, he and his allies – Goths, Franks, Burgundians and others – marched into Gaul. He defeated a Roman-Goth force on the Catalaunian Plains, south-west of Paris, on 20 June 451. The Roman historian Jordanes, writing the following century, claimed that 165,000 men died that day, which is probably more than the strength of the combined armies, but whatever the numbers, the consequences were significant. In crushing Roman power, Attila struck a blow from which the Roman Empire never recovered. Twenty-five years later the last emperor of the West was deposed by Odoacer, who may have been a Hun and who, on taking power, preferred to be known as king, not emperor. The old order had passed.

Two years later, Attila threatened to attack Constantinople. Before he marched with his army, the warrior, now in his forties, took time out to celebrate yet another marriage. It was said that he indulged liberally at his wedding feast and then retired with his young bride. When she woke in the morning, the new bride found the scourge of the gods still lying beside her: he was dead, having suffered some sort of haemorrhage. Attila was buried in a gold coffin enclosed in a silver one encased in iron, but his tomb has never been found. Yet his legend has lived on, told and retold, first among the Romans, then across Europe, where it was eventually set in type and bound between covers, preserved for posterity.

At the beginning of this string of stories, all of humankind lived on the move in a world where human-made barriers were no more permanent than bundles of thorns and branches, or a few rocks piled on top of each other to protect a temporary shelter. Even after the great dream of urban advancement lured people into Uruk, Babylon, Rome and many other cities, most people still lived outside walls and many of them – migrants, nomads and traders – lived on the move. The path picked through ruins, the highway of history, would have us believe that the only notable achievements of the 10,000 years before the Christian Era came from people who were settled. But we know from the builders of Göbekli Tepe through to the Huns who hastened the end of the Roman Empire, nomads, migrants and other people who lived on the move made significant contributions in advancing civilisation, from building the first stone monuments to taming the horse and teaming it with wagons and chariots.

The eternal dance of attraction and repulsion between the two very different ways of living is captured at the end of the *Histories* when Herodotus tells a story about the Persian king Cyrus. After a string of hard-won battles and with his empire stretching from the Indus Valley to the Mediterranean Sea, Cyrus was on his way home when one of his generals, remembering the hardships of their Persian homeland, suggested that they settle where the living was easier. 'Let us emigrate from this small and rugged land of ours,' the general said, 'and take ownership of a different and better one.'

Cyrus found the proposal less than wonderful, for he believed that if they lived in a gentle land they would not be rulers for much longer. 'Soft lands', he explained to them, 'breed soft men. No country can be remarkable for its yield of crops, and at the same time breed men who are hardy in war.'[91] Abel could have said no better. But if the previous millennia, and the stories I have told, revealed anything, it was that the settled needed nomads and nomads needed the settled. When they cooperated, when borders and markets and minds were open, the world was a better place, as St Sidonius, Bishop of Clermont in France, noted a few years after Attila's death. In the lush volcanic lands of central France 'where pastures crown the hill-tops and vineyards clothe the slopes, where villas rise on the lowlands and castles on the rocks, forests here and clearings there, headlands washed by rivers . . .' the saintly bishop recognised that there was room enough for herders and farmers and city people alike.[92] The Persians saw sense in this and so too did the great nomadic emperors who were to come.

PART II

The Imperial Act

When there is a general change of conditions, it is as if the entire creation had changed and the whole world been altered, as if it were a new and repeated creation, a world brought into existence anew.

Ibn Khaldun

The Imperial Act: From the Rise of the Arabs to the Fall of the Mongols

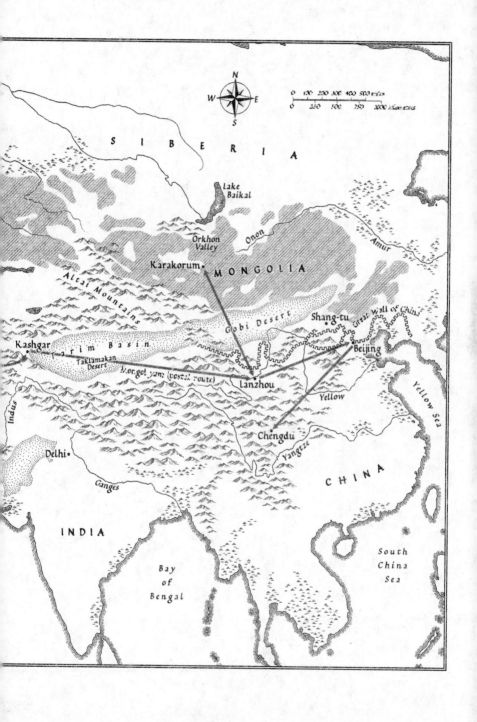

1375: The Castle

The castle of Ibn Salama stood above rolling hills and hard valleys, four or five days' journey south from the Mediterranean and the white city of Algiers. It sat a few miles south of the modern town of Frenda in Tiaret province, Algeria. The farmland between the castle and the sea was rich and produced a surplus. Because it could be taxed, it was called *bilad al-makhzan*, 'government land'. The rich north had sustained glorious civilisations in antiquity and had been home to great people – the Roman emperor Septimius Severus was born at Leptis Magna, Queen Dido ruled at Carthage, Antony and Cleopatra's daughter, Cleopatra Selene, was queen of the rolling riviera around Cherchell. South of the castle was the forbidding *bilad al-siba*, land literally 'running to waste' because nothing could grow there. This *sahra* or Sahara Desert was nomad country where Berber, Fulani, Tuareg, Wodaabe and other wandering tribes roamed free. But if the desert was beyond the reach of government, it was not beyond its interest because 1,250 miles south, across rock and sand and the occasional life-saving oasis, lay the Niger river and Timbuktu where salt, gold, ivory, slaves and other exotic 'commodities' were ready to be moved on foot or by camel across the desert to the coast.

The people of this part of North Africa stood in as much contrast to each other as the varied terrain. But as always with nomads and settled people, their fortunes were inextricably bound together and for most of history they lived in mutual dependence and often also in harmony. This umbilical link between them is perfectly expressed in Arabic, as the writer Tim Mackintosh-Smith points out: 'Arabic, which loves doublets, preferably rhyming ones (Cain and Abel are themselves *Qabil wa-Habil*) characterizes the duality by *madar wa-wabar*, "[people who live in houses] of clay and of camel hair", or "*zar'wa-dar*" "seed-sowing and udder[-milking]".[1]

There were times when differences overwhelmed them and then the bond was broken, harmony disturbed, fratricide ruled. When this happened, it was as well that there was a buffer zone and a castle to offer safe haven to anyone caught between the two. It was at the gate of just such a castle that one of the sultan's courtiers appeared in 1375. Unlike the tax collectors, army officers and other government visitors who arrived from time to time, demanding submission or tribute, this one was travelling with his family, had brought his library, his manuscripts, and he wished to stay.

Wali al-Din Abd al-Rahman Ibn Khaldun was in his early forties when he reached the castle of Ibn Salama and had already distinguished himself as a diplomat and judge. His family story was typical of those whose fortunes were tied to the rise of the Arab Empire. They had moved out of the austere beauty of the Hadramawti valleys in what is now southern Yemen, riding north to the Euphrates with the first armies of Islam in the seventh century. Later, they followed the western sweep of the Arab advance, eventually settling in Seville, where they became leading members of the community in al-Andalus, the Muslim state in Spain. Their fame and fortune continued to grow until 1248. Like many Muslim families, the Christian reconquest transformed Ibn Khaldun's grandfather from grandee to refugee. He had lost his fortune and estates but not his reputation, and back across the narrow waterway in North Africa the Bey of Tunis appointed him minister of finance.

The family fortunes had revived by the time the next calamity struck. Exactly one hundred years after the reconquest, the Black Death swept across North Africa and carried with it Ibn Khaldun's parents, his teachers and a significant number of his friends. The teenager survived and we should be grateful he did. Not because his image appears on a Tunisian banknote or his name graces a university in Indonesia, a Center for Democratic Studies in Cairo, a business hotel in central Tunis or a restaurant in Saudi Arabia, but for the book he wrote in the castle of Ibn Salama.

Ibn Khaldun spent four years living among the Berbers and their hills. Faced with the vastness of the desert, the richness of the farmland, the majesty of monuments, considering the patterns of history and the power of tribal identity, remembering his family's story and his own experiences, the darkness of the fall of al-Andalus, the consequences of the devastation wrought by the Black Death and now, three decades later, the expected arrival of murderous barbarians from the east, he set himself to answer a series of questions that are as relevant now as they were in the fourteenth century. How does the wheel of fortune turn? Why do emperors and their empires rise and fall? Is it inevitable? How are people in cities different from those who live in remote places? Why are some groups of people more powerful than others? What is civilisation and what can we expect from it?

The book in which he began to answer these questions, *The Muqaddimah: An Introduction to History*, is, as the title suggests, a prologue – a three-volume prologue – to his much larger *Kitab al-Ibar: The Book of Warning and the Collection of Beginnings and Historical Information*. But it is the *Muqaddimah* that is the work of genius and, as with Machiavelli's *The Prince*, it has influenced the way we all think today. Described by one twentieth-century Oxford historian as 'the greatest work of its kind that has ever yet been created by any mind in any time or place',[2] the *Muqaddimah* laid the basis for the systematic study both of history and what we now call sociology. It describes the subjects and the areas that needed investigating, and also suggests ways in which those studies might be advanced. Economics is in there as well, for Ibn Khaldun made astute observations about the working of financial systems, the best-known being that 'at the beginning of the dynasty, taxation yields a large revenue from small assessments. At the end of the dynasty, taxation yields a small revenue from large assessments.' This thought was picked up by the twentieth-century economist John Maynard Keynes and turned into theory by Arthur Laffer; the Laffer Curve credits Ibn Khaldun with being the first to notice the inverse relation between tax revenues and power. And that explains why the late US President Ronald Reagan quipped that 'I did not personally know Ibn Khaldun, although we may have had some friends in common!'

The achievement was all the greater because Ibn Khaldun was not writing in Aristotle's Athens, in Alexandria's ancient library or

Baghdad's House of Wisdom, but in a remote castle in turbulent, fourteenth-century North Africa, with darkness and difficulty spreading around him, governments fighting each other, and people left to fend for themselves. It was a time when to move was to risk attack, or infection by deadly disease, when travel was both difficult and dangerous. Most people ventured no further than their nearest market or town centre. In Europe, where the Romans had proudly built and maintained roads, neglect and lack of resources had made anything other than short journeys an ordeal. So if people did travel, it was usually for reasons that outweighed the considerable risks and significant discomfort, mostly either to find salvation by making pilgrimage to sacred shrines at Canterbury and Walsingham, Compostela, Mecca or Jerusalem, or to fight in a crusade. It was in this time of universal difficulty and widespread ruin that Ibn Khaldun set out to do what no one before had done, to describe how humans organised themselves. The resulting volumes are nothing less than the story of civilisation and of the rise and inevitable fall of cities and empires, but they might not tell a story that you know. Unlike Western histories, the *Muqaddimah* presents nomads not as barbarians riding in to destroy what had been created, but as prime movers and king makers. In Ibn Khaldun's world, the sons of Abel are catalysts and creators, and the prime agents of social renewal.

New, Extraordinary, and Highly Useful

'It should be known', Ibn Khaldun opens, with a blare of trumpets that is, for once, justified, 'this topic is something new, extraordinary, and highly useful.'[3]

He did not have access to the works of Herodotus or Sima Qian, but he knew some of the many histories that already existed and he could safely assume that others were being written while he was in the hills. The histories he had read he found mostly ill-conceived because they relied on bad sources or drew wrong conclusions. He had no time for the received wisdom that other historians were happy to accept, and to prove this point he mentions the work of the tenth-century Baghdad-born historian al-Masudi. In his *Meadows of Gold and Mines of Gems*, al-Masudi describes a city in the Moroccan Sahara built entirely of copper and which had no gate: it could only be entered by scaling its walls. Many went in, but no one ever came out. Ibn Khaldun dismissed this story out of hand as being 'the idle talk of storytellers'.[4] Yet he himself was not always entirely accurate. When he wrote about Og, son of Anak, an ancient Canaanite ruler who fought the Israelites, for instance, he tells us that Og was so tall that when he wanted something to eat, he took fish out of the sea and 'held them up to the sun to be cooked'.[5] Ibn Khaldun wondered how anyone could be so naive as to believe that the sun produced heat. 'The sun', he stated without equivocation, 'is neither hot nor cold, but a simple uncomposed substance that gives light.' Fourteenth-century science had a way to go before it had all the answers.

The world view on which Ibn Khaldun's work rests is one in which things do not inevitably improve with the passage of time. This is central to his writings. Instead of there being an 'ascent of man', an upward or even a downward progression, he saw circularity in all things. As his wheel of fortune turns, as the cycle of the months, seasons and years spins, power waxes and wanes, empires rise and collapse, cities are founded and fall, people live and die, all of it dust to dust. Given that he was writing after the fracturing of the great empire of the Arabs, after the fall of al-Andalus, the loss of millions of lives to the Black Death, the many rulers he had seen deposed, the powerful friends exiled or executed, considering all this and the challenges he continued to face – not least the threats from his rivals, which had led him to seek refuge in the castle – it is a wonder that he was not more apocalyptic. From what he had seen on his travels, from what he had read and deduced of the achievements of earlier civilisations, the outlook for human-kind seemed as bleak as the landscape to the south of the castle. But there is one glittering seam of hope running through his masterwork and it is formed by the ability of nomads to embrace diversity and change, and to use this and their energy to revitalise the world.

Ibn Khaldun anticipates Immanuel Kant's observation that 'geography lies at the basis of history' and opens his history by describing the world and considering how landscape and climate shape our character and action. In his geographical categories, the inhabitants of what he calls the middle zones include Arabs, Byzantines, Persians, Israelites, Greeks, Indians and Chinese. He describes them as being temperate by nature and as living in four different ways: in cities, as sedentary farmers in the countryside, as herders and as desert nomads. The first group is self-explanatory. The second group farm and 'are the inhabitants of small communities, villages and mountain regions'[6] and include the majority of Berbers and non-Bedouin. The third group herd sheep and cattle, need to stay on the edge of barren land to be sure of pasturage and close to markets where they can trade the produce of their herding, and they include Berbers, Kurds, Turks, Turkomans and Slavs, and his hosts at his castle, the tribe of Awlad Arif. The final group are camel herders, people who trek deep into the desert in search of grazing and also, he tells us, because female camels need the extreme desert heat to survive the perils of giving birth to their calves. Obliged to live in such hardship, he considers these herders to be 'the most savage human beings . . . on a level with wild, untamable animals and dumb beasts of prey'. They could also be San hunters in the Kalahari, Inuit in the frozen north, Aborigine in the bush, but for Ibn Khaldun, 'Such people are the Arabs.'[7]

There is something elemental and inevitably nomadic about the word *a'rab*. In its original form it referred specifically to people who lived in the desert, to *badw*, the Bedouin as opposed to *hadar*, the settled. The earliest-known use of the word *a'rab* is on an inscription from 853 BCE that records a battle near the Orontes river, in what is now north-west Syria, between the Assyrians and an alliance that included the kings of Damascus and Israel and a leader called Gindibu, who entered the fight with a thousand Bedouin warriors. These camel-mounted nomadic Arabs were a long way from home, but movement was one of their defining characteristics. Indeed, there was a theory that they could only achieve greatness 'if they strap on their swords, tie on their turbans, and ride off'.[8] No greatness was achieved that day by the Orontes river; the Assyrians were victorious.

Ibn Khaldun considered wild Arabs to be the hardiest of all. They were his 'nomads of the nomads' and he thought they were 'closer to being good than sedentary people' because 'the soul in its first natural state of creation is ready to accept whatever good or evil may arrive'.[9] But man, as he knew, 'is a child of customs and the things he has become used to'. These people lived in remote places with neither high walls nor strong gates, which meant they needed to defend themselves: these circumstances inclined them to courage, fortitude and to look out for each other: this is a key claim in the *Muqaddimah*.

Of even greater relevance in our age of environmental breakdown is the way Ibn Khaldun recognised that nomads were bound to the natural world in a way that forced them to recognise that they could only guarantee their survival by respecting their environment. They lived in harmony with their surroundings because they were entirely dependent on them. Their way of life also required them to travel light because they had to pack and carry all their belongings when they migrated. For these reasons, 'they obtain no more than the bare necessities, and sometimes less, and in no case enough for a comfortable or abundant life . . . In spite of this, the desert people who lack grain and seasonings are found to be healthier in body and better in character . . .' Health, hardiness and good character qualified them to be 'the base and the reservoir of civilization and cities'.[10]

This idea of the moral and physical strength of the 'first people' was not new. Plato referred to it in *Timaeus*, in 360 BCE, when he imagined cities being destroyed by floods and their inhabitants washed away to their deaths as civilisation faced elimination by environmental breakdown. The only survivors were nomadic shepherds, rough, unsophisticated people who lived in the highlands and who now went down to repopulate the plain and rebuild the cities. Ibn Khaldun does not seem to have had access to Plato, but he had read the twelfth-century Andalusian philosopher Ibn Rushd, better known as Averroes, and other writers who had read the ancient Greeks. This may have helped shape Ibn Khaldun's belief that civilisation began and was renewed by people with natural goodness and energy, people who understood and respected the natural world, who lived light and on the move.

Before they could be 'the base and the reservoir of civilization and cities' nomads needed to be brought together and inspired by a leader. The group that formed around this charismatic character might be his extended family or his tribe, united by shared blood, but it could also be a disparate group brought together by a shared revolutionary idea or religious belief. He called the force that binds these people *asabiyya*.

The word *asabiyya* appears more than five hundred times in the *Muqaddimah*. Like so many words in Arabic, it has a range of diverse but loosely connected meanings, which include: a she-camel that will not give up her milk unless her thigh is tied; the tying of a turban; a fanatic. But the sense that is most relevant here is: party spirit, team spirit, esprit de corps; tribal solidarity.[11]

Put that way, *asabiyya* sounds similar to the bond that held together an Indo-European *comitatus*. *Asabiyya* might relate to blood-ties, tribal bonds, shared beliefs or devotion to a leader, but whatever the 'glue' that formed the bond, *asabiyya* gave the group a sense of security and a guarantee of mutual support. This was something the twentieth-century British explorer Wilfred Thesiger expressed so clearly when writing about the Bedouin he had travelled with across the Arabian peninsula: 'In times of need a man instinctively supports his fellow tribesmen, just as they in like case support him. There is no security in the desert for an individual outside the framework of his tribe.'[12]

More than individual or collective survival, Ibn Khaldun was fascinated by what happened when the power of *asabiyya* was turned outwards. Away from the family or tribe, it became more powerful than the sum of its individual parts and could be a catalyst to reshape history, to make or break kingdoms and empires, encourage civilisations or force them into collapse. The nature of this group feeling within a state, he realised in what was an original and brilliant perception, dictates the nature of its government and institutions. This may now be, as one political commentator recently called it, 'the fundamental reality of human existence'.[13] And it points to an existence that is constantly morphing, shifting, migrating, nomadic.

Ibn Khaldun says: 'Since desert life no doubt is the source of bravery, savage groups are braver than others. They are, therefore, better able to achieve superiority and take away the things that are in the hands of other nations.'[14] The 'things' Ibn Khaldun refers to that nomads could take were power, royal authority, land and wealth. He also noticed that, however much he might want power for himself, a nomad leader 'cannot completely achieve his goal except with the help of the group feeling . . . Thus, royal superiority is a goal to which group feeling leads.'[15] These pronouncements may seem simplistic, but no one before Ibn Khaldun had made them, nor had anyone arranged them into a theory to explain the rise and fall of states and empires.

Many of the rulers Ibn Khaldun had served in North Africa and Spain had had their fortunes made or destroyed by this process. The Almohads, for instance, were Berber nomads from south of the Atlas Mountains in what is now Morocco, who had had their *asabiyya* shaped by the puritan message of a reforming religious scholar, Ibn Tumart. What started on the desert fringe as complaints against the corruption of the dynasty ruling Morocco soon moved north and became mainstream. Within twenty-five years, the Almohads had established a caliphate that stretched across North Africa and into al-Andalus.

The Almohads showed what nomads could achieve when they channelled the power of the *asabiyya*, but Ibn Khaldun's system to explain the rise and fall of civilisations found a more significant example in the past of his own people. As with many nomad stories, this one starts with 'open lands and pastures grazed by camels',[16] with tribes and trade routes, and with one trader in particular, from a desert city, who claimed to have been visited by an angel.

Seventh-Century Messengers

A messenger rode out of the Arabian Desert heading east to the Euphrates river. At the Persian capital, Ctesiphon, he delivered this message to the Sasanian ruler, Khosrow II: he had been sent by a man who described himself as 'the slave of God' and who called on the emperor to embrace a new religion 'so that you may remain safe (in this life and the next)'. The message concluded with a threat: 'If you refuse to accept . . . you will be responsible for the sins of the Magi.'[17]

Persia's wealth and power had been diminished by its long struggle against Byzantium, the Christian West, and also against nomads to the north, but the Shahenshah still ruled an empire that stretched from the Mediterranean to the Himalayas and included the hard land of Arabia's north. According to al-Tabari, the ninth-century Persian historian, Khosrow was both braver and wiser than most of his dynasty and although his empire was reduced, he still deserved the epithet *Parviz*, Victorious. Khosrow took the message as an insult not an invitation and demanded that whoever composed the message be brought to him for punishment. When the author was told of the emperor's response, he prophesied that Allah would destroy both Khosrow and his empire. As it transpired, this prophecy was fulfilled: the author was not brought before the emperor, but the emperor did die, slowly, on the orders of his own son, and the Persian Empire fell soon after.

A similar message was carried north to Constantinople for the Byzantine emperor. Unlike Khosrow, Heraclius was reported to have been curious about the author, as well he might have been; before long the entire region would be feeling the force of the followers of this man from Arabia.

Muhammad ibn Abdullah was born in Mecca around 570 CE. Although he was the offspring of a culture that was defined by nomads, the people of Mecca engaged in trade and what we would now call religious tourism. Mecca had long been revered for its sacred Zamzam well and the Kaaba, a 15-metre-high cube wrapped in layers of legends. Beneath the Kaaba's roof, supported by three pillars, there sits a black stone said to have been placed there by an angel. The stone has not been tested, but is thought to be either a meteorite or obsidian.

At the time of Muhammad's youth, the Kaaba was rebuilt along the lines of an Ethiopian church. It housed 360 idols including an image of the Christian Virgin Mary and a figure of the Nabataean god Hubal carved from red agate, with a golden arm and surrounded by seven arrows.[18] The Kaaba served both as cult and cultural centre,[19] attracting pilgrims throughout the year and Bedouin tribes en masse for annual gatherings. At these large tribal events, Hubal with his arrows and the other Kaaba gods were consulted for divination. Outside the shrine there would have been all the chaos of a medieval Christian fair or a twenty-first-century Egyptian *moulid* (saint's day). Deals were done, food and other charity dispensed, sermons preached, marriages contracted and, as their Indo-European forebears had done millennia earlier, the fabled poets of Arabia competed for glory with their verses about mighty warriors, noble deeds and hopeless love. The winning lines were said to have been inscribed or embroidered on long strips of cloth and hung, as trophies, from the Kaaba roof, the words literally blowing in the desert air.

At that time, Meccans were pragmatic traders at heart and they welcomed both the settled and the mobile, accepting pilgrims from cities and settlements across the peninsula and bartering with nomads for their wool, animal skins, cheeses and weavings, which they exchanged for grain, metalwork and other settled produce. But it was international trade that made Meccan families rich. At first they lent money and levied taxes on goods passing through their lands. But eventually they organised their own caravans, travelling south into Yemen to load frankincense alongside goods shipped from India, China and elsewhere in the east, and then running camel trains north to sell in Jerusalem, Damascus, Aleppo and Byzantium.

Muhammad was a Meccan trader on the Damascus road and it is believed that on at least one occasion he travelled north into Syria. The journey was demanding, trade was tough and the living far from easy, but it was said that he refused to enter Damascus because a human may only enter one paradise and he was keeping himself for the celestial one. Around his twenty-fifth year, Muhammad's prospects improved when he married a widow, Khadija, fifteen years older than himself and a wealthy trader in her own right. With her capital and contacts and his energy their business should have flourished, and if events had turned out otherwise, we might know Khadija and Muhammad and their six children as an Arabian trading dynasty. But the slow-burning conflict between the Byzantines and Persians had damaged the Eurasian economy and created challenging trading conditions. As money leached from courts and civilians, both the trans-Arabian caravans and the number of pilgrims to Mecca dwindled. At this point, around his fortieth year and with time on his hands, Muhammad took to meditating in caves in the hills around his home in Mecca. On one of these retreats, he is said to have heard a voice. It was the archangel Gabriel.

Recite! the angel instructed.

And the words poured forth, words that *taught man what he knew not*,[20] the final recitation from God.

When the angel had finished and the words were consigned to memory, Muhammad, now the Prophet, sent messengers to Arabs and their neighbours, to the leaders of the Ghassanids, Lakhmids and others as he had done to Khosrow and Heraclius, calling on them

to listen. 'Peace be upon him who follows the right path,' he is said
to have announced. 'If you become a Muslim you will be safe – and
God will double your reward, but if you reject this invitation of Islam
you will bear the sin of having misguided your subjects.'[21]

Neither Khosrow nor Heraclius accepted the invitation, but many
in Arabia did. They accepted because they believed in the message
and in many cases they believed because they were ready to do so.
The recession had left many people on the Arabian peninsula in
need of the sense of unity and belonging that *asabiyya* could offer.
For them, Prophet Muhammad's message was direct and simple: join
the *umma*, the community, and profess that there is only one God,
that Muhammad is his prophet. The message appealed in a way that
nascent Christianity had not, for it came without a hierarchical
priesthood, which appealed both to the settled traders of Mecca and
Medina and to the freedom-loving nomads of the oases and desert.
Unlike the Jewish, Christian, Zoroastrian or Nabataean divinities,
this God also demanded attention because he appealed to nomadic
Arabs in their own language.

Ibn Khaldun knew about the Kaaba and the rival pre-Islamic poets
who 'made poetry the archive of their sciences and their history,
the evidence for what they considered right and wrong'.[22] Applying
his system, he understood how Prophet Muhammad's message had
attracted Arabs and why desert tribes, the sons of Abel or Habil,
had created an *asabiyya* around this charismatic leader. He also knew
about their extraordinary military achievements, although their first
engagement outside the peninsula did not go to plan.

In September 629 CE, a force of 3,000 Muslims rode north to
Mu'tah on the ancient trade road to Damascus, now the so-called
King's Highway in Jordan. They went to avenge the treatment of
one of the Prophet's messengers, who had been executed as he went
north to deliver a message, but the timing of their raid was unfor-
tunate. Instead of surprising a small local force of non-Muslim Arabs,
as they had expected, they arrived at the same time as a large
Byzantine army, sent by Heraclius to regain control of territory east
of the Jordan river.

Until this time, the mostly nomadic Muslims had only faced other

Arabian fighters. Fully armed Byzantine cataphracts on their heavy horses and well-drilled imperial infantry presented a more serious threat. Later Arab accounts wildly exaggerate when they talk of there being more than 100,000 Byzantine troops in the field, but the Arabs were significantly outnumbered and the bloody battle looked increasingly desperate for them. Three of their commanders had already fallen when a brilliant young fighter called Khalid ibn al-Walid took charge. The new general, whom the Prophet would later honour with the epithet 'the Sword of Allah', is said to have broken nine blades during the fight and although that might say more about the state of Arab metalwork (or Muslim hagiography) than about the battle itself, he was clearly a brave and skilled warrior and a survivor. By the end of the conflict, which both sides claimed as a victory, the Byzantines were aware of a new power rising on their southern border.

Prophet Muhammad was reported to have been angry that his fighters returned without a clear victory. Four years later, after the death of the Prophet, Khalid ibn al-Walid was back in action against both Byzantine and Persian armies and four years after that he and his fellow 'caravan-chiefs-turned-tacticians'[23] had brought Mesopotamia, Palestine, Syria and some of Anatolia under their control.

The dramatic rise of Arab Muslim power transformed the existing world order. By the mid-700s, little more than a century after Khalid's victories and the Prophet Muhammad's death, the Roman Empire was reduced to the rump of Constantinople and its Balkan hinterlands while Arab rule stretched from the Indus Valley to the Atlantic Ocean, larger than any previous empire. The most striking thing about this new empire was not its size, but that it had been won by desert people, by nomads, whose habit of movement led to speedy conquests. For while the inner circle of advisers and generals were mostly settled townspeople, some 85 per cent of Arabs and the majority of eighth-century Muslims either lived on the move or were shaped by nomadic tradition. The great success of this relatively small number of Arabian tribesmen, the backbone of Islam's first wave, fighting alongside 'small, reasonably disciplined bodies of soldiers of varying origins',[24] is traditionally explained by their religious conviction – they were fighting for Allah and in the certainty that if they fell they would go to heaven as martyrs. As a ninth-century historian explained, while Persian,

Byzantine, Egyptian and other fighters came looking for things of this world, Muslim fighters' desires and aspirations were all in the hereafter.[25] Ibn Khaldun begged to differ. He ascribed their success to the power of their nomadic *asabiyya*. Arabs were victorious, he believed, because they were closer to the 'natural state' and unencumbered by the trappings of settled life.

Although some of the circumstances and details of their daily lives were different – not least the climate, the scale of the Arabian peninsula and a reliance on camels not horses – there were many similarities between the *asabiyya* of the Arabian nomads and those of the Scythians, Xiongnu, Huns and others off the steppes, just as there were similarities between nomads north and south of the Sahara, mobile groups in Frankish and Germanic Europe and those roaming the American grasslands and the southern pampas. Their identity and sense of self had been shaped by family and tribal bonds as they lived on the move across the natural world. Some also had an understanding of the essential but delicate relationship between Cain and Abel, urban and rural, between citizen, farmer and nomad. Now Arabs faced the challenge of learning how to settle while maintaining the *asabiyya* and holding on to the energy that had made them victorious.

A Problem with Cities

Attila had recognised that the ruler of an empire must build a house, banqueting hall and council chamber. Even though his were made of wood and could be dismantled, they referred to the settled world and taken together they approximated to what we could call a capital. But Attila's personal habits always referred back to his nomadic steppe heritage, just as his personal behaviour relied on the touchstones of nomadic conduct – a sense of personal honour, the value of reputation, of being true to one's word, of loyalty, of tribe, family, *comitatus* – values which had held since the first Indo-European wagons rolled slowly off the steppes and changed the world. Priscus, the Byzantine ambassador who observed Attila first-hand, was surprised that, for all his power and wealth, he had chosen to live simply on the plains and not in a palace in one of the many cities he had conquered. But Attila was still moving forward, still had his eyes on bigger prizes. Had he fulfilled his ambitions and not died aged forty-seven on yet another wedding night, had he succeeded in taking Rome, perhaps then he might have settled. If that had happened, he would have faced the same dilemma as the seventh- and eighth-century Arab leaders. How to balance mobile traditions with the demands of a vast empire and the need for a capital city?

The first Arab imperial centres were transformations of long-established cities and the most dramatic of these was Damascus. The city was conquered for the new religion in 634 CE by the unstoppable Khalid ibn al-Walid and at the beginning of the next century a sumptuous mosque was commissioned to confirm its status as the seat of power, the new imperial capital. The site chosen had previously accommodated a Christian basilica, the tomb of John the Baptist, a Roman temple to Jupiter and the eleventh-century BCE temple of the Semitic storm god Hadad-Ramman. Each civilisation had imposed itself on its predecessor, but the new mosque, owing more to Byzantine than Arab vernacular architecture, could be mistaken for a church.

New cities were also founded in those first years after the Arab conquest and they tell a different story of continuing reference to the Arab nomad heritage. In Tunisia, Kairouan – the 'Caravan' – was at first a trading post more than a city. In Egypt, the conquering Arab army created al-Fustat, 'the Camp', a tent city beside a Byzantine fortress on the Nile that would eventually evolve into al-Qahira, Cairo. Then, in 751 CE, the Arab caliph decided to build a new capital on a site not far from the supposed location of the Garden of Eden. This was not a nomad city, but it owed both its inception and its spirit to a nomadic past and it would derive its wealth from its engagement with the nomadic present.

Settled people lacked simplicity, toughness and many of the other qualities Ibn Khaldun admired in those who lived to move. He thought they were without the essential goodness he found in nomads because people in the city

> become used to laziness and ease. They are sunk in well-being and luxury. They have entrusted the defence of their property and their lives to the governor who rules them and the militia which has the task of guarding them. They find full assurance of safety in the walls that surround them, and the fortifications that protect them.[26]

This reliance, he concluded, made them vulnerable, especially to nomads who were 'better able to achieve superiority and to take away the things that are in the hands of other nations'.[27] This certainly applied to the family of Abbas ibn Abd al-Muttalib.

Abbas ibn Abd al-Muttalib was born in Mecca and was an uncle and close companion of the Prophet. As the Muslim Empire grew and Arabs resettled, some of Abbas's family ended up at a caravan post called Humeima in the Jordanian desert. Ancient Nabataeans from nearby Petra had built an aqueduct there and cisterns provided constant water, but life was hard and apart from passing trade the Arabs relied on herding camels. Some among the descendants had grander ambitions and in 750, just over a century after Abbas's death, his great-great-grandson seized control of the empire and established a new caliphate in his ancestor's name, the Abbasids.

In what might have been a nod to his Bedouin origins al-Mansur, the new Abbasid caliph, moved base four times in the first two years of his reign before deciding to build a new capital. Damascus, the existing imperial centre, was oriented to the Mediterranean world and was dangerously close to the Byzantine border. By contrast, al-Mansur's ambitions lay to the east in Asia and so he preferred to be in Mesopotamia. There was another reason to favour Mesopotamia: empires needed grain and, as Herodotus noted, when properly watered Mesopotamia could be 'the bread-basket of the world'.

Al-Mansur is reported to have sailed up and down the Tigris

looking for a location for his new city. One wonders why, for earlier conquerors had surveyed the river and all had built on the same patch of ground, where the Tigris and Euphrates flowed close together. The most recent of these cities was Ctesiphon, founded in the second century BCE by the Parthians. When al-Mansur took it, Ctesiphon was the capital of the Persian Empire and one of the largest cities in the world, home to around half a million people. The new caliph pitched his tents twenty miles upstream and with the help of a crowd of astrologers and architects, poets and prophets, he laid out the ground plan for a new city.

Al-Mansur was now forty years old. Born and brought up in the desert in Jordan, much of his adult life had been spent on the move and most of that on campaign, where he put 'a multitude of people to death'.[28] Now that he was caliph and emperor, the most powerful person on earth, he wished to express himself by building a place of wonder, a city of superlatives. And yet his nomadic background taught him that cities were a deception, at least in the way they expressed certainty, in their pretence of permanence. He had seen for himself the ruins of some of the great cities of antiquity including Babylon and Uruk – the great city of Gilgamesh that had been home to 80,000 people, but was now little more than dust. He already knew that palaces and cities did not last. He had also recently discovered that not even names endured: he had wanted to call his new city Madinat al-Mansur, al-Mansur's city, but the name had previously been attached to a palace near al-Kufa and instead the new capital was called Madinat as-Salam, the City of Peace. Given the amount of strife it would foster, that now seems wishful thinking. In the end, and for reasons that are not entirely clear, it came to be known more simply as Baghdad.

The ground plan was a circle bisected by two straight roads that formed an X, the outer circular wall pierced by four gates. Al-Mansur claimed credit for the design and for its originality although the idea had really come from his chief architect, Khalid ibn Barmak, and he had several sources of inspiration. The architect may not have known that this image, of a circle cut through by a cross, was the ancient Egyptian hieroglyph for 'city'. But he had grown up in a building with a circular floor plan because his father was abbot of the Buddhist monastery of Nawbahar in Merv (now Turkmenistan), whose circularity reflected the navel at the centre of the Buddhist *mandala*. Ibn Barmak also knew of the Sasanian round palace at Firuzabad in the Fars province of Persia, where he had served two years as governor. His circular capital was intended to be every bit as symbolic as the Buddhist *mandala*, with the palace at its centre, its audience chamber covered by a 120-foot green dome, a hub for the great wheel of empire.

One of many fictions surrounding Baghdad was that its massive walls four miles long, the outer one 60 feet high, the inner wall 90 feet high, would act as a deterrent and keep its people safe. Since when had walls ever kept anyone safe? Not at Troy or Rome, not at Ur or Babylon. The thousand-man garrisons posted at each of the city's four cardinal gates were more of a guarantee of safety. And safety was what was needed for this, al-Mansur is reported as saying, 'is indeed the city that I am to found, where I am to live, and where my descendants will reign afterward'.

No one knew better than al-Mansur that if his line, his capital and empire were to thrive, what he needed was not walls but a fluidity that would allow the easy movement of people and facilitate the sparkling exchange of ideas and the free trading of goods. Baghdad was to be an expression of that fluidity, a triumph of movement, its circular walls a fixed point around which the nomadic world could turn. Its location had been chosen for the fertility of the plain – to guarantee food supplies – and for easy access to the empire's Asian provinces and the trade roads that stretched web-like beyond them. Connected to the Tigris and Euphrates rivers, Baghdad was well located both for the Persian Gulf in the south and Syria in the north-west. It was also close to the old Persian Royal Road, which linked the Mediterranean and the Nile with the central Asian steppes, India and the markets beyond. 'There is no obstacle between us and China,' al-Mansur said, recognising the viability of the Silk Roads; 'everything on the sea can come to us on it.'[29] As the centrepoint in a mobile world, Baghdad became a place of wealth and wonder and for many years, as al-Mansur predicted, it was home to his descendants, most glorious among them being his grandson Harun al-Rashid.

There are contrasting images of Harun. To some, he was an austere teetotal Muslim who devoted his life to bloody jihad and who performed the hajj to Mecca eight times during his reign. But more common is the pleasure-loving Harun, the good-time caliph who ruled over the empire's boom years. This Harun is tall, handsome, eloquent and also arrogant, the caliph of the *Alf Layla wa-Layla* story cycle, *The Thousand and One Nights*. His grandfather had been a frugal man, who had earned the nickname Abu Dawanik, 'Father of the smallest coin in the realm', but had also set the empire's finances on a firm footing, leaving Harun to start his reign with such wealth that he was able to boast to the Byzantine emperor that 'the least of the territories ruled by the least of my subjects provides a revenue larger than your whole dominion'.[30] Unlike his grandfather, Harun was famous for his largesse and for being generous with his hospitality. It was said that on his wedding day he showered his wife with pearls and rubies before serving her the finest banquet ever prepared . . . for a woman. During the feast, guests were invited to help themselves from gold trays filled with silver and silver trays filled with gold. Harun passed this love of largesse to his son and successor because when al-Mamun married, Ibn Khaldun tells us, he sat his wife Buran on carpets woven with gold and embroidered with rubies and pearls, and gave her a thousand 'hyacinths', the word then used to describe rubies. Around 150,000 mule-loads of wood were burned to cook the wedding banquet in the imperial kitchens, while 30,000 boats ferried guests to and from the party. Ibn Khaldun, imagining all this from the austerity of his draughty chamber in the castle of Ibn Salama, assures us that there were 'many other such things'.

Perhaps Harun was hajji, jihadi and generous libertarian, for in some ways that is how he was celebrated in the pages of the *Arabian Nights*. He was the caliph who drank deeply of the cup of life, happy to entertain a small army of companions, singers, musicians, dancers and beautiful women. Large amounts of Shirazi red and other wines were drunk, vast banquets were served and notable debauches enjoyed. 'What is this life', one of his court poets, Muslim ibn Walid, asked, 'but loving, and the surrender to the drunkenness of wine and pretty eyes?'[31] Harun was also said to have been an insomniac and liked to wander the night streets of his capital incognito, accompanied by his vizier Jafar and his executioner, distributing largesse and punishment as he saw fit, catching cheating traders, jousting playfully with poets, chasing beautiful girls, some of whom ended up in the royal harem, others left with significant treasure. If this was him, he was the ideal ruler for a city and empire in harmony with itself, in which nomad had been reconciled with settled, tribes with nations, and in which all worked for the benefit of the whole. It was *asabiyya* on an imperial scale.

Al-Mansur had placed Baghdad's markets inside the circular walls, but things quickly evolved and they were moved to Karkh, a new suburb south of the palace city. One story suggests that the move was not so much because traders needed more space but because al-Mansur had been stung by a comment from a Byzantine ambassador who noted that the caliph had invited his 'enemies' inside the walls. By 'enemies' the ambassador meant foreigners, many of them nomads, but it was they who helped the empire to thrive as people, goods, knowledge and ideas, beliefs, stories, songs, styles of representation and all the myriad other aspects of culture were carried through mountain ranges and deserts, along valleys and steppes, across seas and oceans. In this milieu, Arab civilisation flourished.

Harun knew that the vast wealth and glittering inspiration of the Islamic golden age came not from the safety offered by walls and borders, but by people being in motion and allowed to move freely across an empire that stretched from al-Andalus to Central Asia. Abbasid influence could now be felt south of the Sahara, down into India, up into Siberia, west to the Byzantine border and east into China. The great centres of the Islamic Empire, Fustat/Cairo, Samarkand, Basra, Damascus and Mosul, were open marketplaces. And as the Arabs had turned their backs on Europe, the bulk of the world's trade now moved between the two largest cities in the world: the million-strong Tang Chinese imperial capital Chang'an and Baghdad, home to at least 600,000 by the late 780s.[32] There was nothing new about cities of this size – Rome had probably been home to around a million people in the year 1 CE.

As a result of these exchanges, and the trade between these peoples, under Harun's gilded hand Baghdad lived up to its reputation as 'the crossroads of the universe'. It boasted sumptuous palaces and indulgent pleasure gardens that gave rise to fantastic stories of trees having golden branches and the birds that perched on them being golden automata with voices sweeter than any living creature. The arts and sciences flourished as vast sums were also spent to attract the finest painters and potters from across Eurasia, the best singers and musicians. Male and female poets and storytellers had always been popular among Arabs, but now they became the superstars of this age, reciting old stories and inventing new ones in the halls and hangouts of the new capital and making this one of the great ages of Arabic poetry. Even royal princesses composed verse, among them Lubana the young bride of al-Amin, Harun's crown prince. She was said to have been one of the most beautiful women of her age and she had much to write about, not least that in spite of her beauty and her skills her husband preferred eunuchs. When al-Amin was beheaded by his brother al-Mamun during the succession struggle, the nubile Lubana, married but untouched, wrote these words: 'Oh hero lying dead in the open, betrayed by his commanders and guards. I cry over you not for the loss of my comfort and companionship, but for your spear, your horse and your dreams. I cry over my lord who widowed me before our wedding night.'

However noted Baghdad became for storytellers and versifiers, it was most renowned for the achievements of the many familiars of Bayt al-Hikmah, the House of Wisdom. Like much else in Baghdad, the house was modelled on an earlier Persian institution, which in turn owed much to institutions at Alexandria and Athens. The city's wealth and open doors attracted some of the brightest minds of the age from provinces across the empire and beyond. For those who preferred to avoid the politics of the capital, there were other centres of scholarship in Damascus, Kufa, Basra and Khwarazm (Khorasan). Much of the learning had its basis in the ancient world, with many documents being translated from Greek, Coptic and Syriac, particularly after al-Mamun, Harun's son, wrote to the Byzantine emperor asking for 'a selection of such works on the ancient sciences as had been preserved and passed down in Byzantine lands'.[33] Philosophy, mathematics, law, the Hadiths or sayings of the Prophet Muhammad, texts from other religions – in Greek, Persian, Sanskrit and other eastern languages – were all translated into Arabic. But the House of Wisdom, the epicentre of all this learning, was about more than mere translation. Al-gebra, al-chemy, al-gorithm and many other subjects and disciplines were either created or advanced during this period, as Arab and Persian scholars transformed ancient knowledge and theory with work that would later shape the European Renaissance and Enlightenment.

One key difference between the Abbasid centres of learning and the ancient libraries and *mouseion* was that ideas were now set down on paper, not parchment or papyrus. The secret of paper production, which had long been strictly confined to China, had come west in 751 CE and as so often it came out of warfare. In that year Abbasid and Tang forces had fought an epoch-defining battle at Talas in modern Kyrgyzstan. One result of the battle was the creation of an unofficial border that marked the limit of China's western expansion, which effectively gave the Abbasids control over much of Central Asia and its trade routes. Another outcome was that one of the Tang prisoners showed his Arab captors how to make paper. The technique was trialled in Abbasid-ruled Samarkand that same year of 751 and by the end of the century paper was being produced and used in Baghdad.

The Glorious Age of Settling Down

There was a price to pay for these advances, as Ibn Khaldun knew:

> At the time of the first Umayyad caliphs, the Arabs continued to use the dwellings they had, tents of leather and wool. Only a very few of the Arabs had at that date ceased to live in the Bedouin manner. When they went on raids or went to war, they rode their horses, loaded their nomad households onto camels, brought their dependent women and children . . . Their armies, therefore, consisted of many nomad households.[34]

But in the golden age of the Abbasids, 'the Arab dynasty adopted diverse ways of sedentary culture and ostentation. People settled in towns and cities. They were transformed from tent dwellers into palace dwellers. They exchanged the camel for the horse and the donkey as riding animals.'[35]

Although the original Arab nomad culture continued to shape the thoughts and behaviour of many in the Abbasid world, particularly those who could trace their lineage back to the Arabian peninsula, the empire became increasingly cosmopolitan, multicultural and settled, while the administration was ever more Persian in character.

The transformation from free-moving, free-thinking and free-speaking nomads to settled city dwellers, from tough, light-living desert people to luxury-loving citizens, had been quick and complete. A century stood between the palaces of Abbasid Baghdad and the tents of Khalid ibn al-Walid, 'the Sword of Allah', between the reign of Harun and the time when Arab tribes mounted horse and camel and left Arabia for the Atlantic, the Indus river, the Indian Ocean and beyond. In that time, the rough energy, the strength, devotion and also the violence that had given Arab leaders control of a huge empire and made their new religion one of the most popular on earth, had dissipated. With the leadership settled in Baghdad and the empire administered by Persians and others, Arabs began to realise what they had lost.

It was not just a question of a diluted bloodline, although that would become a critical issue: only three of the thirty-seven Abbasid caliphs were born to Arab mothers. Many Arabs had a sense that they might lose their culture, history and identity. Perhaps it was inevitable that Arabs would be estranged from their past. 'The world', as the eleventh-century poet-philosopher al-Ma'arri would write, 'has intermingled, the people of the plain with the daughters of the mountain.'[36]

Ibn Khaldun identified this estrangement as one of the reasons for the inevitable downfall of the Abbasids. In a section entitled *Dynasties have a natural life span like individuals*, he traced what he saw as an inevitable arc:

1) The generation that establishes the dynasty has a toughness and savagery about it, and is held together by *asabiyya*.

2) Once power and authority are established, the rot begins to set in as 'the second generation change from the desert attitude to sedentary culture, from privation to luxury and plenty'.[37] This separates the ruler from the rest of the group, which leads to the dissipation of the group feeling that made conquest possible in the first place.

3) The third generation, then, has completely forgotten the period of desert life and toughness, as if it had never existed. They have lost the taste for the sweetness of fame and for group feeling . . . Luxury reaches its peak among them, because they are so much given to a life of prosperity and ease.[38]

Ibn Khaldun's scheme for the rise and fall of dynasties easily fits the Abbasids in Baghdad:

1) Al-Saffah and al-Mansur establish the dynasty and the capital.

2) Al-Mansur's son al-Mahdi, the caliph who loses his way on his horse, settles for luxury and plenty.

3) Al-Mahdi's son, Harun al-Rashid, enjoys the peak of prosperity and ease.

'It is in the fourth generation', Ibn Khaldun writes, 'that ancestral prestige is destroyed.'[39] This proved to be the case when Harun's sons, al-Mamun and al-Amin, fought for control of the empire. Conflicting regional allegiances came into play, with Baghdadis, Arab and Mesopotamian forces backing al-Amin and the Persians and other easterners fighting for al-Mamun. The succession struggle lasted two years, until al-Mamun killed his brother, but the conflict between the various factions dragged on for twenty more. Although al-Mamun ruled as caliph in Baghdad, the familial, tribal and political unity, the *asabiyya*, the sense of Muslim community and what Ibn Khaldun called ancestral prestige, Arab pride, disappeared from Baghdad. It was perhaps at this stage that an anonymous poet wrote:

> *I abhor Baghdad; I abhor life there.*
> *This is from experience, after a taste . . .*

And ending with these words about Baghdadis:

> *Abandoning the path of nobility,*
> *They rival each other instead in disobedience and sinfulness.*[40]

One consequence of the loss of pride was a rising wave of nostalgia among Arabs. This had been coming for a while – perhaps ever since Arabs started to be replaced by Persians and others in key administrative positions – and it now inspired scholars to set out to recover a sense of their Arabness. This was not a desire to recreate things as they had been at the time of the Prophet: the religion he had inspired had transformed Muslim society and now had imperial and international reach. The nostalgia felt in the 800s was for pre-Islamic Arabia, for a language and a set of values, *nomadic* values, that had been lost as the Abbasid world became increasingly settled, agricultural and urban. As a result of this nostalgia, in the ninth century, in what became known as the Age of Setting Down, scholars and poets from Baghdad and elsewhere set out to recover that original *Arab* identity many felt had been lost in the rush to empire. They did so literally by setting out to recover it and the place they looked first was Basra.

Basra had become an important trading post because its location, on the Shatt al-Arab, the waterway created as the combined Euphrates and Tigris rivers head to the Persian Gulf, gave access to Arabia and Persia, and made the site strategically and economically important. It remains today Iraq's economic hub, as well as its hottest city. The city also became culturally important during the Age of Setting Down for the reason that it was closest to Arabia.

Bedouin from the peninsula traded at Mirbad, a souk a few miles outside Basra, and whenever they pitched camp, poets were soon to be heard. So Mirbad was a good place to be if you wanted to meet a poet or travelling singer. Eighth-century Arab poets such as Farazdaq and Jarir had 'flyted' or traded insults in verse at Mirbad while their tribespeople were trading commodities. This habit of jousting with words with as much passion as others fought with weapons was still popular a century later. But the difference in the 800s was that rival poets now found themselves with an audience of scholars from Baghdad, who followed the verbal jousts in the hope of finding 'rare and obscure words', the old Arabic that had been lost in Persianised cities. Women of the tribes were also interviewed in the hope that words lost to the cities were still common among Bedouin.

As this movement grew, some more ambitious scholars extended their search south into the desert and to Arabia itself. One of the most famous of these intrepid researchers was Abu Amr ibn al-Ala, the Quran reciter of Basra, who had a particular passion for Bedouin poetry. He was famous for the relentlessness of his questioning, as this vignette suggests:

'What tribe do you come from?'
'From the Asads.'
'Which, in particular?'
'The Nahd.'
'What region are you from?'
'From Oman.'
'And where does the purity of your speech come from?'
'We live in an isolated land.'[41]

This was no longer something the Quran reciter could say, in any language. Nor could the caliph, or any of his Arab family or entourage. Ibn Khaldun's cycle of dramatic rise and steady decline still had some way to go before it was done. But even the Abbasid Empire, created and shaped by nomads and revolving around the circular city of Baghdad, would inevitably decline and fall.

Heaven Smiles

Worlds on worlds are rolling ever from creation to decay, the poet Shelley writes, *like the bubbles on a river, sparkling, bursting, borne away.* But where does circularity begin – the cycles of seasons, of years, the

movement of people, the circularity of the city – when its beginning is its end, and the end a beginning? Shelley gives us clues:

> *The world's great age begins anew,*
> *The golden years return,*
> *The earth doth like a snake renew*
> *Her winter weeds outworn:*
> *Heaven smiles, and faiths and empires gleam*
> *Like wrecks of a dissolving dream.*[42]

As a courtier, Ibn Khaldun may have been the definitive city
man, but four years in a Berber castle writing the *Muqaddimah*
were enough for him to recognise circularity in the passing of
seasons, the growing of his children and in his own ageing. They
were also enough for him to consider a question that is as fundamental today as it was in the 1370s: if humans strut from tottering
first steps to teetering last ones, if everything that sprouts also
withers, if the sun that rises must inevitably set, why should social
and political structures not do the same? *Asabiyya*, dynasties,
cultures, civilisations – all must inevitably fall as certainly as they
rise, but they could then rise again, for, as Ibn Khaldun knew, the
vital energy necessary for a new beginning came from people who
lived on the move and in the natural world, from Abel not Cain,
Enkidu not Gilgamesh.

Nomads, hunters and others who lived in the natural world were
aware of these truths, although they might not know them, aware
of them through the instinctive measuring of their lives against the
waxing and waning of the moon, the shifting of the sun through
the latitudes, the evolution from bud to fruit to fall. But those who
aspired to power were to become aware of the dissolving dream, as
those worlds-on-worlds, the empires that Shelley refers to, rolled
inevitably from creation to decay.

The inevitability of decay lay in their inability to move. Cities
and walls might protect against danger from the natural world and
against threats from outsiders, but what was gained from this security was lost in a lack of flexibility. When Scythians were faced
with the overwhelming might of the Persian army, they simply
moved away from it: 'We have no cities,' the Scythian king explained

as he kept his people ahead of the Persian army, 'nothing that we need worry you might capture. We have no crops – nothing that we need worry you might destroy.'[43] Eventually the Persians gave up and went home. When climate change arrived on the Eurasian steppes in antiquity, Indo-European nomads did as the Scythians had done and moved away to find new grazing. It became increasingly difficult for people to do this if they were walled up in a palace.

'Something of this sort', as Ibn Khaldun puts it, some inability to adjust in the face of their decline, overwhelmed the Abbasids. The dazzling surge of nomadic energy that had brought them power in the first place and allowed them to establish an empire to the glory of Islam across half the world began to seep away almost as soon as they settled behind the circular walls of Baghdad. No amount of 'setting down', no recovery of pure Bedu Arabic or Arab heritage, could stop the creeping decline. It was too late for that: their *asabiyya* had gone and without it they were – or would become – politically and militarily weak. Unable to command the loyalty of their own group and to rally them to arms, Abbasid caliphs became dependent on the support and the might of others, on Persians in the administration and Persians, Turks, Seljuqs and many other nomadic people in their armies. 'Then', as Ibn Khaldun describes it – and you can feel the grinding inevitability in his words – 'the Persians (non-Arabs) and clients gained power over the provinces of the realm. The influence of the dynasty grew smaller, and no longer extended beyond the environs of Baghdad. Eventually, the Daylam (Persians living south of the Caspian Sea) closed in upon that area and took possession of it. The caliphs were ruled by them.'[44]

Because we know that nothing stands still, because as the Greek philosopher Heraclitus noted we can never step into the same river twice because rivers are ever-changing, it comes as no surprise that the Daylam were soon overwhelmed by Seljuqs, a Turkic tribe who, like Huns, Persians and others before them, had ridden south off the great steppeland beyond the Caspian Sea. Tribes moved in waves, pushed – in what we now recognise as an eternal cycle of human migration – by changing climate, shortage of grazing, a spike in population, shifted by invasion, inspired by a leader of passion, or sometimes just because they could. Ibn Khaldun knew of these nomadic shifts from his reading and from his own experience of the North African dynasties and of the Umayyads in Andalusia, with whom his family had been involved. But his particular take on the wheel of fortune could just as easily apply to the Tankish kings in what is now Sudan, whose people were the migrating pastoralists of the Beja tribe. Or the Duguwa kings of Kanem in Central Africa, nomads who lived in simple reed huts, probably similar to the way the Wodaabe live in Niger today. Or Serbs, Slavs, Vikings and Sami in Europe. It also applied to the early Aztecs of Central America, whose lives were dictated by migration until their god Huitzilopochtli commanded them to look for a place where an eagle perched on top of a cactus, eating a precious serpent. There, Huitzilopochtli commanded, they were to settle, which they did. The place was called Mexica.

Ibn Khaldun knew that the third or fourth generation usually lost touch with – and therefore the support of – the *asabiyya*. This happened when they settled behind walls and were softened by luxury. This had happened inside the walls of Baghdad. The Abbasid caliphs and princes had lived in glorious safety, but they lived divided from their people and the *asabiyya* they had inspired had withered.

'Finally', Ibn Khaldun wrote of the remains of their great Islamic Empire, 'the Tatars closed in.'

Temujin

It was said that his people were descended from a buck fallow deer and a blue wolf, and that they had lived on the other side of the great water before moving to the vast mountain-enclosed valley on the eastern steppes of Eurasia.

It was said that he was conceived by a ray of divine light touching his mother's belly and was born with a knot of blood in his hand. But beyond myths of immaculate conception, we know that he was born around 1162 CE. The Crusades were ongoing, Thomas Becket was Archbishop of Canterbury, the English were occupying Brittany and Frederick Barbarossa, the Holy Roman Emperor, had just sacked Milan, destroying public buildings and dismantling its fortified walls.

His early life, like much else, is wrapped in legend. We cannot know if there really was a knot of blood in the infant's hand, even though it was widely accepted as a sign that he would conquer and that there would be bloodshed. But some facts are secure. He was called Temujin, which means 'blacksmith', a common enough name among nomads who relied on horses and were taught to ride as soon as they could walk, to shoot a bow as soon as they could ride. These nomads had a tradition of agreeing marriage contracts long before the betrothed was of marriageable age, especially if the tribe might benefit from the alliance. But here too there is legend: when nine-year-old Temujin was sent to his bride Borte's family, his future father-in-law had a dream in which a gyrfalcon clutched the sun and the moon. Shamans interpreted the dream as another sign that Temujin would rule the world. But dreams did not always come true and this one must have seemed unlikely, never more so than when the boy's father was killed by rival nomads and his family's sheep and horses rustled. He returned to his family home and spent years enduring extreme hardship.

It was said that soon after the death of his father, he was captured and put into a form of stocks, a wooden board fitted over his head to make it impossible to escape or to retaliate against the humiliation. Yet he did escape to the mountains where he was nourished by a gyrfalcon. He was also nurtured by a desire for revenge, for it was there that he vowed to restore his family's fortunes.

In 1178, Temujin was able to marry his fiancée, Borte, both of them still teenagers. But soon after their marriage, she was abducted by another nomad tribe. For some eight months, Temujin suffered her loss, his bed 'made empty', as it was recorded in the Mongol chronicles, his breast 'torn apart'. It is at this stage of the story that Ibn Khaldun's view of the rise and fall of dynasties applies, for Temujin now gathered a group of supporters around him to bring back his wife. These men regarded him as their *khan* and their devotion to him was the beginning of an *asabiyya*. By the time he was twenty-four years old, in 1186, Temujin's fortunes had turned full circle: Borte had given birth to several sons, he had killed the nomad leader who had humiliated him and his *asabiyya* was increasingly strong.

He would prove to be a good leader, elevating those who served him well and rewarding all who were loyal, whatever their original standing and irrespective of their tribe or religious beliefs, just as he was stern with those who he thought deserved punishment. And he was a good judge of men and women, with an eye for an exceptional fighter. So when an archer from a rival tribe almost killed him with an arrow, Temujin had him captured and brought to him. The man expected to be executed, perhaps have his flesh peeled off or his orifices sewn up and then be thrown into a river. Instead, he was made one of Temujin's most trusted advisers. The man repaid this faith by becoming one of the greatest and most loyal of steppe generals. But although he could be generous in friendship, Temujin was a terrifying opponent, fierce in battle, though not always victorious, and relentless in the pursuit of a grudge. Some of the people he turned against were chased across vast tracts of land for many months before they lost their lives.

Twenty years after becoming khan of his tribe, and thanks to a combination of shrewd alliances, relentlessly bloody campaigning, his own forceful character, the wise counsel of Borte, a ruthless streak, good timing and a period of warm, wet weather over the Mongolian steppes, Temujin was master of 2 million people. Most of these were migratory nomads, whose actions had always been guided by the twin forces of tribal network and expedient allegiance. Under Temujin, they now found themselves driven by expansive ambitions and bound by a new, pan-Mongol identity. This was the secret that held their *asabiyya* together. With the tribes united, or at least with opposition suppressed, Temujin's word became law over a thousand-mile swathe of Central Asia, east to west from China to Kazakhstan, six hundred miles north to south from Lake Baikal to the Gobi Desert.

In the Year of the Tiger, 1206, Temujin consolidated his position by calling a *quriltai*. These periodic gatherings of 'the people of the felt-walled tents'[45] were an important opportunity for Mongol tribes to come together to resolve grievances without bloodshed, agree new rules or laws, lay plans for the future and, as in this instance, acknowledge a new leader. The *quriltai* of 1206 took place at the tribe's spiritual base, by the headwaters of the Onon river, near where the Russian, Mongolian and Chinese borders meet today. This is a beautiful, harsh landscape of *taiga* where the air is clear, the wind biting, the valley slopes covered in Siberian larch and pine. This was where Temujin had been raised and where his mother, so vividly described in the Mongol chronicles, had foraged for food:

> *Pulling firmly her tall hat*
> *Over her head,*
> *Tying tightly her belt*
> *To shorten her skirt,*
> *Along the Onan [sic] River,*
> *Running up and down,*
> *She gathered crab apples and bird cherries,*
> *Day and night she fed*
> *Their hungry gullets.*[46]

Now in his early forties, back in his childhood homeland, his nine-pointed white banner raised in front of his white tent, Temujin was transformed from the head of a tribe and of the Mongol people into the future emperor of the world. The exact translation of his new title remains contentious – it could mean fierce or universal leader – but the intent was clear, just as it was clear that the gyrfalcons had read the character of this man, this Genghis Khan, sent by the gods to lord over all.

Genghis Khan spent the following weeks 'setting the Mongol people in order'.[47] He renewed family and tribal bonds, organised his fighters into ninety-nine groups of a thousand, rewarded those who had supported him and considered the way forward for the years ahead. Until this moment, Mongols had mostly kept to themselves and avoided regional confrontations unless absolutely necessary. Now that they were a regional power, Genghis Khan laid out a long view and a well-conceived plan to expand their empire. They would reach out over the entire world, first east, then west, in what would become one of the high points of nomad influence in the world.

But why would he have wanted to break with Mongol tradition and leave the region of his birth? Why not settle for control over Central Asia, which had been vast enough to contain most rulers' ambitions? Western histories compare this inflection point in Genghis's life with Julius Caesar pushing north into Gaul and then England, or Hitler moving into Czechoslovakia and Poland. Seen that way, it appears as a political move backed by a desire or need for greater resources or revenue. But Genghis's plan was not the whim of a tribal leader who feared what would happen if he stopped moving forward. According to the wider Mongol view, the move was not even of his choosing. It had been ordained and was sanctioned; making it happen was more than just a declaration of war, it was fulfilling the will of Tengri, Lord of the Blue Sky, the Sky Father.

Genghis Khan is one of the few nomad leaders from any time in history whose name resonates around the world today, along with Attila the Hun who lived eight hundred years earlier, and Tamerlane, 170 years later. If Genghis Khan's name sounds more familiar than the others it might be because, at least in the West, he is remembered as the bloodiest and most vengeful of killers, a cruel man who left smouldering cities and a swathe of scorched earth across Eurasia, a butcher with the blood of 20, 30, perhaps even 40 million people on his hands. None of this is necessarily wrong, although the figures are disputed and impossible to prove either way. But like so much about the man and his people, there is more to consider and much to correct. He is often presented as an impetuous barbarian warlord, but the record of his careful strategising says otherwise. He is remembered for vengeance, yet when he tracked down and killed the nomads who had abducted his young wife Borte, he was doing no more than Homer's Greek heroes had done when they launched a thousand ships to rescue Helen of Troy.

More than this, more than the legends around his sexual appetite and the generous way in which he spread his DNA across the world – as many as one in every 200 males alive today carry his DNA – we should remember him for his achievements. He created an empire that was more than twice as large as the Roman Empire. He enforced what became the *pax Mongoliana*, a peace that was at least as transformative as the *pax Romana*. He could be welcoming and open-minded. And most important because of the way it runs against prejudice, his vast empire was administered according to a rule of law. At one end of the Mongol legal scale, murder and adultery were punished with death. The other side of their law tolerated and even encouraged freedom of worship: within the vast Mongol-administered territories, one was free to practise as a Buddhist, Muslim, Confucian, Zoroastrian, Jew, Christian, animist or indeed no religion.

Edward Gibbon, who could peddle prejudice as well as the next, was particularly struck by the Mongol acceptance of freedom of conscience, writing that 'it is the religion of Zingis [*sic*] that best deserves our wonder and applause.' Gibbon knew that at the same time as Genghis Khan's Asia was flourishing thanks to his open borders and freedom of conscience, the French monarchy was sending armies to suppress what it and the papacy considered the heresy of Cathar Christians: this crusade to southern France led to the death of at least 200,000 Christians, perhaps five times that number. 'The Catholic inquisitors of Europe,' Gibbon continued, 'who defended nonsense by cruelty, might have been confounded by the example of a Barbarian, who anticipated the lessons of philosophy, and established by his laws a system of pure theism and perfect toleration.'[48]

Like a Flock of Birds

Whether by the grace of God or the power of *asabiyya*, ten years after the great 1206 *quriltai* on the Onon river, Genghis Khan was master of the migratory world and much of China as well. Mongol fighters were happiest in the saddle, which made sense given how much of their lives on the steppes, herding or hunting, required them to ride. Mounted on steppe ponies, which grazed happily on grass and therefore did not need fodder, they were deadly with their composite bows and particularly effective on open land, where they could manoeuvre at speed. They were less skilled at other sorts of warfare. Sieges were difficult for everyone involved, but nomads faced the extra challenge of finding grass for their horses, a problem made more acute by each Mongol horseman travelling with several mounts. For this reason, among others, Mongols were often generous to towns and cities that conceded without a siege. It also explains why they devastated towns that defied them, as many Chinese cities did, among them the central capital at Dadu, now known as Beijing, which was levelled in 1215. This ruthlessness against cities that defied them was not some Mongol love of blood; it was intended to dissuade other cities from resistance.

With the fertile Yellow river floodplain under his control, Genghis Khan turned the bulk of his armies away from China, west into Central Asia. Here, as elsewhere, there would be savagery and leniency, and extraordinary success. Even the Uighurs, who might have provided fierce opposition, accepted his sovereignty.

Alliance with the Uighurs was hugely significant for the conqueror, not least because they had previously lorded over much of what was now Mongol territory. As their power had declined, Uighurs had settled north of the Tarim Basin, above the Taklamakan Desert, from where they controlled one of the main trade conduits along the Silk Roads. Exposed to the influences and ideas that moved east and west with trade, Uighurs had also comfortably embraced diverse religions, including Buddhism and Nestorian Christianity. Their leaders now showed themselves to be politically astute by aligning themselves with the coming power; they were the first non-Mongol people to do so. On his side, Genghis Khan recognised that Uighurs could provide his hitherto insular people with a more sophisticated world view. They also had an unusually high literacy rate and would serve the new empire as scribes, administrators, record-keepers and teachers – Genghis's own sons were tutored by a Uighur called Tatar Tonga (T'a-t'a T'ung-a). With the Uighur khanate on side, the Mongols continued westwards and hoped for similar success from their diplomatic advances towards the Uighurs' neighbour, the Sultan of Khwarazm.

The Great Khan was learning to curb his steppe instinct to return agricultural land to pasture, an early form of rewilding. Those of his advisers who had experience at the Chinese court had helped him see the advantages of allowing settled people to continue in their own way, not least the wealth to be had in trading with them. It was with the intention of establishing this sort of trade link that Genghis exchanged messages with the Shah of Khwarazm, Ala ad-Din Muhammad II. In 1218, he sent envoys bearing gifts to the shah, the most notable being a nugget of gold that had been mined in China and was so large it needed a special cart to carry it. Along with gifts, the Mongol envoys brought a suggestion that in return for grain and cloth from the Muslim west, Genghis could offer access to Mongol and Chinese markets. Tell the Shah of Khwarazm, the khan instructed his envoys, that 'I am the sovereign of the East, and you are sovereign of the West! Long may we live in friendship and peace . . . and [long may] ordinary goods of my land be transported to your land and vice versa.'[49] Along with his envoys, Genghis financed a trade mission of five hundred camel-loads of goods and, out of respect for Khwarazmi sensibilities, he chose Muslim traders. They were accompanied by a light escort of a hundred Mongol horsemen because what could possibly go wrong?

The caravan's first stop in Khwarazm territory was at the city of Otrar, now in Kazakhstan. Otrar sat in an oasis on the Syr Darya river, the ancient Jaxartes, which had marked the northernmost extent of Alexander the Great's empire and had long been an important trading post between the steppes and the caravan cities. The city's governor was a relative of Shah Muhammad's. When the caravan arrived, he ordered it to be seized. It is not clear whether he had a problem with foreigners in general, or Mongols in particular, whether he was driven by a desire to relieve them of their goods or whether he had instructions from his master. Whatever the motive, the entire trade mission was charged with spying against the shah. As the accusation was levied by the governor, there was no way for the Mongols to appeal the charge, or the sentence of death. As sometimes happens on such fateful occasions, there was a survivor: a camel driver who had gone to relieve himself at the exact moment that the governor's soldiers arrested the traders. His absence went unnoticed and when he returned he saw what had happened.

The camel driver escaped the Otrar trap and hurried across the border to the court of the Mongol khan. When Genghis Khan heard his account his response was unusually calm. Instead of vowing bloody revenge, he gave the Khwarazmis an opportunity to make amends. He sent a Muslim envoy, again out of respect for Khwarazmian religious persuasion, and two Mongols to ask that the Otrar governor be handed over for punishment, but Shah Muhammad had other ideas. The Mongols were executed and the others, the Muslims, sent back to their master after suffering the humiliation of having their beards shaved off.

Perhaps Shah Muhammad had been emboldened by a string of

recent military victories that had left him master of much of the old Persian Empire, by his fine army, his many strongly defended cities. He certainly knew that the Mongols had no great skill in siege warfare. Perhaps he was also encouraged by the silence that followed the second insult without any response from the Mongols. But in 1219 Genghis Khan crossed the border at the head of a force of as many as 120,000 men.

Western history usually presents Genghis Khan and his Mongol horde as bloodthirsty killers whose idea of fun was to eviscerate babies and flay men alive, burn cities and devastate farmland. But *The Secret History of the Mongols*, the official Mongol history, presents another side of the mighty khan's character and relates that Genghis responded to news of the Khwarazmi insult by asking, 'How can my "golden halter" be broken?' This 'golden halter' was the bond between Genghis Khan and those who owed him allegiance. The Mongols viewed the bond as sacred because it was sanctioned by the gods and therefore if it was broken, it had to be repaired, order must be restored. So, in their own words, the Mongols went:

> To take revenge,
> To requite the wrong . . .[50]

Before Genghis Khan set out, *The Secret History* tells us, one of his wives suggested that he consider his mortality and think about who might succeed him as Great Khan. You are not eternal, she told him, so:

> When your body, like a great old tree,
> Will fall down,
> To whom will you bequeath your people
> Which is like a tangled hemp?
> When your body, like the stone base of a pillar,
> Will collapse,
> To whom will you bequeath your people
> Which is like a flock of birds?[51]

Genghis then spoke to his four sons to settle the succession and they all set off to requite the wrong and restore order.

Muhammad Shah knew how formidable Mongol fighters could be on a broad field where their horsemen and archers were most deadly. He is quoted as saying that they 'are brave and fearless and that nobody can vie with them in courage, staunchness before hardships of war, and their skills in piercing with a spear and striking with a sword'.[52] But he also knew that they were nomads and always struggled to maintain a siege. What he did not know – and his spies had not reported – was how much Mongol commanders had learned from campaigning in China. Among the great migrating army now moving towards Khwarazm, 10,000 men had specific skills in siege warfare. The trailing caravans of ox-carts that stretched beyond the horizon, creaking and rumbling down tracks from the steppes towards Otrar, were carrying huge crossbows and mangonels to shoot flaming arrows and other incendiaries over high walls, catapults to sling rocks the size of men, all the materials necessary for making siege towers, ladders for scaling walls . . .

Muhammad Shah had also not been idle and during the hiatus he had levied extra taxes to pay to strengthen urban defences and hire mercenaries to fill his ranks. Recent campaign successes had added significant territory to his empire as well as the cities of Samarkand and Tashkent and the Fergana Valley. But there had also been bad judgements, as when he had marched on Baghdad only to lose a significant part of his army in snow in the Zagros Mountains. So it should have come as no surprise that, for all their bravado, the Khwarazmis were ill-equipped to withstand Mongol determination and skill. Their armies were routed and there was huge loss of life, although that was just the beginning. Samarkand, which had fallen to Muhammad Shah in 1208, had quickly become Khwarazm's political capital and one of the great trading centres of the Silk Roads. Bukhara, one of the largest cities in the Islamic world, was the empire's religious centre and a refuge of scholarship. Gurganj had earned immense wealth from its pivotal position on the north–south and east–west trade routes. Before each city, Mongol leaders paused to demand that the city's governor open the gates. The terms offered were always the same: acknowledge sovereignty and pay tribute, usually in the form of gold, and the city and its people would be safe. But the governors were confident that their cities could withstand the brunt of Mongol arms and they did not concede.

Arrows and flaming balls of naphtha rained on the cities day and night without respite until the walls were breached, or the moat was filled in and the city gates forced. In Gurganj in 1221, the second year of the campaign, the Mongols diverted the river, using the force of its flow to undermine the city walls. Then the first wave of the assault force appeared, many of them Khwarazmi prisoners who were being used as a human shield to draw fire. After the initial bloodletting, Mongol fighters moved in and the outcome was always the same bloody mess. When the city fell or was about to fall, elders and imams would beg for peace. They were usually spared long enough to see the consequences of their earlier refusal to cede. Artisans and artists were sent east where their skills were in demand, beautiful women were sent to the many noble and royal harems or raped by soldiers, or both, while the rest of the population, those who had not managed to flee or hide, were killed, tens of thousands, sometimes hundreds of thousands of them put to the sword. That, at least, is one version of what happened. But it is more likely that only those who resisted and hid in the citadel or mosque were slaughtered, and that Genghis Khan 'did not disturb the [other] inhabitants in any way'.[53] Not that things were easy for those whose lives were spared, for they risked being conscripted into the Mongol army or used as labour.

The definitive violence in Khwarazm was intended in part to send a message east towards China where there was still resistance to Mongol advances, north into Russia and west beyond Persia and the Arab lands into Europe. It was a message to the world that resistance to the Mongols was futile. Temujin believed he had been sent by the Lord of the Blue Sky to claim the whole world as part of his empire, although most people who faced him regarded him as just another conqueror. If religious conviction was not sufficient reason to align oneself with the new masters of the world, the head count of those who died in a few blood-soaked years might have been. That, and the knowledge that some of Central Asia's richest

provinces had been reduced to wasteland, fertile farmland allowed
to rewild, some of its strongest cities levelled, some of the glories
of Afghanistan gone, along with those of the Persian heartland,
including the fabled underground canals. Hundreds of thousands,
perhaps millions of people were forced to flee ahead of the Mongol
wave. 'O would that my mother had never borne me,' the Arab
chronicler Ibn al-Athir wrote, echoing common sentiment, 'that I
had died before and that I were forgotten.' The consequences of
the 'disaster' of the Mongol attack were worse, he thought, than
anything that had happened in the world before and seemed to hit
Muslims hardest of all. 'The Anti-Christ', he went on, would at
least only kill enemies, but the Mongols 'spared no one'.[54]

Al-Athir's statement obviously does not stand up to scrutiny.
There was immense bloodshed, but there was also clemency,
especially for people of use or value to the Mongols. Before the
city of Kiva was besieged it is said that Genghis Khan sent a
message offering safe passage to Shaykh Najm al-Din Kubra, the
founder of a Sufi order. The shaykh refused the offer and said he
would prefer a martyr's death, but he allowed his disciples to leave
while he is reported to have taken part in the fighting. He was
eventually beheaded, his remains interred in his hometown of
Gurganj. But the story suggests that the headlines of bloodlust
were exaggerated by writers, most of whom did not witness the
events they described but were happy to stoke prejudices against
Mongols, who were regarded by many Arab, Persian and European
writers as barbarians.

Whatever the body count, the Mongol invasion certainly created
chaos. Out of that chaos came change and some of the greatest
human achievements. Among the multitude on the move was a
man called Baha ud-Din Walad, a mystic and jurist from Balkh
in what is now northern Afghanistan. Like many in Khwarazm,
Baha ud-Din decided to leave home rather than risk his life and,
followed by some of his disciples, he and his family moved west.
They went first to Baghdad and from there, on pilgrimage to
Mecca, later travelling north through the Fertile Crescent into
central Anatolia, which they hoped would keep them far from
the Mongol reach. On the journey, Baha ud-Din met a man

named al-Attar, the pre-eminent Sufi poet. Al-Attar is said to have watched the traveller and his teenage son coming towards him and remarked that he could see a sea followed by an ocean. The 'ocean' was Baha ud-Din's son Jalal ud-Din, who would soon win fame for his mystical poetry. Sufis and many others have called him *Mevlana*, 'our master', but he is more commonly known as Rumi.

Rumi understood the dangers inherent in the cyclical nature of all things. But unlike Ibn Khaldun who believed the wheel would inevitably turn, and who found relief and solace in the promise of return, Rumi urged his followers to look at things in another way and to 'step out of the circle of time'.

Nomad Empire

They were still nomads, but by 1223, after four years of campaigning in the west, the Mongol Empire stretched 4,500 miles from the Caucasus and the shores of the Caspian Sea to Korea and the Pacific Ocean. At that point, Genghis Khan could have installed himself in one of the many palaces he had captured, or lorded it over Gurganj, Samarkand or the many other great cities that now formed part of his empire and which were again thriving, in spite of the reported massacres. He could have conquered Constantinople or Rome, at which point the 'emperor of the world' title would have sat very lightly on his shoulders. He could have followed the Abbasid example and built a new capital. But instead he did what nomads do and he returned to his summer grazing in the Orkhon Valley, to an old familiar camp known as the 'black tents', Qara Qorum.

There are scant remains in Qara Qorum (Karakorum as it is more commonly known) today. Waves of conquerors, the most recent being Russian-backed Mongolian communists of the late twentieth century, have finished what time and weather started, and the once-glorious nomad city has been levelled. But for thirty years from 1223, this was the centre of Mongol power and therefore – as London was for some of the nineteenth and twentieth centuries – the capital of the world. Although the empire offered many better connected and richer places to site an administrative centre, the choice of Karakorum is a reminder of Genghis Khan's sound judgement.

The valley in which it sits is surrounded by stubby hills and cut through by the meandering Orkhon river. It is blessed with an ideal microclimate and had reliably good grazing for Mongol horses and herds. But perhaps most important for Genghis, it enjoyed sacred status among the nomads. A thousand years earlier, the valley had been the homeland of the Xiongnu. After them, nomadic Gokturks had made it their capital, as had eighth-century Uighurs who displaced them. The Uighurs had built a large centre at Ordu Baliq, 16 miles north-west of Karakorum, to serve both as a marketplace and royal residence, complete with a fabled golden tent. It is impossible now to know whether any rocks in the Orkhon Valley had religious significance, or if a sign or omen had once been seen in that place, but there must have been some reason why the valley was the long-time physical and spiritual home of eastern steppe nomads. Now it belonged to the Mongols.

Establishing himself in the Orkhon Valley helped the new emperor reinforce tribal identity and strengthened his *asabiyya*. Unlike the Abbasid caliphs in Baghdad, in his new capital the Mongol khan lived with his people. 'I, living in the barbaric north,' he wrote to a Chinese sage, just as Attila the Hun might have done eight hundred years earlier, 'wear the same clothes and eat the same food as the cowherds and horse-herders. We make the same sacrifices and we share the same riches.' Genghis's description of a life lived without what he called 'inordinate passions' was confirmed by foreign visitors to the capital who saw the Great Khan eat what his court ate – hare, deer, wild pig, marmot or antelope if they had been hunting, and otherwise fish from the Orkhon river and mutton from the herds.

In spite of the vast wealth and power that Genghis had amassed in the twenty years since the *quriltai* of 1206, Karakorum was mostly just a camp of nomad yurts that was put up ahead of his arrival and removed once the conqueror moved on, as he did in 1226. This time he headed east to the Yellow river to consolidate his hold on the heartland of China. He returned to Karakorum the following year, and this time he had come to stay for ever because, as *The Secret History* puts it, 'he had ascended to Heaven'.[55]

As with so much about Genghis Khan, there are a number of explanations for his death. One account suggests he suffered that most nomadic of accidents, falling from a horse. A Tibetan chronicle records that he died after having sex with one of the princesses of Xixia, the Chinese state he was attacking: she had hidden a blade in her vagina and he subsequently bled to death.[56] But more probable, as Marco Polo reported, is that he died of battle wounds.

The Mongols had by this point perfected a process for selecting the Great Khan which was to some degree democratic: the princes and nobles who attended the *quriltai* held at Kode'u Aral on the Kelüren river the following year, 1229, mourned Genghis's passing while also voting for his successor. Although there were no hard rules, Mongol tradition favoured succession to the youngest son. But election did not give him the power to rule over the entire empire. So while Genghis's youngest son, Tolui, took control of the Mongol homeland, the rest of the empire was divided between his brothers, with one ruling over Transoxiana, another over the eastern territories, another over the far west in what is now Russia. A second *quriltai* was held two years later and this time the princes and nobles agreed that Ogodei, ruler of the east, would assume the title of Great Khan.

Ogodei, Genghis's third son, was a man of great energy. He also had a great appetite for life and all its pleasures, hunting and drinking among them. Over the next ten years he used the small army of artisans and craftspeople captured during the many campaigns to turn Karakorum from a yurt camp into a permanent city of imperial stature. Solid structures were built and decorated, the lower, wider stretch of the Orkhon Valley was farmed and the city's food supplies were guaranteed by the creation of regular traffic routes from China.

Most people in Christendom regarded Mongols as nomadic barbarians with all the obvious exaggerations of depravity, savagery and cruelty that hung around the label. But whatever the truth of their barbarism, Mongols were now masters of the world, which is why a succession of European ambassadors were sent east. Beyond a desire to share in the great wealth that was being created within the Mongol Empire, there were other significant motives behind these European embassies.

The first was the memory of what happened in 1241, when Ogodei ordered the Mongol armies into Europe. The Rus principalities, Hungary and Poland were devastated – half of Hungary's population was said to have died in the campaign after the Mongols crossed the Danube – while a second Mongol column fought its way to the Dalmatian coast. There had been no significant field army ready to confront the eastern invaders and Vienna was exposed. But the conquest of Vienna had to wait till the spring because winter was coming. The Mongol armies pulled back across the Danube and set up their winter camp on the great Hungarian plains, ideal for grazing their horses and convenient for gathering intelligence for the spring campaign. But the spring campaign never started, leaving many Christians believing they had been saved by an act of God. There was another reason. In December 1241, Ogodei left Karakorum to go hunting, riding with his companions in the hills above the Orkhon Valley. When it was over, he celebrated with a long night of partying and heavy drinking. The following morning, 11 December, he was dead. As Mongol princes were required to be present when the new khan was elected, they postponed their invasion of Europe, left their armies in winter camp on the Hungarian plains and returned to the Orkhon Valley. The exposed Christian West was saved not by God but, as one British historian put it, by Mongol democracy.[57]

Another reason for the embassies to Karakorum was that European rulers hoped to persuade Mongol leaders to redirect their armies towards the Middle East, where the Crusades had failed to secure a

Christian kingdom and where Mamluks, slave soldiers from Caucasia, had taken control of Egypt and much of the Holy Land. Putting aside their age-old prejudices about Asian nomads, the pope and Europe's Christian kings hoped these Asian nomads would find common cause against a mutual Muslim enemy. One reason they thought this might be possible was a belief widely held in Europe that Ogodei was a Christian. Genghis Khan and Ogodei had both been animists in the great steppe tradition, worshipping the One God – Sky Father or Tengri – while holding the sun, moon, earth and water to be sacred. Like his predecessors, the newly elected Great Khan – Guyuk – was happy to welcome all religions because freedom of conscience remained a keystone of Mongol society. Europe, however, was not so accommodating; England was expelling Jews at this time and cancelling all debts owed to them. News of a significant Christian presence in Karakorum convinced some in the West that there must be a Christian king among these nomadic barbarians. His name, they said, was Prester John.

The name of a Prester or King John had been mentioned in European courts for at least the previous century. In 1145, the Bishop of Syria had appeared in Rome to share the good news with Pope Eugene of the rise of a Christian priest-king in Asia. According to the bishop, Prester John now wished to emulate his ancestors, the Magi, and travel to Jerusalem. For this reason, if for no other, he was prepared to assist the Crusaders. A letter circulated in Rome and Constantinople at the same time, purportedly from the king himself, claiming that he did 'surpass all the kings of the entire world in wealth, virtue and power'. That might have rung true, but it is surprising that no one expressed doubts when the report went on to state that 'milk and honey flow freely in our lands; poison can do no harm, nor do any noisy frogs croak. There are no scorpions, nor serpents creeping in the grass.'[58] It is a sign of their desperate need for Mongol help, and the extent to which their campaign against Muslim power in the Middle East was failing, that the Christian heads of Europe convinced themselves that Guyuk Khan and Prester John were one and the same. To persuade him of their cause, European ambassadors risked their lives, travelling for months, some even years, to reach Karakorum.

Crusaders refused the Abbasid sultan's offer of a peace treaty and instead prepared to attack Cairo. Their defeat brought an end to the Fifth Crusade and yet the myth and the misunderstanding persisted.

Two years later, in 1224, a vast army blazed through Georgia and the Russian states.[61] The King of Hungary wrote to the pope that these strangers carried crosses in front of them and so he assumed 'a certain King David or, as he is more usually called, Prester John'[62] had arrived to fight against Muslims. Such was the depth of delusion that even after reports filtered through that this strange king had slaughtered 200,000 Christians, the Hungarians were offering explanations – perhaps, they suggested, those who died were heretic Georgians of the Greek Orthodoxy, so King John was merely cleansing the Church. The contemporary Novgorod Chronicler was more sober as he captured the sense of anxiety and bewilderment that 'for our sins, unknown tribes came, whom no one exactly knows, who they are, nor whence they came out, nor what their language is, nor of what race they are, nor what their faith is; but they call them Tartars.'* And who were the Tartars? 'God alone knows.'[63] But eventually everyone in Eurasia would know that these were not people from some mythical Christian kingdom in the east; they were Genghis Khan's Mongols and, having made their mark on eastern Europe, they left the land and cities they had captured, and they returned home. And that too left Europeans baffled, not just about who these barbarians were, but what they wanted.

The savagery that was believed to characterise Mongol behaviour did not deter the pope and Europe's monarchs from sending more ambassadors east. Fifty years after the first papal envoy disappeared, a regular convoy of missions shuttled eastwards to consult with the khans, among them Hungarian friars Riccardus and Julian, a Dominican friar Ascelinus, Benedict the Pole and Simon of Saint-Quentin. And there was John of Piano Carpini, another papal envoy, who returned with one of the most revealing accounts of life among

---

* Tartar or Tatar is used to refer to Mongols as well as people of the Volga and Crimea.

the Mongols. At the same time, the Mongols sent envoys to the west. One of them, sent by the Mongol commander in western Asia, encouraged the Christian kings in Europe to continue their crusading and suggested that the current Mongol khan was a grandson of Prester John, who had common cause with them now that he had converted to Christianity.

Guyuk, however, was not a Christian and was clearly annoyed by some of the ambassadorial proselytising. In 1246 he wrote to tell Innocent IV that the papal envoy had suggested that the khan should convert to Christianity. 'This petition of thine', the khan continued, 'we have not understood.' Instead of converting, he affirmed his belief in 'the Eternal Sky'. Calling himself 'the Oceanic Khan of the whole great people', Guyuk then demanded that 'the great Pope, together with all the kings, must come in person to do homage to Us'.[64]

Partly in response, another Dominican, Andrew of Longjumeau, was sent east, this time by Louis IX of France and with gifts that included fragments of the True Cross and a purple portable tent-chapel for celebrating Mass. Longjumeau and his companions got about halfway to Karakorum, into what is now Kazakhstan, before they were diverted into the mountains. The reason for the detour was that Guyuk was dead and his wife, manoeuvring to have their son elected as Great Khan, thought an embassy from a European monarch would help the child's claim. Longjumeau returned to France with a letter from the young man thanking Louis for the gifts and inviting him to send more. It was clear that the young khan saw the gifts as a sign that the French king acknowledged Mongol superiority, for why else would Louis have sent tribute?

The most successful Western visitor to Karakorum at this time was a resilient Flemish Franciscan, Friar Willem van Ruysbroeck. William of Rubruck, as he is known in English, had already been on crusade with the French saint-king and he was present when Andrew of Longjumeau reported back to Louis, which was how he learned that there were Christian slaves in the Mongol heartland who were without the support of the Church, something he thought he could rectify. He had also heard that these nomads were tolerant in matters of religion and it was with optimism – and gifts – that he sailed into the Black Sea in 1253 just after Guyuk's succession had been settled and another of Genghis Khan's grandsons, Mongke, was elected Great Khan. Friar William was armed with Bibles, 'fruits, muscadel wine and dainty biscuits',[65] a letter from the French king, a sharp eye and the unshakable religious zeal with which he hoped to win the new master of the world over to Christianity.

It was a long road into what the Fleming described as 'another world'. It was also slow, with ample time to record the places he passed through and the things he learned on the way. Friar William's detailed description of Central Asia was the first to note the size and inflow of the Caspian Sea, the courses of the Don and Volga rivers, the first to prove that what the Greeks and Romans had called Seres was China (the case is now made that Seres refers to the silk-producing parts of Asia, which includes China and India), and the first to describe Tibet, where the Mongols had made further land gains. At a time when many in Europe still believed, as Herodotus had done 1,700 years before, that the Far East contained dragons, people with one eye and others with goat feet, his account was revolutionary and was not improved upon until the nineteenth century.[66] It provided details of how these nomadic people lived in circular houses made of sticks, covered with white felt, how some of their houses were thirty feet wide yet even the largest of them could be mounted on an ox-drawn cart, how the door always faced south and the master always sat in the north. These barbarian nomads, he reported, wore Chinese silk in summer and coats of fur, and they padded their trousers with silk in winter. They had been taught the ancient Sogdian script by Uighurs, and had learned mantras from Tibetan Buddhists – he was the first to describe the *Om mani padme hum* mantra.

Friar William was a heavy man and the sweet wine and biscuits he had brought on the journey suggest that he was fond of his comforts. The second part of the long Karakorum road must have seemed a penance as the Mongol guide kept the Europeans moving all day, only allowing them to stop to eat at night. Even then, all they were offered was seared mutton, which the guide spiced with stories of the terrors and torments on the road ahead.

The Mongols were not without their suspicions of Friar William. The election of Mongke as Great Khan had shifted power from one branch of Genghis Khan's family to another and the atmosphere was febrile, especially as the new khan had eliminated anyone who threatened his position – even the royal widow Longjumeau had met had been executed. But as he drew closer to Karakorum, there was some relief in hearing that the new khan was eager to establish closer relations with Europe's rulers.

It took almost a year for Friar William and his companions to reach Karakorum. Khan Mongke was camped a little way outside his capital for, like his grandfather Genghis, he seemed to prefer tent life. It was late December and the priest and his party were exhausted, cold and considerably lighter than the previous winter when they had left the Palestine coast, thanks to short rations on the gruelling journey. The Great Khan was disappointed to learn they were not an official French embassy, but he still allowed them to stay because they might have useful information to share. Before they were granted an audience, they were questioned by the emperor's chief scribe on their country, the journey and news of their world. Did the scribe or his master believe all they heard? We cannot know, but the good friar certainly did, for alongside the solid facts he gives us, there is the odd wild story. My favourite is his report of creatures which lived to the east of China, who had human features but were no taller than your forearm and had legs that could not bend. They also had an appetite but no tolerance for alcohol, so Chinese hunters would leave mead out for them and the little creatures would cry 'Chin, chin', drink and then pass out. The friar then showed himself even more credulous when he reported that, once unconscious, the hunters opened a vein in the creatures' necks and extracted a few drops of blood. The blood was used for dyeing purple, and the creatures became known as *Chinchin* . . .

A week after his arrival, Friar William was granted an audience with the khan. What must he have thought as he was escorted through camp? He was surrounded by nomads whose mere appearance had been known to rob adversaries of the power to speak and to raise a sword or shield, whose bloody brilliance had taken the lives of millions of people and whose name was whispered to children in the West to scare them into behaving. Now he was to meet their leader, whose reputation seemed to justify all the prejudices settled people had ever levelled against nomads.

Before he was allowed into the khan's presence, the friar was thoroughly searched for hidden weapons; even in the Mongol heartland, there were fears of the Assassins, the radical Shi'a sect whose followers had already killed a number of prominent figures without being caught. After being searched, the heavy tent-flap was pulled aside and the European walked into what he described as 'another world'. The yurt was huge, hung with gold cloth and warmed against the icy winter by a fire of wood and dung. Mongke was enthroned on a couch covered in sumptuous fabrics near the centre of the yurt. He was short, middle-aged and snub-nosed, dressed in sealskin and attended by many women. His first gesture, in Mongolian, was to offer his visitors a drink. What would they have: wine, rice wine, fermented mare's milk or mead? It was at this early stage that Friar William discovered how little of the Mongol language his interpreter understood. Even providing an answer to which drinks they would prefer was beyond the interpreter's abilities, made more difficult partly because he was already drunk. At the end of the audience, the Europeans were told they were welcome to stay two months among the Mongols, until the cold had passed and they would be able to travel in more comfort. It was perhaps a recognition of the Europeans' frailty and the rigours of the journey. They were still among the khan's tented entourage on Palm Sunday, late March, when Friar William and his companions blessed some trees that had no spring buds. After that, at long last, the court and the European visitors approached the solid mud walls of the capital.

The transformation of Karakorum from an enlarged yurt camp to imperial capital was most clearly encapsulated in the khan's new residence. The riverside Palace of Ten Thousand Tranquillities was a seismic shift away from the gold-lined yurt in which the khan had received the Europeans. Friar William described it as the place where Mongke held his 'drinkings', state occasions on which he reinforced *asabiyya* among his followers with public displays of largesse and heavy intake of alcohol. With the massed ranks of Mongol nobles crammed into the palace, Mongke handed out promotions, titles, domains, furs and gold to his companions. It was at these sessions that dividends were shared – for in the same way that twenty-first-century shareholders benefit from the profits of the companies they have invested in, so Mongols shared in the profits generated by their imperial success, receiving 'taxes and tributes from regions that were under the direct supervision of the Great Khan'[67] and were distributed during *quriltai* and other tribal gatherings.

We know that these gatherings were well lubricated from the journal of another visitor, an Armenian, who wrote that

> wherever possible they ate and drank insatiably, but when it was not possible, they were temperate . . . To drink *kumiss* [fermented mare's milk] or wine, one of them first takes a great bowl in his hand and . . . sprinkles the liquid to the sky, then to the east, west, north and south. Then the sprinkler himself drinks some of it and offers it to the nobles.[68]

To provide drinks for the khan's many guests, the palace's most notable feature was a huge tree. Planted just inside the palace entrance, this tree needed no blessing to encourage it to blossom for it was fashioned of pure silver, the ultimate accessory for a generous, free-drinking thirteenth-century ruler. It had been created by a French master goldsmith, William Buchier, who was captured in the Mongol conquests but had stayed in Karakorum of his own free will, attracted by the possibilities of working in the world's richest court. Buchier was certainly being well paid for his skills, although Friar William's estimation of the goldsmith's latest commission at what today would be over £14 million may have been an exaggeration. But his description of the silver tree has enough detail to be convincing. It was clearly a thing of wonder, its four branches symbolising the four rivers of paradise, each one flowing with a different kind of alcohol. The roots were guarded by four silver lions from whose mouths flowed mare's milk. Above them, topping the tree, a silver angel sounded a trumpet when one of the reservoirs was about to run dry, a sign for servants to bring more goatskins of alcohol.

Mongke may have ruled the largest empire in the world, but he was still a nomad and he only stayed in the capital and his palace when he passed through on migration into or out of the Orkhon Valley. Perhaps he already knew what Ibn Khaldun was to discover, that cities posed existential risks, that their temptations could overwhelm the *asabiyya* and nomads could lose their identity. But Karakorum was unlike other cities. It had no distinct palace quarter – rich and poor lived alongside each other, some in palaces, others in hovels – and the four gates were named not after the direction they faced, or a person who had lived or died there, but according to commodities for sale: sheep and goats in the west, grain in the east, oxen and carts in the south, horses in the north. It was a reminder that the imperial capital was still a market.

In other ways, Karakorum was similar to imperial capitals from any age, the population reflecting the huge reach of empire as Mongols, Chinese and Turks, Hungarians, Alans, Ruthenians, Georgians, Armenians, Arabs and many others rubbed shoulders in the city's alleys and shared benches in its taverns. Genghis Khan had sought out carpenters, jewellers and other skilled craftspeople in the cities he conquered and had sent them back to Mongolia. In the process, he and his successors had gathered not just a unique mix of people, but also a great resource for building and filling their new capital, not unlike Darius drawing craftsmen to build Persepolis. There was an area of Karakorum for Chinese craftspeople and traders. In another zone, workshops of metalworkers brought from the West created swords, stirrups, cauldrons, axle rings and arrowheads, as well as spindles, which suggests that Mongols were spinning wool and weaving their own carpets. Kilns fired roof tiles and finials, sculptures, plates, platters and glass. And jewellers fashioned beautiful objects out of gold, silver and precious stones. Wherever the jewellers came from – and William, the Parisian goldsmith, was just one of many – they worked within an ancient tradition, for archaeologists at Karakorum have found gold and other jewellery from this period that is similar in style and technique to pieces worn by Scythians, a thousand years earlier.

Ideas and beliefs mixed in Karakorum just as much as manufacturers and traders, and if one detail captures the spirit of the place, and the empire at this time, it is the range of religious buildings to be found along its lanes. There was a mosque, Buddhist temple and Nestorian Christian church among the twelve main places of worship, and some of the khan's family converted to these imported religions. Even the Great Khan himself was happy to be blessed by Friar William. In this way, he took the idea of freedom of conscience to an extreme, allowing the Nestorians to pray for him, Buddhist priests to chant mantras and Muslim imams to recite their *salat*, yet all the while he retained his belief in the sanctity of the earth, with its profusion of sprites and spirits, and he trusted his shamans, astrologers and soothsayers to find meaning for him in the movement of stars and the entrails of beasts. As well he might have done for he, like many Mongols, still believed that their glory had been foretold in a dream in which a gyrfalcon held both the sun and the moon in its claws, a prophecy that in one part was about to be fulfilled.

The Tears Will Tell You

About the time Friar William left Europe on his long journey east, one of Mongke's younger brothers, Hulagu, rode out of Karakorum at the head of a large army of nomads. Their mother had been a Christian and Hulagu was later to adopt Buddhism, but for now he was a nomadic animist out of the Orkhon Valley. Mongke, it was reported, had seen signs on his brother's forehead that told of conquest, sovereignty, royal majesty and fortune. Perhaps it was to keep him away from Karakorum that Mongke set Hulagu the task of asserting Mongol power over western Asia and Mesopotamia, just as he sent away another of their brothers, Kubilai, to subdue China.

And if the promise of glory and the Mongol reputation in war were not enough to spur Hulagu to victory, he was also fighting for his own future, since Mongke had agreed that Hulagu could rule whatever land he conquered.

Hulagu's first significant engagement was in north-west Persia with Nizari Isma'ilis. This radical Shi'a sect was led by a Grand Master who was said to drug his followers and promise them entry to paradise and the attention of nubile virgins before sending them to kill political opponents. The adepts were popularly known as *hashishin*, Arabic for people who smoke hashish, although it is more likely they acted out of religious devotion. For more than a century the *hashishin*, whom we know as the Assassins, operated as an independent force in the Middle East, at times fighting alongside Crusaders, at others standing with their Muslim adversaries. Their actions were directed neither by religious nor racial preferences but by political expediency: they simply fought for their survival. Their independent highland state was serene, secured by some fifty castles or strongholds, while the world around them became increasingly unstable and bloody, in part made more so by Assassin blades or poison, which claimed the lives of a Christian king and a patriarch in Jerusalem, Crusader knights including Raymond of Tripoli, two caliphs in Baghdad, the sultan in Cairo, another in Damascus and the *qadi* (judge) of Isfahan. Death was not inevitable, however, as the Crusader Edward 'Longshanks' discovered when he survived a poisoned Assassin dagger blow and went on to become King of England, where he reigned for thirty-three years. Even the tent of Saladin, the great Arab leader, was infiltrated and a message left pinned by a poisoned dagger to a table near where he slept. The Mongols also knew all about the Assassins – that was why Friar William was frisked before being allowed into the Great Khan's presence. If Hulagu was to establish Mongol supremacy in the former Persian Empire, he would have to eliminate these stealthy killers.

The Assassins had built bases in some of Syria and Iran's most remote places, none more so than near Qazvin in the Elborz Mountains, in north-west Persia. Alamut Castle was fashioned out of the summit and saddle of a huge rock that stands like a lone tooth on the edge of a fertile valley. The remains today are impressive, cut

into the summit and built up above it, equipped with outer fortifications, deep wells, equally deep storerooms that would keep
food cool and, my guide assured me when I visited, also made for
a convenient place for *hashishin* to talk in confidence. The castle's
name is Persian for 'eagle's nest', for once no exaggeration and
also perfectly apt, for like birds of prey these mobile predators had
built a defensive stronghold that took its strength from its natural
setting.

When you stand at the uppermost level of Alamut's fortifications,
looking down onto long, sheer cliffs and out across the Elborz
Mountains and their lush valleys, it is easy to imagine how awe-
inspiring it was to live in such a place. It is also easy to imagine
how desperate the Assassins would have felt seeing Hulagu and his
horde arrive, their numbers bolstered by the khan's vassals in the
region, although the Abbasid caliph in Baghdad had chosen not to
answer the call.

Hulagu approached Alamut with the care appropriate for such an
enemy and a stronghold that was considered impregnable. First he
approached some of the more vulnerable Assassin fortresses in the
area and in one of these he found twenty-six-year-old Imam Rukn
al-Din Khurshah, the sect's new Grand Master. When the imam
was captured, Hulagu persuaded him to order other Assassin strongholds to surrender, which he did, recognising the inevitability of
defeat and hoping, perhaps, to spare lives. The great Assassin story
came to an abrupt and less than glorious end when even Alamut
surrendered. The Grand Master was sent to Karakorum. He had
been given assurances for his safety but was executed nonetheless.
The contemporary Persian historian Juvaini, who was with Hulagu
at the time, described all this as divine punishment upon 'the her-
etics [at] the nest of Satan'.

Juvaini also recorded for posterity that the Mongols 'came, they
sapped, they burnt, they slew, they plundered and they departed',[69]
which was clearly not true because here as in Baghdad and elsewhere
– and contrary to tales told in the West – the Mongols did not
destroy everything. Before the fortifications of Alamut were dismantled, the library was secured and sent east. So too were some scholars
who had been living with the Assassins, the most famous being

Nasir al-Din Tusi, a mathematician, philosopher and astrologer, who was the first to write about trigonometry. Hulagu enlisted Tusi as an adviser and later settled him in the khan's new capital at Maragheh, now in Iran, where he built him what was then the world's most advanced observatory. The Maragheh observatory was the most sophisticated of its age and the model for observatories in Samarkand in the fifteenth century, Constantinople in the sixteenth and India in the eighteenth century, but it was no pet project. At Maragheh, Tusi was able to make more accurate astronomical tables, which were essential for the astrological predictions on which Hulagu relied to inform his decisions.

The people of Baghdad might not have ridden out to join the Mongols, but they did cheer the fall of the Assassins for reasons that might resonate today: the Abbasid caliph was a Sunni and had had his own problems with the fanatical Shi'a in the mountains. But their joy was short-lived. The previous year, one of the great poets of the age, Shiraz-born Saadi, had written that 'the leopards have given up their leopard-like behaviour'.[70] In 1258, the leopards began moving towards Mesopotamia and they were hungry.

Hulagu wrote to the Abbasid caliph al-Mustasim in Baghdad:

> You have doubtless learnt from men of high rank and low what punishments the Mongol armies have inflicted on the world and its peoples from the time of Genghis Khan to the present day: the humiliation, thanks to eternal God, of the dynasties of the Khorezmshahs, the Seljuks, the sovereigns of Dailam, the Atabeks and other princes renowned for their grandeur and power. Since the gates of Baghdad were not closed to any of these races . . . how then can entry to this city be forbidden to us, we who possess so many forces and so much power?[71]

Hulagu's argument had a persuasive logic to it, but seeing that the caliph was unmoved, he warned that if the people of Baghdad rallied to fight, the Mongols would strike with 'righteous anger' as the hand of God.

> *I will bring you crashing down from the summit of the sky,*
> *Like a lion I will throw you down to the lowest depths.*

I will not leave a single person alive in your country,
I will turn your city, lands and empire into flames.

What better illustration could there be of Ibn Khaldun's wheel of fortune in motion, than the young Mongol dynasty, its *asabiyya* strong, its nomad energy potent, threatening to overwhelm the corrupted older dynasty, the power of its *asabiyya* eroded by generations of being settled?

Al-Mustasim was in the sixteenth year of his reign as caliph when the massive Mongol force appeared around Baghdad. He has been called an imbecile, weak, miserly, vain, incompetent and cowardly. He found excitement in hunting and took pleasure in his harem, but had little interest running what remained of his empire and his reign had been far from glorious.[72] To make matters worse, his council was divided over the best way to meet the nomadic challenge. Years of underspending had reduced the Abbasid armies and left their cities defenceless. Many argued they had little choice but to capitulate. Others harked back to the glory of the first caliphate and to their Arab ancestry and they urged al-Mustasim to fight.

The bulk of Hulagu's army were Mongol fighters, including the renowned horsemen, but they had been joined by Armenians, Georgians, a detachment sent from Antioch and the elite Chinese siege corps. Hulagu described his army as being 'as numerous as ants and grasshoppers' and it is estimated at somewhere between 100,000 and 300,000. Even the lower figure should have made the most deluded of Baghdadis wonder how long they could hold out.

Contrary to their image as barbarous nomads, the Mongols did not wish to destroy Baghdad, which was why the khan sent a final demand to the caliph. Submit to us, his letter urged, and you and your family will live, your city will flourish, your people thrive. The Mongol Empire would also thrive.

But Hulagu knew that the caliph would resist and in words that might have come straight from the pen of Ibn Khaldun, he wrote: 'The love of great things, riches, pride, the illusions of fleeting happiness have so completely seduced you that the words of well-intentioned men make no impression upon you . . . Now all you can do is prepare for war.'[73] But even the caliphate's war preparations were compromised, with many Abbasid troops deserting, some even defecting to the Mongols.

In the middle of January 1258, al-Mustasim's generals sent a force of 20,000 across the Tigris river in a pre-emptive strike. The Mongols were ready for them. In a classic nomad move, they retreated, luring the Abbasid force further from the city than they had intended, at which point Mongol sappers broke the dykes and flooded the plain. Most of the expeditionary force was drowned. Hulagu quickly seized the advantage and took up positions outside the famous circular walls. Another twelve days and then his siege engines and battering rams went to work at the gates and walls. While they were slowly breaking down the barriers, a variety of catapults lobbed rocks and pots of naphtha into the city and storms of arrows flew from Mongol composite bows. Some of these arrows carried notes addressed to judges, sheikhs and merchants, promising to spare them and anyone who had not yet taken up arms; as ever, the Mongols were keen to minimise casualties and the time it would take to enter the city. Meanwhile, they were building pontoons across the Tigris, both up- and downstream from the city, to cut off defectors.

Before it was over, but when the fight was obviously lost, al-Mustasim sent a delegation to the Mongol leader. His sons and viziers brought lavish gifts and an offer to surrender. But Mongol custom stated that the time to talk was before the fighting started. Once the fight was underway, it must end in the destruction of one side or the other. Soon after the delegation was sent, the caliph's commander-in-chief was captured along with seven hundred guards. 'The caliph was led by his destiny,' the commander-in-chief protested, a line that could have come from the Mongol leader's mouth, but neither excuse nor petition could spare the commander's life nor those of his men.

Twelve days after the assault began, al-Mustasim, the thirty-seventh caliph and successor to the Prophet Muhammad, walked out of the gates of what had been the greatest city on earth followed by his sons and many dignitaries: their walls had not protected them. They made their surrender in Hulagu's camp, but this did not ensure their safety because that was not the Mongol way. According to Hulagu's own account, some 200,000 Baghdadis were led out of the city to their execution, although one contemporary historian put the figure at four times that number. A thousand of the caliph's eunuchs and seven hundred women from his harem were also put to the sword. After the executions, Hulagu allowed his men to sack Baghdad and to rape or kill as they wished. Then the city was put to the torch and much of it burned, including the House of Wisdom. The great library had suffered many depletions over the centuries and yet had remained one of the world's great repositories of knowledge. Its fate that day is still disputed but, having saved the Assassin library at Alamut, it would have been inconsistent for Hulagu to have destroyed the contents of the larger and more significant Baghdad library.

There are several versions of what happened to the caliph, who was held in the Mongol camp after his surrender. Persian and Arabic sources suggest that Hulagu forbade him access to food until he begged to be fed, at which point he was served three platters, one loaded with gold, another with silver and the third with gems. When he protested that this was not food, Hulagu is reported to have chastised him. 'Since you knew these were not fit to eat, why did you make a store of them? With some of these you might have sent gifts to propitiate us and with others you could have raised an army to serve you and defend yourself against us.'[74] Perhaps at that moment al-Mustasim remembered an earlier message he had sent the Mongol leader. 'The prince forgets', the caliph had said before the siege, 'that from the east to the west all the worshippers of Allah, whether kings or beggars, young or old, are slaves of this court and make up my armies.'[75] That, at least, was what should have happened, and what would have happened had the caliph attended to his *asabiyya*. But as Ibn Khaldun understood, like many of his forebears the caliph had lived apart from the people who could have protected him, and the group feeling that had brought the Abbasids to power had long since dissipated.

The Mongol punishment for refusing to capitulate was death, but Hulagu had qualms about shedding the blood of a descendant of the Prophet. Perhaps his Sunni advisers warned of dire consequences, although Nasir al-Din Tusi, the astrologer who had been spared at Alamut, the Assassin stronghold, and who was a Shi'a, reminded the khan that nothing of consequence had followed the beheading of John the Baptist or the deaths of the imams Ali or Hussein. Nor indeed the death of the Assassin Grand Master, Imam Rukn al-Din Khurshah.

It was said that Hulagu did not want to burden any of his men with having to kill the caliph and that he thought it wrong to spill such a man's blood, so an unusual end was devised. Al-Mustasim, Prince of the Faithful and last of the caliphs, was rolled in a carpet along with his son and heir and the carpet was then ridden over, again and again, by Mongol horses, perhaps by the caliph's own horses. The story may not be true but then again perhaps it did happen because there was something appropriate for a ruler who had strayed so far from his nomadic roots to die beneath the hoofs of steppe ponies. Appropriate too his being wrapped up in a carpet, the signature possession of the migrant community.

Before he lost consciousness, did al-Mustasim experience a moment of clarity? Did he see, as Hulagu had seen and Ibn Khaldun would later see, where things had gone wrong for him? Did he rue the moment his people gave up their mobile way of life, or when they were seduced by palaces and softened by city ways? And as the caliph was being trampled, did Hulagu have a moment of reflection where he wondered what might lie in store for himself? Would he eventually settle?

With the caliph dead, the Abbasids' great treasury was emptied and divided in two. There was certainly enough for Hulagu to share with his brother the Great Khan, for one contemporary chronicle describes how they 'sank under the weight of the gold, silver, gems and pearls, the textiles and precious garments, the plates and vases of gold and silver, for they only took those two metals, the gems, the pearls, the textiles and the garments'.[76] After half of the hoard had gone to Mongke in Karakorum, Hulagu had the rest shipped to Shahi Island in Lake Urmia, near his new capital, Maragheh. Hulagu would follow soon enough for he died seven years later, in 1265, and was buried in one of the last of the great nomad interments with a herd of sacrificed horses and a mass of his hard-won treasure.

As Baghdad burned, one of Hulagu's commanders pointed out to his khan that it was in their interest that the city continued to function. For the settled caliph, Baghdad had represented security, power, stability, and to destroy it would show his people that they could not defend themselves against nomad power. But for nomads, the commander argued, Baghdad was a marketplace and meeting point.

Hulagu was convinced and soldiers were sent to put out the fires and to clear rotting corpses from the city. Perhaps as a nod to his mother's religion and a reminder that Mongols celebrated freedom of conscience, Hulagu gave one of the caliph's surviving palaces to the Nestorian patriarch, along with a large plot on which to build a new church. The surviving inhabitants were placed under the governorship of the Persian historian Juvaini, who began the huge task of rebuilding the city and the lives of its inhabitants. Many remained inconsolable at the fall of the caliphate, at the loss of Baghdad's prestige as Islam's great city and at the end of their *asabiyya*, their sense of belonging, their shared cause.

'Oh seekers of news about Baghdad,' the contemporary poet Ibn Abi al-Yusr lamented, 'the tears will tell you':

> *No benefit from remaining here, the beloved has departed.*
> *Oh visitors to al-Zawra, please do not come here.*
> *Baghdad is no longer a refuge; no one is here any more.*
> *The crown of the caliphate, the great monuments,*
> *All has been burned to ashes.*[77]

Hulagu, meanwhile, continued his march west, now heading for the Mediterranean coast. From Syria down to Egypt, the rich Mediterranean farmland of the Fertile Crescent was controlled by Mamluks, many of whom had been born along the edges of Mongol territory. Mamluks had pushed the Crusaders onto the coast, but the Christians still held the key ports from Tripoli to Jaffa. Hulagu's appearance added to the complexity of the long-drawn-out drama of the Crusades. Choosing his route according to the availability of fodder, he first led his Mongol army north from Baghdad, following the fertile Euphrates and Tigris valleys. From there he moved west – both Aleppo and Damascus refused his demands (unlike Homs, which capitulated) and were devastated – and he was preparing to continue south to confront the powerful Muslim Mamluk army.

Had he done so, he might have defeated both the Mamluk and Crusader armies and taken control of the region. That, in turn, would have changed the course of history, and the destiny of the

Middle East, perhaps also of Europe, might have been very different. But before that could happen, in August 1259, Mongke died and, like the Mongol princes on the Hungarian plain when Ogodei died eighteen years earlier, Hulagu was obliged to return to Central Asia for the election of a new Great Khan. Without him, the reduced Mongol army struggled and in September 1260 they were heavily defeated by the Mamluk leader Beibars at Ayn Jalut near Nazareth. The Mamluks followed up their victory by pushing the Mongols north-east towards Azerbaijan, where Hulagu had established his powerbase. By the winter of 1260, Beibars controlled much of the Fertile Crescent and was installed as Sultan in Cairo. The title of one of his Mamluk successors would have better suited him, for now he really was 'the Powerful, the Dreadful, the Punisher of Rebels, the Hunter of Franks, Tatars and Armenians' and, last but not least, the 'Snatcher of Castles from Rogues'.[78]

1271

Thirteen years after the fall of Baghdad and six years after Hulagu's early death, which had been foretold by a comet, a teenager set off from Venice on a journey to the court of the Great Khan Kubilai. Thanks to him, and others, we know something about the significant achievements of the Mongols' immense empire, an empire based on the twin pillars of freedom of movement and freedom of conscience.

Marco Polo was travelling with his father and uncle, both of them traders who had already made the journey across Eurasia. Their experience made the road no less arduous, nor any quicker: twenty-four years would pass before the son returned to Venice. Three years after that, he was caught up in a naval dispute between his hometown and their Genoese rivals, at the end of which he was imprisoned. Enforced seclusion proved to be a blessing for he had time to gather the stories of his journeys and he had a fellow inmate to write them down. Because his journey was remarkable, but also because his adventures were written and published, Marco Polo is regarded as one of the most famous travellers of all time, with even the airport in his hometown now named after him. And, yet, what was all the Eurocentric fuss about? It was said that in those years a virgin could cross the vast nomad empire without fearing for her modesty, her life or her fortune, even if she was carrying a golden bowl on her head. What could a group of armed European men have to fear?

For the century after the fall of the caliphate, Eurasia was dominated by competing, migrating tribes. Marco Polo's account of his travels has remained significant because it is a great tale, but also because it is a rich source of detailed information about the new masters of the world.

Life under the new Mongol ascendancy was different from life under Genghis Khan. Kubilai Khan had left Karakorum and established his winter base at Khanbaliq, now Beijing. In the summers, he still preferred the cool of the nearest steppe and, some 220 miles north of Beijing, at a place called Shang-tu, he settled on a beautiful site surrounded by hills of pine forests in which falcons nested. The valleys had fat grazing for his horses and the land was good for agriculture. There, in the poet Coleridge's words, Kubilai decreed 'a stately pleasure-dome' be built, a summer palace whose gilded rooms and beautiful grounds were something 'you regard with delight and astonishment'.[79] Those last words were written by Marco Polo, who saw rather than imagined the place. At Coleridge's Xanadu, Alph, the sacred river, ran. At Marco Polo's Shang-tu, the gardens were bright with sinuous rills and meadows, fountains and brooks, all enclosed within a 16-mile-long wall.

Mongols now ran the largest empire the world had ever seen. Kubilai, founder of the Yuan dynasty, was the first non-Han ruler of China. Hulagu was *Ilkhan* (Viceroy) of an empire that stretched westwards from the Indus to the Bosphorus and included Persia, Mesopotamia and Anatolia. The descendants of another of Genghis Khan's sons, Chagatai, ruled the core of Central Asia – including the Silk Road cities of Bukhara, Samarkand, Kabul and the land as far east as the Altai Mountains. Their cousin Berke lorded it over the Golden Horde, an alliance of Mongol, Turkic and other tribes who controlled a vast swathe of the original Indo-European steppe-land north of the Caspian Sea. The combined Mongol domains covered four thousand miles east to west from the China seas to the Himalayas, across much of what is now Russia and down through Iran and Iraq to the Euphrates river. In a century when European states were fighting among themselves, while also launching six crusades into the Holy Land, all of which ended in defeat, the Mongols opened their markets and welcomed trade and movement across their lands. In the process, they would change the world.

They would also welcome strategic marriages and, just as the royal families of Europe were linked by blood in the nineteenth century, Mongol leaders were connected by a web of marriages that linked them to sultans, kings and emperors, from the Tatar Ilkhanate of Persia and Iraq to the Yuan emperor in China, the Khan of the Golden Horde, the emperor of the Mamluk lands of Egypt and Syria, the Byzantine emperor, the empress of Trebizond and the houses of Savoy, Brunswick and Genoa.

The people who lived under this grand nomad-inspired alliance, from Yuan Chinese in the east to Turks and Persians in the Ilkhanate west, were as diverse as the land they called home, but they now also shared much in common, not least the laws of Genghis Khan. There is continuing controversy regarding the *Great Yasa*, the legal code that Genghis Khan decreed into being in the *quriltai* of 1206.[80] Whether or not there was ever a written set of laws, it is clear that from the early thirteenth century Mongol princes governed according to a set of commonly acknowledged values intended to suit their subjects living both on the hoof and in cities. Freedom of conscience gave Christians, Muslims and Buddhists the same status as animist steppe people. Freedom of movement must have seemed an obvious necessity to nomads who migrated each year in search of pasture. And freedom to trade, in our own time a fraught issue, had always been essential for nomads. The great change was that this had now been imposed over a vast empire.

Protecting these rights had often been the catalyst for nomadic action, whether it was Attila the Hun moving on the Roman Empire to protest the closure of frontier markets or the Xiongnu punishing the Han Chinese for closing trading posts along the Great Wall. Guided by these principles and the overwhelming desire of Mongol khans to cooperate with others, the nearest thing the world had ever seen to frictionless trade flowed and in volumes that were previously unimaginable. The Mongol peace, more even than the *pax Romana*, connected the world through trade, and many people became very rich, including those native people whom Mongols had chosen as their tax collectors.

The stability and security provided by the Mongol ascendancy made the century following the fall of Baghdad the golden age of the Silk Roads. Fifty years after Marco Polo told tales of such wonder that many doubted whether what he said could ever be true, trade between Italy and the East was a commonplace. So much so that a Florentine mercantile agent, Francesco Balducci Pegolotti, wrote a *Book of Descriptions of Countries and of Measures Employed in Business*. Pegolotti had never been further east than Armenia – he probably did not even reach that far – but that did not stop him from including the route from the Black Sea to China in his guidebook for traders. 'The road you travel from Tana [Azov in the eastern Black Sea] to Cathay is perfectly safe, whether by day or by night,' he blithely advises his readers, and then adds the caveat, 'according to what the merchants say who have used it. Only if the merchant . . . should die upon the road, everything belonging to him will become the perquisite of the lord of the country in which he dies . . .'[81]

The risks, it seemed, were outweighed by the fortunes to be made thanks, in part, to low transport charges. Pegolotti calculated that an Italian trader setting out with 25,000 gold florins-worth of goods, helped by two servants, with a dragoman as guide, interpreter and agent, would need to spend no more than 400 florins getting himself and his goods to China and back. Mongol khans made east–west trade even more attractive by reducing tariffs and waiving local taxes on international goods.[82] Duties on goods passing through Black Sea ports were also kept low, perhaps no more than 3 per cent of the cargo's value; transit through Egypt, by contrast, could attract a levy of 30 per cent. As a result of this, gold, pearls, spices, curious medical cures, musical instruments, gold-embroidered damask fabrics and damascened steel flowed along the thick Mongol-protected arteries of Eurasia from the Middle East. Silver, amber, furs and fighters were traded from Russia, otter skins and paper from Korea, wools, swords and glass from Europe, textiles from central Asian cities such as Nishapur and Tabriz, and endless bolts of silk and crates of porcelain, among many other products, from China. Global trade had never been so attractive nor so successful.

News also travelled faster than ever before as Mongols expanded the *yam*, their thirteenth-century take on the ancient Persian Royal Road or the old Roman messenger system. Rivers were spanned, wells dug, routes widened and maintained and, most striking, post-houses were built every twenty-five to thirty miles along the main routes out of their capital and maybe every forty miles along less travelled tracks. The khan settled keepers to manage each way station, where they were obliged to grow food and maintain a herd of horses that could be used in relay. These were not run-down caravanserai or flea-ridden Mongol motels: Marco Polo described them as 'the most splendid proof of magnificence and greatness that ever was given at any time by Emperor or King, or by any mortal whatsoever'.[83] There were ten thousand post-houses across the empire, he estimated, 'all richly furnished' – that seems to have included silk sheets on the 'splendid beds' – supported by a large family who also grew food to support themselves and to serve to travellers. Between them they maintained 200,000 horses ready for imperial messengers and envoys to ride.

Some of those details are probably exaggerated. Polo had a habit of adding an extra zero to many of his estimates, but he still captures the scale of the effort and funding that was devoted to creating the messenger system and keeping it running smoothly, and that speaks of the importance the Mongol khans put on connecting the great landmass they now controlled. And they succeeded. Under Mongol rule, a person carrying an oval token called a *gerege*, also known as a *paiza*, could travel the length of the empire enjoying the facilities of post-houses as well as the protection and support of local rulers. Different levels of service were on offer depending on whether you were touting a gold, silver or wood *gerege*. A wood *gerege* ensured you would receive food and a fresh mount. A gold one would get you a feast followed by a night in a good bed with silk sheets. There is an important point here beyond silk sheets and it relates to the way trade moved between east and west Eurasia.

A thousand years earlier, the *pax Romana* had helped Chinese silk and porcelain find a market around the Mediterranean. But Chinese merchants were not seen, because it was easier to move goods than people. Now that roads had been built and maintained, accommodation offered, security ensured and profit margins boosted by low tariffs, it seemed as though the whole of Mongol-controlled Eurasia was in flux and it became unsurprising to find Venetians in Beijing/Khanbaliq competing with their great rivals the Genoese, just as Mongols were to be seen in Egypt and northern England, a French silversmith happily at work in Karakorum, and traders from Lucca and Siena driving hard bargains in Tabriz.

But trade and traders were not the only things set in motion. Christian priests scattered across Eurasia show that religious influences were also passing along the various Silk Roads. The popularity in Europe at this time of Saints Barlaam and Josaphat, legendary martyrs whose life story is a Christian reworking of the life of the Buddha, is evidence of eastern beliefs travelling west. Technology, culture, science, skills and habits also shifted more easily across the great Asian mountain ranges and north and south of the Gobi and Taklamakan deserts. At times this had surprising consequences as, for instance, with the use of something as apparently innocuous as cobalt oxide.

Cobalt ore had long been mined in several places in Persia, and since at least the tenth century Persian potters had been heating it to create cobalt oxide, which they used to colour glass and as an underglaze for pottery. Under the Mongol supremacy, Persian pots were sold into Chinese markets, but so too were cakes of dried cobalt oxide. Chinese potters then began to experiment with this Persian or 'Muhammadan blue'. At the same time, they also experimented with arabesque and 'Islamic' patterns, which were drawn on their beautiful white porcelain bowls. These Chinese 'Muhammadan' bowls and vases were then shipped back west to be sold in Persian and Egyptian markets. When Persian ceramicists recognised what the Chinese were doing, and when they saw how popular their goods were, they copied the Chinese copies, and sold them along the trade routes. These Persian copies of 'Chinese Muhammadan' cobalt-coloured porcelain would later influence Ottoman Turkish potters. In Iznik and elsewhere, they copied Chinese patterns onto bowls, jars and tiles, but added flamboyant orange tulips to the cobalt-blue designs, creating what is now recognisably Turkish ware. There were two further extensions to this cobalt-blue chain. In the seventeenth century, Dutch potters copied these Persian/Chinese designs onto their own tin-glazed Delft earthenware and sold them around the Mediterranean. A century later, British potteries such as Minton and Spode responded to the success of Delft ware, and to the Chinese originals, by creating what is known as Willow Pattern china, or Blue Willow, still in widespread production and extremely popular to this day.

While it is possible and fascinating to track the movement of cobalt across Eurasia, it is harder to follow the equally widespread movement of ideas, beliefs and knowledge. But 'Muhammadan blue' was certainly not the only thing that bounced between east and west as people across Eurasia found themselves connected to each other in a way that had never been felt before. Under the Mongols, a babel of tongues wagged in caravanserais and post-houses between the Yellow Sea and the Mediterranean. Through their talk and trade, whether they knew it or not, they stirred into being what would eventually become a revolution of ideas and gossip, conventions and behaviour that would transform the world and nourish the European Renaissance.

Some of the changes brought about were local and also relatively small-scale: the religion of the Great Khan, for instance, on which European leaders had pinned such great hopes during the Crusades. Kubilai had been brought up an animist, worshipping the old steppe gods like his forebears. In his late twenties, before he assumed power, he was influenced by Tibetan holy men, who encouraged him to convert to Buddhism. Although an insistence on freedom of conscience was central to Mongol culture – practise what you like, or nothing at all – and although Tengriism, Zoroastrianism,

Christianity and Islam spread across the empire, there was an importance to the fact that the Great Khan was a Buddhist, even more so
later when the khans converted to Islam.

Other transferences and transformations are there to be glimpsed
– in the surprise at the idea of meritocracy, at Mongol democracy
where the leading figures chose their leader, at the strength of Mongol
belief in codified law whether it was written down or not, at the
stories of universal education – of boys at least – among the Great
Khan's subjects. There was surprise when large sheets of paper travelled west for the first time, just as there was when paper money,
already in use in China for several hundred years, was first distributed
in Persia in 1291. There was amazement in 1331 when sixteen knights
rode in the opening procession of King Edward III's first London
tournament at Cheapside, amazement because they were dressed in
clothes and masks *ad similitudinem Tartorum*, to look like Tatars
(Mongols), inspired perhaps by Marco Polo's descriptions. Or when
the same king, seventeen years later, commissioned gold-embroidered
Mongol-inspired cloth as part of the regalia for the knights of his
new Order of the Garter. Or when women in Europe began to copy
Mongol ladies and wear the *boghta*, a headdress whose origins lie in
the tall conical hats worn by ancient Saka and Scythian women.
Mongol *boghtas* were originally made of two-foot-high cones, kept
upright by a frame of wood and birch bark, and covered with felt.
As the empire generated wealth and enriched noble Mongol families,
boghta wrappings became more elaborate, felt was replaced by silk or
brocade, now decorated with pearls and feathers. In Europe, these
hats inspired the *hennin*, the *capuchin* and a range of other impractical
headgear worn for centuries by ladies of grander houses.

In some ways, none of this should come as a surprise because the
idea of the East had been transforming the European imagination
since at least the beginning of the thirteenth century and probably
much earlier. As the French historian Georges Duby pointed out, the
Mongol ascendancy forced Europeans to recognise that 'the world
was infinitely larger, more various and less docile than it had seemed
to their forefathers; it was full of men who had not received the word
of God, who refused to hear it, and who would not be easily conquered
by arms.'[84] Three especially significant developments came out of this

realisation. The first was a freeing of the European imagination, a freedom that is most beautifully expressed in the shape and ambition of Europe's great cathedrals of the age, from Chartres and Canterbury to Burgos in Spain and Budapest's Matthias Church, commissioned to celebrate the end of the Mongol invasion. These churches and cathedrals expressed something of the new world order in their structures, their great spires pointing to the heavens, their interiors flooded with light, in their funding which came from trade and in the mathematics, inherited from Arab scholars, which made their construction possible. The second development was an acceptance of the nomadic Mongol ascendancy. As Duby explained, 'Why persist in struggling against all those infidels, those expert warriors, when it was more advantageous to negotiate and attempt to insinuate oneself in those invincible kingdoms?'[85] But perhaps most significant, because it would lead to the transformation not just of Europe but the world, was the way that Mongol power and their domination of the vastness of much of Asia, inspired Europeans to broaden their horizons, to look east to India and across the Atlantic in the west. The voyages of explorers such as Vasco da Gama and Christopher Columbus were in response to the stranglehold on goods by central Asian nomads.

The cross-fertilisation of culture made possible by the Mongol peace would transform the other end of Eurasia as well. China had long been known for the insularity of its kingdom, but now, ruled by a nomad khan from the landlocked, horse-dominated steppes, it emerged as a naval superpower. Kubilai Khan had initially thought his new fleet of four-masted junks would help bolster his campaign against his sea-facing neighbours in Japan and Korea. But when that plan failed, he repurposed the ships to create what may have been the world's largest armada prior to the Second World War.[86] This new merchant navy was so immensely successful that it allowed China to take control of the sea trade between the East China Sea and the Red Sea. The benefits of this were not lost on Marco Polo. The Italian had spent four years travelling overland to China, but when he and his fellow travellers left for home, they cut their journey time in half by sailing under the protection of fourteen Chinese ships from Guangzhou to the Persian coast.

The new Chinese junks were the seaborne equivalent of Silk

Road caravans. Each one was manned by a crew of three hundred (this might be another Polo-esque exaggeration, although he did see it with his own eyes) and had sixty cabins for traders and their goods. The trade they generated was so profitable that even nations who had resisted Kubilai's military assaults – Indian states, for instance, Viets, Cambodian Khmers, the Sukhothai and Chiang Mai kings in Thailand – were prepared to acknowledge Kubilai's sovereignty in order to be part of his maritime network. Between the maritime routes and the Silk Roads, the Mongols had stimulated the nearest thing the world had ever seen to a global trade network and it generated wealth in Europe as well as in the East. That, in turn, required another adjustment for many Europeans. Until this time the East had appeared on European maps as a place of hideous creatures, one-footed freaks and barbarian hordes. But with the success of east–west trade, it was now seen as a place of immense wealth and where the roads, markets, security and much else were more advanced than in Europe.

The khan of China was thought to live in a gold-lined pleasure palace surrounded by the sort of seductive splendour European monarchs could only envy. In a story told by one of Kubilai's contemporaries, the Ilkhanate vizier and historian Rashid al-Din,

> one day, when he [Kubilai] had laid the foundations of Qaraqorum, he went into the treasury and saw nearly a hundred thousand bars [of silver]. 'What benefit do we derive from all these stores?' he asked. 'They have to be constantly guarded. Have it announced that every-body who wants a bar should come and take one.' The people of the city, high and low, rich and poor alike, all rushed to the treasury, and everyone got an abundant share.[87]

This sounds like something out of a fairy tale, but it has the ring of truth about it, for Kubilai was acting no differently from bankers in Europe then, or now, who recognise that capital must be kept moving and who give seed money in the hope that the ventures will become profitable. But there was more to this than a capital handout. As one scholar puts it, silver, like other luxuries, 'is better viewed as the receptacle or medium of something immaterial. In the Mongol conception, the circle of redistribution brought happiness.' What's more, redistribution was 'the key to maintain social order, and to repair social disorders. It is hard to reconstruct how the medieval Mongols defined collective happiness, but they certainly believed that the circular movement of things was crucial in producing it.'[88] For a century and more, there was happiness as well as significant return on capital as trade routes remained busy and markets thrived. But Ibn Khaldun knew it could not last. It would not last.

Writing from the safety of the Algerian hinterlands, Ibn Khaldun, who was born forty years after Kubilai Khan's death, described the Mongol ascendancy as an eruption out of the steppe. This was one of the great stories of his time. He knew how the empire had developed, how it had been divided after the death of Genghis Khan and how his sons and grandsons had enlarged it. He also knew about the tensions between the different lines of the Great Khan's family and he now used their story as an example to support his theory of the circularity of dynasties.

He identified five steps in the cycle from rise to fall:

'The first stage is that of success, the overthrow of all opposition, and the appropriation of royal authority from the preceding dynasty.' This is achieved thanks to *asabiyya*.

The second stage consolidated power and royal authority in the hands of the leader, but to the exclusion of the group – the aim, here, is 'to blunt the aspirations of the people who share in his group feeling'.

In the third stage, the leader settles for a life of peace and luxury, decrees laws, commissions buildings, equips a fine army and hands out largesse to his own people and to foreign ambassadors.

Next comes a phase of contentment in which the new ruler mimics his predecessors, lives in peace with his royal peers and 'thinks that to depart from tradition would mean the destruction of his power'.

Finally there is the downfall, in which 'the ruler wastes on pleasures and amusements (the treasures) accumulated by his ancestors'.[89]

Considering all five stages of a dynasty, Ibn Khaldun concluded that 'God is the best heir'. That may have been so, but Genghis Khan had had children, a vast number of children.

For a century after Genghis's death, his heirs had lorded it over land and sea from China to the Near East, confounding their nomad origins by building spectacular monuments, flourishing towns and cities across Eurasia, which they filled with some of the most skilled artists and the finest minds. When, as had happened, sparks of jealousy or suspicion had set the regions ablaze, the khans had still maintained sufficient order across the empire for trade to flow east and west. But Ibn Khaldun had outlined the inevitable process at work here, how the corruption of cities and the weakness of their *asabiyyas* had led, in the 1330s and 1340s, to the disintegration of the Golden Horde, the fragmenting of the Ilkhanid state in Persia, which was consumed by a series of civil wars, and the splitting of the central Asian khanate into two very distinct kingdoms. The nomadic world, which had so recently dominated the globe and shaped it to its ways, had failed and as Ibn Khaldun wrote, the rule of the descendants of Genghis Khan 'came to an end'. In that he would prove to be wrong, for there were more of Genghis's descendants to come. But first something came along that proved to be more deadly to Mongols than disunity and more deadly to Europeans than the Mongols.

Nothing that Should Delight Me

When the great Moroccan traveller Ibn Battuta visited the Crimea in the 1330s, the port of al-Kafa was still a place where you could feel the nomad 'bounce'. Surrounded by Turks to the south, Rus and Mongols to the north, and Christians to the west, al-Kafa was somewhere the Mongol peace had brought wealth and a previously unknown cultural openness. On its quays one might meet Genoese, Venetians, Greeks, Armenians, Jews, and a variety of Mongol and Turkic people. Among its houses, as Ibn Battuta's biographer noted, 'doctors of Islamic law studied the fasting habits of Christian ascetics; [whilst] in an Armenian monastery church, a font could pass muster as an Islamic prayer-niche'.[90]

Al-Kafa was important because it gave the Genoese and their Venetian rivals easy access to the edge of the great steppes, it was relatively well defended and just a short sea voyage from the Mediterranean. Trade had made al-Kafa what Ibn Battuta called one of the world's 'most celebrated' ports and he reckoned there were two hundred cargo vessels and warships in harbour when he was there, as many as he saw in the greatest port in China. He also describes the town's fine bazaars, although he fails to mention the slave market, which was then the largest on the Black Sea. Al-Kafa was also where the North African heard church bells for the first time and 'never having heard them before I was alarmed at this'.[91] In panic, he had the Quran chanted from the top of the mosque's minaret to ward off whatever terror was to come, 'but no evil befell us'. Some twelve years after his visit, evil would arrive.

The local mint issued coins which perfectly expressed the dual nature of the place, with an inscription of the nomad khan in Arabic on one side and the seal of Genoa's Bank of St George on the reverse. Competition between the two turned to conflict in the 1340s when Jani Beg, the khan of the Golden Horde, chased Europeans out of other Black Sea trading posts. In 1345 he began a long siege to force them out of al-Kafa.

'See how the heathen Tartar races, pouring together from all sides, suddenly invested the city of Caffa,' wrote Gabriele de' Mussi, a contemporary notary from Piacenza, 'and besieged the trapped Christians there for almost three years. There, hemmed in by an immense army, they could hardly draw breath, although food could be shipped in, which offered them some hope.'

With autumn came help from an unexpected quarter: one by one, the fighters besieging the Italians began to drop dead.

'But behold,' de' Mussi continues, 'a disease . . . overran the Tartars and killed thousands upon thousands every day. It was as though arrows were raining down from heaven to strike and crush the Tartars' arrogance . . .'[92]

This idea – that the Mongols were being punished by Heaven, that this was an act of God – was repeated in the coming years but for different reasons. As the death toll mounted, the Mongols responded in a way that might have seemed practical to them, but which had dire consequences for all. They gathered the corpses of their many dead fighters, loaded them into siege catapults and launched them over the walls into the city. Whether they intended it or not, they had just invented biological warfare.

'Mountains of dead' and rotting Mongol corpses began to pile up inside the city, polluting the air and water. When the situation became intolerable, the healthy European survivors took to their ships and sailed from al-Kafa, from the Mongols and from the plague. Or so they believed. But

> as it happened, among those who escaped . . . by boat were a few sailors who had been infected with the poisonous disease. Some boats were bound for Genoa, others went to Venice and to other Christian areas. When the sailors reached these places and mixed with the people there, it was as if they had brought evil spirits with them.[93]

The evil spirit was *Yersinia pestis*, more commonly known as the Black Death, the world's most devastating disease. Exactly where it first incubated remains a matter of contention – even today, no one wants the blame – but it may have first appeared in northern China in 1331, where outbreaks claimed the lives of 90 per cent of the population. It could also have come from the great Eurasian steppe, described as 'one of the world's great plague basins'[94] and the ideal environment for the deadly bacteria to propagate. Wherever it started, it spread along the Silk Roads – one unwelcome aspect of a joined-up nomadic world – carried by fleas that infested rats, camels and humans as well as food and clothing. In 1335 it took the life of Abu Said, the last of Hulagu's descendants to rule his empire, whom Ibn Battuta had called 'the most beautiful of God's creatures'. It was also deadly around Lake Issyk Kul, now Kyrgyzstan, where three grave-stones mention that the deceased died of plague in 1338–9.

Between the 1346 al-Kafa outbreak and 1350, when it began

to dissipate, the disease swung through the world like the Angel of Death and took 75 million lives – 25 million in Europe, which was a third of the population. But the Italian observer de' Mussi was wrong to claim that it was the Genoese who spread the disease. They were certainly carrying it when they fled from al-Kafa in 1346, but the disease managed well without them and moved more easily along trade routes than a caravan stowaway. By 1347, it had decimated Near East cities such as Trebizond, Constantinople, Tabriz and Baghdad. The following year it surged and spread south to Mecca, across North Africa from Cairo and Alexandria to Tunis, and into Europe. First to Sicily, then Venice, Genoa, Marseilles, into Spain and up through France. In June the following year, the disease shipped across the Channel to England – carried by a Gascon, according to one contemporary source – making a first appearance at Melcombe Regis (Weymouth) on the River Wey in Dorset.

Everyone suffered from the Black Death, although some nomads may have suffered less because the plague flea seems to have had an aversion to horses. In Venice, as many as three-quarters of its citizens died. Some Egyptian towns lost 90 per cent of their inhabitants. Peasant farmers died, but so too did the King of Castile, the Queen of Aragon, a Byzantine prince and French and English princesses. The population of England was reduced from 7 million at the start of the plague to 2 million fifty years later.

The manner of suffering was also universal. The Italian writer Giovanni Boccaccio, who was thirty-five years old when the plague struck (he survived), relates in his masterpiece *The Decameron* that the authorities in his native Florence removed 'enormous amounts of refuse and manure', forbade the sick from entering the city and issued many instructions as to how citizens might stay healthy, and yet still they fell. 'It began', he explained, 'with swellings in the groin and armpit, in both men and women, some of which were as big as apples and some of which were shaped like eggs, some were small and others were large.' Infected people usually survived no more than three days, while most animals died instantly. Boccaccio recorded at least 100,000 people dying in Florence between March and July 1348. He also noted that 'huge numbers of men and women abandoned their rightful city, their rightful homes, their relatives and their parents and their things, and sought out the countryside . . . as if the wrath of God was aroused against only those who unfortunately found themselves within the city walls.'[95]

Boccaccio's contemporary, the poet Petrarch, was forty-four when the pandemic hit Parma, where he was living. He lost his patron and many friends, and then his beloved Laura died and he knew 'there is nothing left in the world that should delight me'.[96] In a letter to his brother, he wondered: 'When has any such thing been even heard or seen; in what annals has it ever been read that houses were left vacant, cities deserted, the country neglected, the fields too small for the dead . . .'[97]

We now have a clear idea of what caused this terrible disease, how it is spread and why it killed, just as we each now know for ourselves the terror of a pandemic; but in the fourteenth century, no one knew what caused these deaths and that left them free to guess. Boccaccio and Petrarch echoed many when they assumed the 'great mortality' was the wrath of God. Was this the end of the world? And if it was, could it be delayed − or avoided altogether − through prayer, or sacrifice, or if they acted or dressed differently? Would avoiding society help? Or should they be partying every night? Should they abstain from sex, or indulge massively in it? All expediencies were tested. The pope in Avignon obviously believed it was God-sent and encouraged penitence, although like the Mongol khans, he also consulted astrologers, who pointed to a conjunction of Saturn, Jupiter and Mars. Across Europe, church bells pealed in the hope that the sound might drive away the illness. Both Christians and Muslims took to mortifying their flesh, some flagellating themselves, others fasting. Along the North African coast and through the Near East people prayed and fasted in the hope that Allah would live up to one of his ninety-nine names, *al-Karim*, the generous. He did not.

The Black Death did more than cast a shadow over Ibn Khaldun's life and the world in which he lived: it may have provided the inspiration to write the *Muqaddimah*. In 1348, when he was seventeen years old, it killed his parents, teachers and many of his friends. 'Civilization both in the East and the West was visited by a destructive plague which devastated nations and caused populations to vanish,' he wrote in the *Muqaddimah*. 'It swallowed up many of the good things of civilization and wiped them out . . . Cities and buildings were laid waste, roads and way signs were obliterated, settlements and mansions became empty, dynasties and tribes grew weak. The entire inhabited world changed.'[98] The world and everyone in it, including himself, and it was that change which caught his imagination.

He contemplated the causes and consequences of the Black Death over the next thirty years and from this, as much as from his exposure to North African court life, the rise and fall of his family's fortunes, and the sight of ruined monuments scattered across North Africa, he found the motivation to write his history because – and this is central – the idea of circularity in all things offers hope not, as we believe, of progress, but through renewal: 'it is as if the entire creation had changed . . . as if it were a new and repeated creation, a world brought into existence anew. Therefore, there is need at this time that someone should systematically set down the situation.'[99]

This was why he had sought refuge in the castle of Ibn Salama. The setting had clearly agreed with him. For four years, he 'was inspired by that retreat, with words and ideas pouring into my head like cream into a churn, until the finished product was ready'.[100]

The Ant-hill of the Human Species

When he left the hills, towards the end of 1378, Ibn Khaldun set in motion a sequence of events that led inexorably towards the fulfilment of a prophecy. Twenty years earlier, as a twenty-six-year-old scholar in Morocco, Ibn Khaldun had met a seer in the great al-Qarawiyyin Mosque in Fes. The seer spoke of 'a powerful one who would arise in the north-west region of a desert people, tent dwellers, who will triumph over kingdoms, overturn governments, and become master of most of the inhabited world.'[101] He also predicted that the young scholar would be a witness to the man and his deeds.

From the castle, Ibn Khaldun returned to the Mediterranean coast and his old home in Tunis, settling his differences with the Hafsid caliph and starting to teach again while continuing to write. But his return stirred up old rivalries, and the jealousy both of courtiers and some of the city's key scholars, including the powerful imam of the Great Mosque, convinced him he must leave. This was easier said than done because he was a courtier and therefore not free to come and go as he wished. Eventually he requested permission to make the hajj to Mecca and even if some in court suspected his motives, the request was difficult to refuse. At the end of 1382 he took ship for Alexandria in Egypt with a plan to establish himself in Cairo and send for his family.

The Egyptian capital had been decimated by the Black Death, which had taken the lives of 200,000 of its 500,000 inhabitants. Things had got so bad according to al-Maqrizi, one of Ibn Khaldun's future pupils, that 'a person might walk all the way from the Bab Zuwaylah to Bab el-Nasr without even being jostled'.[102] The lack of jostling on Cairo's famously crowded central street was as shocking then as it would be today. But as Ibn Khaldun knew, calamity was also opportunity, every decline was eventually followed by a renaissance, and by the time he reached Cairo the process of renewal was underway. There were crowds in the streets and the city overwhelmed him with its energy, grandeur and sophistication. He described it as 'the metropolis of the world, garden of the universe, assemblage of the nations, the ant-hill of the human species, the portico of Islam, the throne of royalty, a city embellished with palaces and arcades . . . and lighted by the moons and stars of erudition'.[103] It was also ruled by a new sultan, Sayf ad-Din Barquq, who had seized power the previous year and now occupied Saladin's old palace up on the citadel, from where he could survey his capital, the Nile and the Pyramids on the horizon.

Barquq was a Circassian, born between the Black and Caspian seas, who had been sold in one of the Black Sea slave markets – perhaps even al-Kafa – and shipped to Egypt. Much of his life had been one of soldiering and now, in his mid-fifties, Barquq was fighting to protect his sultanate. This struggle brought out his most ruthless side, so that alongside the glories of Cairo, Ibn Khaldun also noted its dangers, none more deadly than falling foul of the volatile ruler. Barquq had tortured one wealthy citizen on the rack to reveal where he had hidden his fortune, while another had been nailed to his camel's saddle and left to die on the hoof. But Barquq could also be generous, especially to those who were useful, and he recognised that Ibn Khaldun had the qualities and experience that he needed. Within two years of his arrival in Cairo, the sultan had appointed him one of Cairo's main judges. The appointment did not last, but the respect did and it was as an adviser to the sultan, and as an historian, that he arrived in Damascus in 1401. It was there that the seer's prophecy would be fulfilled.

The Mongol Renascence

The Black Death had damaged the Silk Roads – the huge loss of life had shrunk Asia's economy and markets, as it had Europe's. But so too had the instability caused by a hundred years of conflict between the English Plantagenets and French Valois, and the equally long-standing struggles between various Mongol dynasties. Kingdoms and empires fractured. In western Asia, the Mongol collapse created a power vacuum that pulled Turkic tribes and other nomad groups west off the steppes. In China, Kubilai's century-old Mongol dynasty was overthrown by a monk-turned-commander, Zhu Yuanzhang, from eastern China, and the great Chinese merchant navy of some 3,500 ships was unrigged and scuttled as the Middle Kingdom chose once again to retreat and hope that its Great Wall would keep out the nomads and other barbarians. The golden age of the Mongol khans had tarnished and dulled. 'Little by little,' as one British expert on Central Asia puts it, 'the road that had once joined the Pacific to the Mediterranean fractured and stilled.'[104] For Ibn Khaldun, this decline was as inevitable as the fulfilment of the prediction he had heard in Fes regarding the nomad leader who would rise out of the steppes, gather his group and overwhelm the settled world.

By the time the judge-scholar met this new conqueror, Timur was master of the East, Asia was in his hands, his armies were invincible, his ambition boundless. Once again Mongol forces took control of the old Persian Empire, the Sultanate of Delhi and much of India, Mesopotamia and Afghanistan. Yet Timur was still not ready to settle. He had modelled himself on Genghis Khan and he planned to restore the old Mongol Empire, which meant that he still needed to conquer the Near East and China.

But he was not Genghis Khan. For one thing, Timur was of humble birth which is why, even after thirty-five hard years campaigning in the saddle and having acquired titles such as Lord of the Fortunate Conjunction (a reference to the happy alignment of stars at his birth), Conqueror of the World, Unconquered Lord of the Seven Climes, Warrior of God and the Shadow of God on Earth, he only ever called himself *Amir*, lord. He was never khan or caliph.

It was said that on the night of his birth, somewhere near Samarkand, a helmet was seen fluttering in the sky. When the helmet fell to earth, it covered the plain and city with burning embers. When the newborn opened his hands, his palms were covered in blood, something the diviners of dreams interpreted as a sign that he would be a soldier, a thief, a butcher, an executioner. 'Events', his biographer wrote soon after the man's death, 'decided the issue.' Timur was all of those things as he fought his way to become what the Moroccan seer called 'master of most of the inhabited world'.

He had started simply enough, belonging to a tribe that travelled 'hither and thither', a nomad. He was clearly a horseman, as he was described as 'one of those who know the points of a horse and can distinguish at a glance by the outward shape between good and bad stock'.[105] And at some point he was a sheep rustler, for it was while rustling sheep that he received an arrow to the hip, which left him dragging his right leg. He was tall for the time – some five feet eight – and broad-shouldered, but while it did not show in the saddle, he was also crippled, which is why we remember him as Timur-i Lang, Timur the Lame. Tamburlaine.

The sixteenth-century British dramatist Christopher Marlowe would later coin another label for him, 'the scourge and wrath of God/ The only fear and terror of the world'. Marlowe presents Timur as heir to the Scythians, and to Genghis Khan, and opens his *Tamburlaine the Great* by promising:

> *We'll lead you to the stately tent of war,*
> *Where you shall hear the Scythian Tamburlaine*
> *Threatening the world with high astounding terms,*
> *And scourging kingdoms with his conquering sword.*[106]

Marlowe was gay, an atheist, perhaps also a spy. As an Elizabethan social rebel, he may have admired what has been called Timur's 'transgressiveness', even his nomadism.[107] But it is his image of Timur as a bloodthirsty killer that has survived and long coloured our view. Building on long-held prejudices which go way beyond ancient anxiety about Scythians, Timur is remembered, in the West at least, for the destruction he caused, the lives he took, for the cruelty of his fighters who piled victims' skulls into massive pyramids or catapulted them over the walls of besieged cities, for the rivers of blood, for the many once-great cities reduced to ash. Timur appears as the archetypical barbarian and, in part thanks to Marlowe, is remembered more for his treatment of his rival, the Ottoman Turk sultan Beyazid I, than for some of his finer achievements. Beyazid had attracted Timur's displeasure by claiming parts of Anatolia that had previously shown allegiance to the Mongols. In the showdown between the two nomad forces, Timur's army overwhelmed the Turks and Beyazid was taken alive.

Most of what has been written about this captivity, as with much else about Timur, is laced with age-old prejudices against nomads. All that is known for sure is that Beyazid was Timur's prisoner for nine months, that he died in captivity and that his body was returned to be buried with imperial pomp in Bursa. Less secure is the claim that Timur kept Beyazid in a cage and that the cage was dragged behind the victor as he moved east. Christopher Marlowe presents the story of the cage as a morality tale, as if this confinement was the price the Ottoman paid for his ambition. He also plays up Timur's savagery and finds a nobility of spirit in Beyazid. But Marlowe might have been encouraged along this line by the recent opening of profitable trade between England and the Ottoman Empire. And as Edward Gibbon points out in *Decline and Fall*, like many an ancient ruler on the Eurasian steppe Timur's main objective was neither to sate bloodlust nor confine a rival: 'the conquest and monarchy of the world was the first object of the ambition of Timour [*sic*].'

An equally important ambition was 'to live in the memory and esteem of future ages'.[108] This desire had been motivating nomads ever since the first Indo-European leader gathered his band of brothers around a steppe campfire, made them swear allegiance and promised them that however short their lives might be, if they fought bravely, their names would be remembered around the fires for generations to come. Glorious renown was the reason that Achilles returned to the fight during the Trojan War. If you are going to give your life for a cause, the least you can hope for is that people will speak of you after your death. The cult of the hero was paramount. But the way Timur ensured his posterity sets him apart from many other nomad rulers. More lasting, more certain and more tangible than the pyramids of skulls and destroyed cities were his efforts to encourage the arts. Robert Byron, British gentleman-scholar and aesthete, recognised this when he wrote of a 'Timurid Renascence'.[109] In the 1930s, Byron travelled through much of what had been Timur's empire in search of the origins of Islamic architecture. He described

Timur as 'a free-booter in search of a kingdom', but he also understood how Timur's desire to live in the memory had expressed itself in construction and how that desire had ushered in an age of humanism.*

Timur began in a small way by leaving a mark on the landscape. To commemorate an early campaign in what is now Kazakhstan against the leader of the Golden Horde, who was himself one of Genghis Khan's descendants, Timur had a block of basalt roughly incised with eleven lines of script, in Uighur and Arabic. It reads:

> In the country of the seven hundred black Toqmaq in the Year of the Lamb, in the middle of the spring moon, the sultan of Turan, Timur Beg, marched with an army two hundred thousand strong, of the name of his family, seeking the blood of Toqtamish Khan. On reaching this place, he raised up this stone, so that it would be a sign. 'May God show justice! If it pleases God! May God show mercy on the people! May He remember us and bless us!'[110]

The stone was carved as 'a sign' in 1391 and although it took Timur a further four years to defeat his adversary, the stone still stands as a memorial. Other more impressive, eloquent and long-lasting memorials were to follow in Timur's Renascence.

Timur appointed scribes to record the civil and military transactions of his reign and for good reason. He was confident that he was about to make history and he knew that history would be kind to him because he would write it, or have it written for him. To this end, he was said to be 'constantly accompanied by turbaned lords, *sayyids* [descendants of the Prophet Muhammad], *ulema* [the learned men of Islam] and jurisprudents, and by people of learning and wisdom, Uighur *bakhshis* [scribes] and secretaries'. One of his biographers was certainly exaggerating when he claimed that these scribes wrote down and 'verified every deed and word that issued from His Majesty and everything that happened to the domain and subjects'.[111] Nizam al-Din Shami, an historian who

---

* There are echoes here of Edward Gibbon seeing, for instance, 'a singular conformity' between Genghis Khan's legal code and the work of the Enlightenment philosopher John Locke.

survived the carnage at Baghdad in 1393 by offering his services to Timur, remained with the conqueror throughout and although he was not the only witness to Timur's reign, his *Zafarnama* (The Book of Victory) was the first biographical account to come from inside the Mongol camp and, as Timur would have wished, it has served 'as a memorial upon the face of time'.[112] But it has done so uncritically. Ahmad Ibn Arabshah, another witness, looked at Timur and his actions from a very different viewpoint when he wrote his biography. Ibn Arabshah was an eleven-year-old in 1400 when Timur and his vast army began the siege of Damascus that would end with the death of some of the author's family and with Ibn Arabshah himself being marched east as a slave. It is unsurprising therefore that his *Life of Timur* lacks objectivity. The chapter headings referring to Timur as a tyrant, deceitful one, villain, demon, despot, viper and bastard are a gauge of the author's feelings towards his subject.

From these accounts, and from those of Ibn Khaldun and the foreign ambassadors, we know that Timur had none of Genghis Khan's asceticism. He lived much of his life on the move and was happy to sleep under felt or canvas. But where his predecessor had lived a simple life, Timur enjoyed luxuries and when he was not on campaign, he feasted royally, drank to the full, had his many tents, pavilions and palaces decorated in exquisite tilework and lined with gold fabrics, silks and ermine. His tables were fashioned from gold and silver. 'In diverting the flow of Persian culture to their own enjoyment,' Robert Byron notes, Timur, his wife Bibi Khanum and his family 'were concerned with the pleasures of this world, not of the next'. Out of their delight in this world, they created something extraordinary and beautiful. And that 'something' is more than merely a Mongol copy of Persian culture or architecture. Byron summed it up perfectly as 'the action of a new mind from Central Asia on the old civilization of the plateau'. Out of this action came a perfect union, 'a procreation by nomadic energy out of Persian aestheticism'. The offspring of this procreation between old Persia and nomadic energy was the Timurid Renascence.

Genghis Khan had avoided the great cities he captured, but

Timur took a more settled view and committed himself to building and embellishing on a grand scale, nowhere more gloriously than in Samarkand where he claimed, 'Let he who doubts our power look upon our buildings.' A story that gauges the extent of Timur's sensitivity towards Samarkand has the conqueror becoming angry when the famous Persian poet Hafez wrote:

> *If the Shirazi Turk would only grant my heart's desire,*
> *I'd give up Samarkand and Bukhara for the poorest part of her.*

How, Timur wondered, could Hafez dare to give up Timur's great cities for so little?

To which the poet replied: 'Alas, O Prince, it is this prodigality that is the cause of the misery in which you find me.'

Timur was said to have been calmed and charmed by the poet's wit and sent him away with gifts.

That story is almost certainly apocryphal, but it does show how close Samarkand lay to Timur's heart. He was said to have loved the city like an old man loves a young mistress[113] and it was there, nestled between hills on the banks of the Zerafshan river, and in his birthplace Kesh – the 'heart-pleasing' – some fifty miles away, that he and Bibi Khanum, whose influence over his artistic vision was as clear as it was over the running of his empire, lavished the vast resources of their new-conquered domains as they commissioned palaces, gardens, mosques, tombs and bazaars. As Ibn Arabshah noted, Timur 'gathered from all sides and collected at Samarkand the fruits of everything; and that place accordingly had in every wonderful craft and rare art someone who excelled in wonderful skill and was famous beyond his rivals in his craft.' In Kesh, the Ak Saray, the White Palace, Timur's stately summer pleasure dome, was decorated by craftsmen captured in Khwarazm and Persia. He commissioned tombs there as well, the most striking being a resting place for his eldest and favourite son, Jehangir, who had fallen from his horse at the age of twenty. Timur took this work seriously: it was the work of his heart.

He also encouraged a new golden age in the production of portable objects, always most prized by nomads, as the central Asian cities produced exquisite textiles, rugs, ceramics, jewellery and metalwork – not for nothing did the British poet James Elroy Flecker refer to the *golden* road to Samarkand. This apogee was in part stimulated by the quality and design of objects coming out of Ming China. The Chinese capital was a mere six-month journey from Samarkand, according to the Castilian diplomat Ruy González de Clavijo, although two of those months were spent crossing what he calls a desert country, inhabited only by nomads driving herds in search of fodder – traders followed them across this vast and harsh terrain. Just before the Spaniard reached Timur's court, a caravan of eight hundred camels had arrived at the end of this exacting journey. Silk, musk, diamonds, rubies, pearls and rhubarb came from China, leather and linen from Russia, cinnamon, nutmeg, cloves and many other spices from India. Timur made Samarkand one of the fourteenth century's great trade metropolises and Clavijo has survived as one of its finest chroniclers.

Clavijo had left Cadiz in May 1403 charged with establishing good relations with the great amir of Asia. His was not the first European embassy, nor even the first from Castile: an earlier one had been welcomed in Samarkand and the ambassadors had returned to Castile with a variety of gifts including two Christian women (one of the ambassadors ended up married). Did the thought of future nuptials maintain Don Clavijo on his sixteen-month journey across Asia? In September the following year, he finally reached Samarkand. His first imperial audience took place at the Baghi Dilkusha, the Garden of the Heart's Delight, where Timur was

seated under what might be called a portal, which same was before the entrance of a most beautiful palace that appeared in the background. He was sitting on the ground, but upon a raised dais before which there was a fountain that threw up a column of water into the air backwards, and in the basin of the fountain there were floating red apples. His Highness had taken his place on what appeared to be small mattresses stuffed thick and covered with embroidered silk cloth . . . He was dressed in a cloak of plain silk without any embroidery, and he wore on his head a tall white hat on the crown of which was displayed a balas ruby [rose spinel], the same being further ornamented with pearls and precious stones.[114]

Clavijo's description of Timur, his court and the hospitality he enjoyed stands in stark contrast to Marlowe's imagined portrait. As dazzling as any fifteenth-century encounter, it was fuelled by feasts of whole spit-roast horse and sheep. There were gold platters laden with melons, peaches and grapes. There were songs and games. And because they were Mongol nomads, a large quantity of alcohol was drunk, wine as well as fermented mare's milk. Clavijo, it turns out, was not a drinker and preferred his mare's milk sweetened with sugar, which he thought was 'an excellent beverage'[115] in the summer.

The only hint of the great lord's darker side in Clavijo's record, the side that may have taken as many as 15 million lives, occurred on the occasion of a royal wedding. The entire trading population of Samarkand – 'those who sold stuffs and those who sold jewels, with the hucksters and merchants for sale of goods of all and every sort – were "encouraged" out of the city to display their wares to the Horde of Mongol horsemen.' They were instructed to stay 'until they had received his Highness's leave and permission',[116] which might have been longer than they would have wished, for Timur then ordered a gallows to be set up in the middle of the trade stalls. He would not only 'gratify and give enjoyment to all the common-folk at his festival, he also intended to give a warning and example of those who had offended him and done evil deeds'. The mayor of Samarkand was the first to be brought out, judged and hanged. The many high lords who had pleaded for his life were soon swinging beside him. Hanging, the Castilian observed, was reserved for persons of rank, although they were occasionally hung from the feet until dead. Only common people were beheaded because 'they hold decapitation to be a dreadful deed and a matter of much dishonor . . .'[117]

One consequence of the absolute nature of Timur's rule was that travel across much of Asia was once again safe; because punishments were so summary and extreme, 'the whole country is now at peace', Clavijo noted. Stability always encouraged trade, especially under the patronage of an amir who, although a Muslim, still upheld the Mongol respect for freedom of conscience, and whose nomad back-ground had taught the importance of open borders and easy movement. Trade routes flourished, perhaps as never before. At the eastern end of the Silk Roads, the Ming dynasty enjoyed one of the greatest periods of Chinese creative output. In the west, the naval might of Venice and Genoa facilitated the movement of people, ideas, goods, beliefs, knowledge and money between the Levantine coast and Europe.

Damascus

Ibn Khaldun had not wanted to travel to Damascus, but circumstances forced him there. His patron Sultan Barquq had died seventeen years after the scholar's arrival in Cairo and although succession among Mamluks was supposed to be by election, Barquq was succeeded by his ten-year-old son, al-Nasir Faraj ibn Barquq. Many people saw opportunity in the young king's elevation, including Ibn Khaldun's rivals, who soon undermined his position so that he was replaced as one of the city's judges. Timur also saw opportunity and seized this moment of Mamluk weakness to march his army on a loop through northern Syria. When Aleppo resisted, he devastated the city and built pyramids out of the skulls of his slain enemies, 20,000 faces staring out as a grim warning to those who would dare resist Mongol demands. In 1400, Timur turned his force towards the world's oldest continually inhabited city, Damascus.

The first city of imperial Islam was no longer of any great political significance, but it had value as one of the last strategic strongholds on the road to Mamluk Egypt. The army of Timur encircled the city's walls and sixty massive catapults were raised. Timur was confident of his military strength, but he hoped that diplomacy – and the memory of what had happened in Aleppo – would be more effective and less costly.

Ibn Khaldun found favour with the Mamluk sultan Faraj, as he had with Barquq, and although he was no longer a judge he was still renowned for his histories and his command of Islamic law. So as the young sultan prepared to lead the Mamluk army to Damascus to face the Mongols, he requested that the scholar accompany him. Ibn Khaldun must have recognised that this might lead to the fulfilment of the prophecy that he would witness the coming of a great conqueror.

The Mamluk force reached Damascus in December 1400 to the joy of its citizens and the many refugees who had escaped there from Aleppo, Antep and other cities that Timur had taken. Ibn Arabshah described how the Egyptian-led army 'filled the plains and made the earth glitter and shine'.[118] But the glitter did not last because early in 1401 the sultan heard of a plot to overthrow him and he returned to Cairo, leaving Damascus to its fate. Ibn Arabshah usually kept his best lines for Timur, but of the young Mamluk sultan's hasty exit he wrote that it 'proved the truth of Timur when he denied that they [the Mamluks] knew how to rule and administer a state'.[119]

But Ibn Khaldun did not return to Cairo. Instead, he installed himself in a twelfth-century Quran school, the Madrassa al-Adili, a fortress of a building close to the great Umayyad Mosque. The scene outside his door was not encouraging. The massive walls of Damascus had been built by Romans and restored many times since, more recently by Saladin to resist the Crusaders. The strong gates were barred, stores of food were significant, water sources had been filled and the citadel secured. But Ibn Khaldun estimated the Mongol horde outside the walls to be a million strong. Whatever slim chances the people in Damascus had of resisting that army were soon undermined when divisions appeared between the city's military commanders and their civil leaders. The military were in favour of fighting, but the city elders wanted to negotiate. Ibn Khaldun was among the latter. After a meeting in the great mosque, the judges and notables agreed to send a delegation to the great conqueror.

Timur received them warmly, promised their safety and repeated his demand that they open the gates and allow one of his amirs to rule the city. Timur said he had also heard that a great scholar, Ibn Khaldun, had come from Cairo and he asked if he might see him.

Tensions were now high inside the walls, and there was passionate disagreement as to how to proceed. Ibn Khaldun, who was known to favour submission to the inevitable Mongol victory, feared for his life. Worried that those Damascenes who wanted to fight might get to him before the Mongols could, he decided to leave the city and seek out Timur. On the icy morning of 10 January he was helped over the walls by a group of judges. Once outside, one of Timur's representatives was waiting to take him to the amir's audience tent. As if in anticipation of Christopher Marlowe's lines, here was 'the stately tent of war,/ Where you shall hear the Scythian Tamburlaine/ Threatening the world with high astounding terms'.

'When my name was announced,' Ibn Khaldun wrote, 'the title "Maghribi Malikite Cadi" [North African Maliki judge] was added to it', although he was no longer officially a *cadi*, for he had been dismissed from his position in Cairo. And so begins one of those rare meetings – similar, as the historian Robert Irwin has suggested, to the moment when Napoleon met Goethe, or Alexander the Great sat down with Aristotle[120] – when a prophecy is fulfilled and a great conqueror meets someone who can put their deeds in context and explain, to them and to us, the meaning of their achievements. It was also a moment when the scholar might have lost his head, as so many others were doing around him.

There was nothing menacing in Ibn Khaldun's first view of Timur for it was mealtime and the amir 'was reclining on his elbow while platters of food were passing before him which he was sending one after the other to groups of Mongols sitting in circles in front of his tent'.[121] The scholar offered effusive greetings, bowed and kissed the hand that Timur stretched before him. Instead of offering Ibn Khaldun the food that had been brought, Timur ordered a dish of *rishta*, macaroni and milk, from his own tent. Ibn Khaldun appeared to enjoy it, which impressed the amir because it did not often appeal to many non-Mongols. Ibn Khaldun is likely to have drunk it more out of terror than appetite for he tells us he was 'overcome with fear', perhaps because another cadi had just been imprisoned and put up for ransom. 'Because of this fear, I composed in my mind some words to say to him which, by exalting him and his government, would flatter him.'[122] He started with the truth, explaining that he had waited thirty or forty years to meet Timur.

'You are the sultan of the universe and ruler of the world, and I do not believe that there has appeared among men from Adam until this epoch a ruler like you.' He then went on to explain about nomadic energy and *asabiyya* and how Timur commanded more of it than anyone before him. He omitted to explain his theory of circular history and the inevitable fall of every dynasty, including Timur's.

The flattery worked and Timur clearly enjoyed the encounter, but he had another reason for wanting to meet the scholar. He now questioned him about North Africa, in particular about the road from Egypt to Tunis and Fes, the landscape, the ports and so on. Ibn Khaldun saw salvation in offering to write down what in essence was a manual for an invading army.

The audience was interrupted by news that one of the city gates had been opened and cadis and elders were standing outside it, ready to surrender in return for his promise of safety. Timur was unable to stand on his own 'because of the trouble with his knee' and so he was lifted. 'Placed upon his horse; grasping the reins, he sat upright in his saddle' and rode towards Damascus 'while the bands played around him until the air shook with them'.[123]

Ibn Khaldun made his own way back to the city, returning to his room at the madrassa where he spent three days writing his account of the Maghreb for Timur. His conscience must have been pricked by the consequences of what he was doing, because he then also wrote a letter to the sultan in the west warning about the Mongol conqueror. Three days later he was back in Timur's camp.

In all he spent over a month with Timur, sitting on his right side where he witnessed acts of generosity and of brutality. He took

part in debates and on one occasion, when a claimant to the caliphate came to ask for Timur's support, Ibn Khaldun was called on to
pass judgement. He saw enough to know that when the siege, the
catapults, the vast army and biting winter had had their effect, when
the people of Damascus accepted Timur's amnesty in return for
their wealth – 'entire vaults of money' – the promise of safety was
only ever going to apply to some of the city's inhabitants. He
himself pleaded for the safety of cadis and other scholars, but many
others were not so fortunate and when one of the emissaries sent
to negotiate with Timur began to flatter him, the conqueror stopped
him: 'You are lying, because I am the scourge of God appointed
to chastise you, since no one knows the remedy for your iniquity
except me. You are wicked, but I am more so than you are, so be
silent!'[124]

Once the ransoms had been paid, the tensions that had simmered
between the cadis in the city who had favoured negotiation and
the military inside who had wanted to fight erupted. While Timur's
soldiers celebrated what they thought was a quick end to the
conflict, some of the Damascene soldiers saw an easy target and
attacked them. According to one report, a thousand Mongol
fighters were killed and beheaded, no doubt in revenge for what
had happened in Aleppo. Timur's response was instant and
disproportionate.

'As ravening wolves rage against teeming flocks of sheep' is
how Ibn Arabshah described the Tatar response, and although
the image was borrowed from nomadic life, it fails to encompass
the tragedy that descended on Damascus as the colour of the
banner fluttering above Timur's tent was reported to have been
changed from white, implying mildness, to the red of anger and
blood, to the black of destruction. 'His spear, his shield, his horse,
his armour, plumes,/ And jetty feathers menace death and hell,'
as Marlowe put it.

For three days and nights, Damascenes were tortured, raped and
slaughtered. Their buildings were stripped of anything of value
and then burned, the wind whipping the flames until they reached
the city's beating heart, the eighth-century Umayyad Mosque. This
first great monument of the Umayyad Islamic Empire, built over a

cathedral and earlier temples, a place of worship for as long as people had lived in that place, now caught fire. 'The flames mounted to its roof,' wrote Ibn Khaldun, melting the lead on it, and the ceiling and walls collapsed, the golden mosaics shattered, the white marble splitting in the heat.

No sooner was Damascus won than Timur announced he would be leaving. Perhaps he would march towards Cairo, where the walls were being strengthened. Or perhaps he would go north again. Ibn Khaldun saw this as the moment to request permission to return to Egypt.

During this audience, Timur delivered the most unexpected question of Ibn Khaldun's life: did the scholar have a mule and, if so, was it a good one?

When Ibn Khaldun said it was good, the conqueror asked to buy it.

'May God aid you,' was the response and, in a mix of terror and irony, 'one like me does not sell to one like you.' In return for the 'gift' of the mule, Timur granted Ibn Khaldun's request to depart – this seems to have been at the same time as Ibn Arabshah and many of the learned, the skilled and the beautiful people of Damascus were starting the long walk east to Samarkand. Timur even recommended the scholar to one of his sons 'who was about to travel . . . to the place of the spring pasturing of his animals'.[125] But Ibn Khaldun explained that he would prefer to travel directly to the coast, a decision he soon regretted for he was attacked, near Safed in Palestine, and stripped of everything he was carrying, left only with his thoughts and memories.

Timur did not follow Ibn Khaldun down the Cairo road and nor did he use Ibn Khaldun's insights and march on northern Africa. Instead the horde moved towards Baghdad, where the inevitable siege began in the midsummer of 1401, to be followed by the inevitable bloodletting in stifling heat. Ibn Arabshah gives details of the carnage and of how the Lord of Fortunate Conjunction commanded each of his soldiers to bring him the heads of two Baghdadis as the Mongols turned the City of Peace into what Ibn Arabshah calls 'the house of surrender'. Only mosques, hospitals and colleges were spared. At the end, while his men were gathering the 90,000 heads they had severed and constructing 120 towers out of them, while vultures wheeled over the smouldering city on sweltering summer thermals, Timur went to pray to Allah at the shrine of Abu Hanifa, the eighth-century Sunni jurist.

The following year, Timur defeated the Ottoman sultan Beyazid and sacked Smyrna, a city that had held out against Crusaders and Ottomans. At that point, he could have pushed west into Europe. Who could have stopped him? The Ottomans had recently defeated the combined crusading forces of Europe, and now the Mongols had routed the Ottomans. They and their allies were unstoppable.

But perhaps guided by an alignment of the stars, perhaps because he could see nothing worth fighting for in Europe, at least nothing that called to him as loudly as China – and perhaps, also, because he did not wish to disrupt the lucrative trade into Europe – Timur chose instead to go home.

In Samarkand, he celebrated a two-month-long *quriltai* in the meadows outside his home city – it was this gathering, including the execution of some of the city elders, that the Castilian ambassador Ruy González de Clavijo so vividly described. At the very start of the following year, 1405, the sixty-eight-year-old Timur set out to fulfil his destiny in the East and take possession of China. But after a few weeks' march, when they had got no further than Otrar, the frontier city where Genghis Khan's merchants and envoys had been assassinated, the climate intervened and the severest winter anyone could remember brought the Mongol army to a standstill. The winds howled, hail and then deep snow fell, and it became so cold that some of Timur's men froze in their saddles, which seems a uniquely nomad death. In a chapter entitled 'How That Proud Tyrant Was Broken', Ibn Arabshah enjoys the small satisfaction of having the last word over the man who had forced him, his family and countless others out of their homes and into slavery. As temperatures plummeted, the Damascene explained, Timur was swathed in furs and yet he was still cold. He ordered *arak* to be served, but not even alcohol could warm the old conqueror. As the big chill continued, the strength went out of him until, at last, as Ibn Arabshah wrote, Timur 'coughed like a camel which is strangled'[126] and was dead.

The Wheel Turns

Timur's vast empire pivoted around trading cities, particularly around the Silk Road hubs of Khiva, Bukhara, Balkh, the south Asian power centres such as Delhi and Multan, and Basra, Baghdad and Aleppo in the Near East. But the central pivots were the cities of Mashad, Herat and above all Samarkand, where Timur had lavished so much time and care and such vast sums. But in spite of the obvious importance and magnificence of its cities, Timur's empire remained nomadic in character during his life and after his death. Its nomadic character can be seen in tribal structures and traditions, in the regular *quriltai* and migrations, in the way Timur chose to live in tents and on the hoof, in the organisation and structure of his armies, in the power that his favourite wife, Bibi Khanum, and other women continued to have both in decision-making and in tribal matters, in the prominence given to free trade, and in the way his governors encouraged freedom of movement and conscience, which allowed Buddhism, Christianity, Islam and other religions to spread.

The open nature of the empire saw vast amounts of wealth flow through the markets of Eurasia, and from China to northern Europe many people grew rich. Some of the most obvious signs of that wealth can be seen in the exquisite monuments that remain. Mongol amirs also invested in science, and although the West pays them little attention today their scientists deserve to stand alongside the ones we do recognise – Timur's grandson the great astrologer Ulugh Beg, for instance, is one of the exceptions and rightly honoured alongside the likes of Galileo by having a moon crater named after him. Asia's Timurid patrons also sponsored poets, artists and the creators of beautiful objects, all part of a significant cultural flourishing.

Yet Timur's passing was not widely mourned. By the time news of his death reached Egypt, the Mamluk amirs were absorbed in another power struggle and, as the balance of power tilted one way, then another, they had little time to worry about events elsewhere. The ruling sultan, now nineteen years of age, had been deposed, then reinstated, leaving those who had been so indiscreet as to cheer his downfall feeling exposed. In this febrile atmosphere, Ibn Khaldun briefly returned to the courts as a judge, but was soon dismissed again, so that by the time of Timur's death he was back with his manuscripts, meditating on the rise and fall of cultures, on how nomads could create powerful new movements, but could not maintain them once they settled.

He knew, as a poet would later write, that Timur and his like were some sort of solution. But he was also aware that the wheel would turn. So although heaven had smiled on the Mongols, although he had seen their 'faiths and empires gleam',[127] he knew that the wheel would continue to turn after Timur's death and that his great empire would become a dissolving dream for some, a fading nightmare for many others.

What he did not know was that the time would come when the wheel might stop turning completely, when the world would be shaped by something beyond *asabiyya*, when nomads would be powerless and would turn from being feared and hated, to become the subject of fascination and even admiration.

PART III

The Act of Recovery

The bigger, fuller picture is never as stark as 'nomad' versus
'settled', tribes versus people. It never has been. But the
dichotomy does seem to lie at the heart of history.

Tim Mackintosh-Smith, *Arabs*

The Past is Unpredictable

If you have used a mobile phone or a computer, browsed the internet or trawled social media, if you have worn a pair of jeans or a suit, listened to Dolly Parton or the Beatles, Eminem or Adele then you are among the majority of people in the world who, knowingly or not, have used American and British ideas or inventions, sung their songs or adopted their dress code. In a similar way, people in fourteenth-century Europe adopted the skills or were influenced by the ideas of the most powerful people in the world, who were nomads. But then what happened to them?

Mongol khans exerted extraordinary power when they built their empire across Eurasia and fostered and controlled the routes that connected China and India with the Mediterranean. But their soft power had even greater reach and more lasting significance. They achieved this by fostering open markets and global trade, inevitable consequences of the nomadic insistence on movement and migration. They redistributed capital to create new ventures and help older ones to flourish. And they championed freedom of conscience and a specific though limited kind of democracy. And yet . . . by the seventeenth century Mongols in particular and nomads in general had disappeared from the European view. The word *nomad* was so little used by the eighteenth century that it was not considered worthy of inclusion in the first English dictionary. What had happened between the Mongol ascendancy and the Age of Reason? How had nomads disappeared? What made nomads and nomadism irrelevant?

We have followed the achievements of some of the greatest empires and cultural flourishings the world has seen, and we now know there is more to nomad empires than tents and herds, battered walls and pyramids of skulls. We have traced the arc of their military dominance across two thousand years from ancient Scythia and Xiongnu to the Mongol ascendancy, and we know that there was nothing gratuitous about their conquests, that they were acting to fulfil a divinely ordained vision. We know that beyond military abilities, nomads placed great importance on their role in the natural world, if only because of the need to feed their animals. Perhaps because of that, they showed reverence for the natural forces they believed shaped the world. They prayed to them, made offerings, recognised them as central to their well-being.

We know that each of *our* own versions of history leans toward our achievements and the fulfilment of our visions. Whether in China or the United States, the UK, EU or elsewhere in the world, the history we are taught in school omits a large part of the human story. But we are of and in an age when some of what has been edited from view is being restored, from the domestication of horses and the development of the cart and chariot to the creation of trans-Asian post and trade routes, the evolution of nomadic social structures, the championing of individual liberties . . . Try to imagine the world if we take away nomads and all the others who live lightly. Without them, we would have a much harder path to follow to reach an understanding of what it is to be human and of our place in the natural world.

But does that matter? Had those nomads not run their course and run out of solutions?

Ibn Khaldun thought the wheel of fortune, not a ladder, was a fitting symbol for a world in which the rise and fall of nations and empires merely reflected the heavenly cycles of sun, moon and stars, the earthly seasonal cycle of bud, leaf, blossom and fall, a woman's menstrual cycle, the animal world's migratory cycle and the matching human cycle from birth to death. Empires rose on Ibn Khaldun's wheel because *asabiyya* channelled nomadic energy towards charismatic leaders. Empires fell as the wheel began its downward turn, as the descendants of the imperial founders were softened by sedentary city life and the energy of their *asabiyya* drained away. Looking back over the previous two thousand years, the great scholar understood that being closer to the uncluttered, freethinking, free-moving first state, living in tune with natural cycles led nomadic people to extraordinary achievements. It also allowed them to defeat the settled.

One thing he did not imagine was that the cycle would come to an end, that circular time would stop.

Ibn Khaldun's view that the world did not necessarily get better over time was once a commonplace. It was widely accepted because it fitted neatly with the belief that things *do* go round and round, that every rise leads to a fall, every advance to a regression. This assumption was only challenged in the centuries after Ibn Khaldun's death. But before we look at the end of nomadic ascendancy and the age of scientific revolution, we should examine the rise of three nomadic powers that emerged from the wreck of Timur's empire and survived into modern times.

The Grand Turk

Ibn Khaldun had calculated that it would take a generation or more for a dynasty to bring about its own downfall, but in this as in much else, the Timurids were an exception. Three years after Timur's death – and not long after Ibn Khaldun had been carried out of Cairo's Gate of Victory to be buried in the northern cemetery – Timur's successor Pir Muhammad was murdered by his vizier and one of the greatest of all empires began to fracture. The new realms that rose from the shards of Timur's empire would help to shape our world and all of them were nomadic in origin.

The Ottoman Turks were already carving out space for their herds and their ambitions during Timur's life. Like their great adversaries the Mongols, they were Eurasian nomads who had been pushed westwards across the steppes by the occasional disastrous winter or by threats from another migratory tribe. Searching for grazing and access to new markets, in the ninth century they moved onto the Mesopotamian plain, where their skill in the saddle and with bow and arrow were in great demand. Before long, Turkish horsemen were a common sight in Abbasid Baghdad in the same way that Scythian archers had been a feature of ancient Athens. One consequence of this service was that they were initiated into Islam by Arabs. They also learned how to run an empire from the Persians in the Abbasid court. In the early fourteenth century, a Turkic *bey* called Osman emerged out of this melange to raise his banner near the city of Bursa in Anatolia and create a dynasty that would dominate much of the Near East, eastern Europe and North Africa for the next six hundred years.

Ottoman historians describe Osman's origins as being obscure: 'His right to the lands he held is shrouded in myth,' says one, 'and he did not report to the nominal Mongol suzerain of Turkic Anatolia.'[1] Osman was a nomad by descent and although the demands of leadership had curtailed some of his freedom of movement, like his predecessors he preferred to summer in tents among the herds on upper pastures than to stay in palaces. Osman's independence and free spirit, and his sense of being the first among equals, attracted a large and eclectic following. Among his *asabiyya* were Turkish nomadic herders, refugees from Mongol and Abbasid lands, chancers, warriors, Muslim mystics, Byzantine malcontents and a Greek called Köse Mihal, Michael the Beardless,[2] who was governor of a small community near the Black Sea, a couple of hundred miles east of Constantinople. Like many officials in Anatolia, he had long been neglected by his Byzantine lords. When Osman arrived and began rallying people to his banner, Mihal became one of his most valuable recruits, joining Osman's army, converting to Islam and persuading other Christian governors to cross over. He also created a new force of *Akinji* or irregular cavalry. Mihal, like the rest of the original Ottoman *asabiyya*, was animated by Osman's dynamism, his inclusivity and a view of Islam that was generous towards all People of the Book.

Osman died in 1326 just as his Ottoman army captured its first city, Bursa, where he was buried. Within sixty years, his successors had control of the western half of Anatolia and much of Byzantine Europe. Their greatest coup came on 29 May 1453 when they took the holy city of Constantinople, the new Rome. The siege had been long but the wait worthwhile for the city became the capital of an empire and therefore a bridge between traditional nomad grazing lands in the east and their ambitions beyond the nomad Balkan Mountains in the west. Renamed Istanbul, the city became more than a bridge, for it did what Ibn Khaldun warned cities often do to nomadic people: it sapped their vital nomadic energy and it broke the bond of their *asabiyya*. While the empire remained nomadic both in spirit and in practice, the imperial family settled behind the walls of the opulent Topkapi Palace with their ministers, janissaries, harems and servants, each of whose job made it more difficult for their imperial majesties to remember what happened on the outside.

Nomadism in the empire was dictated, as always, by terrain. Most Ottoman European provinces lay in the Balkans, a Turkic word for 'a chain of wooded mountains', mountains that were good for herding. The Carpathians, Pindus and other east European ranges were best suited to pastoral nomadism and although there was farming in Asian Anatolia, much of that land was dominated by the Taurus and Pontic mountains. So while the Ottoman leaders and their administration settled, the majority of their subjects had little choice but to keep on moving between summers on the high pastures and the plains in winter. The empire also controlled a large number of islands and these too could be reached, with great pleasure, during summer, but were isolated by winds and winter storms. 'Between October and April', historian Jason Goodwin explains, 'the mountains and the seas closed down, like the bazaars at night; and the empire half slept, like a hibernatory beast.'[3]

Nomad tribes were as varied as the empire's terrain. In the European west, there were Orthodox Christian groups – Black Vlachs, Limping Vlachs, Aromanians and others who moved their flocks around the Balkans, slept in goat-hair tents and spoke in a language laced with Latin and ancient Greek. Between them, they created 'the substantive essence of the Balkans', which Patrick Leigh

Fermor, who knew the area well, described as being 'compounded of sweat, dust, singeing horn, blood, nargileh*-smoke, dung, *slivo*, wine, roasting mutton, spice and coffee, laced with a drop of attar of roses and a drift of incense'.[4]

The far east of the empire belonged to Anatolian Kurds and Yoruks, whose name translates as *to walk*. They and the many nomadic tribes who lived between them shared a common identity that was forged out of two factors: they all performed seasonal migrations and they were all the sultan's subjects. But status in the empire came at a cost. Each year nomads swelled the imperial treasury, paying the sultan's tax on every head of livestock, and swelled the ranks of the imperial army, for each nomad family was bound to send two sons to serve the sultan, even though they were needed to feed and shear the herd or for leading the migrations. Even when they were not on active duty, nomad soldiers continued to serve their emperor by forming a mobile buffer between the Ottoman heartlands and those of Europe and Asia. All this was done knowingly. But there was one significant service Ottoman nomads performed without even being aware of it.

The basis of Ottoman identity, their *asabiyya*, was not to be found in Istanbul, Edirne, Bursa or in the other glorious cities they embellished with mosques, palaces and bazaars. Nor did it reside in the significance of the caliphate, the right to lead the Muslim *ummah* or community, a right the Emperor Selim the Grim claimed in 1517 after his conquest of Egypt and the Holy Places of the Hejaz – the last Abbasid caliph had himself presented Selim with the sword and mantle of the Prophet Muhammad. The basis of their identity was to be found in tents and horses and in the nomadic origins of Osman, the founder of the dynasty. For centuries, in what might have been a self-conscious way of reconciling mutually exclusive impulses, Ottoman sultans referred to their nomadic past even as they lived an interior life ever further removed from it. In the sixteenth century, for instance, at the peak of Ottoman power and splendour, Suleiman the Magnificent chose to receive homage from the Hungarian king John Sigismund not at the Topkapi or in the splendour of another palace, but in front of a magnificent tent. The

---

* Waterpipe.

artist who recorded the moment presented the sultan on a throne in front of a tent with a golden dome and brocade cover and a spectacular carpet with a flowering border at his feet. It was a tent for a palace-raised tent-dweller, but a tent none the less.

Jump forward a couple of centuries and, in a repeat of the Abbasid age of setting down, when the caliph's scholars travelled south to Basra and on to the desert in search of Arabs who were still nomadic, herding camels deep in the desert, untouched by the temptations of the city, the Ottoman sultan sent teams of historians and artists to gather proof of their nomadic roots. Even if they were not living a mobile life, the idea of nomadism was still of vital importance to their sense of identity.

Half the World

The family origins of Sheikh Safi ad Din, a Persian Sufi, are as obscure as those of Osman, founder of the Ottoman dynasty; both are lost in the grasslands of the steppes. But as with the Turk, we know that the sheikh's people were certainly nomads, most recently from Anatolia. Early in the fourteenth century, while Osman was rallying followers to his Ottoman banner, Safi ad Din was creating his own *asabiyya*. With a reputation for remarkable feats of body and mind and as a miracle-worker, known for piety but also for his political astuteness and trading skills, he was soon master of his own

Sufi order. The Safaviyya, as his followers were called, were based in Ardabil near the Caspian Sea, his place of birth in north-west Iran, and initially were mostly notable for wearing red caps with twelve black tassels, one for each of the Shi'a Imams. But by the early 1500s, they were also known for the size of their following and for the power they wielded. As Timurid power crumbled, the sheikh's descendant Ismail established Safavid sovereignty across western Iran, the Tigris and Euphrates basin and Azerbaijan. The next generations were even more successful and with the support of a confederation of nomadic tribes – the Afshar, Shamlu, Rumlu, Tekelli, Zulqadar, Qajar and many others – Shah Ismail's Safavid descendants ushered in a new golden and predominantly nomadic age in Persia.

Early Safavid rulers followed their nomad heritage and the example of ancient Persian rulers and resisted the idea of a single capital city. Instead, they moved around their large country, resting at a succession of palaces and walled gardens. But as with Ottoman sultans, this changed at the beginning of the seventeenth century and it happened during the reign of Shah Abbas, who chose to establish Isfahan as his imperial capital. With enthusiasm and impatient energy, the new shah built a garden city, earning his new capital the label 'half the world'. He concluded trade deals both in the Far East and Europe, welcomed foreign diplomats, traders, jewellers and craftsmen, and an economic boom flourished. From visitors we know that within the city's 24-mile perimeter, there were 162 mosques, 48 madrassas, 182 caravanserais and some 173 baths – this at a time when most people in London bathed once each spring. Shah Abbas resettled 300 Chinese potters in the city, which turned out to be a smart move because when China closed its market to foreigners in 1659 Isfahani ceramics, which carried Chinese designs in Persian blue, became a sought-after replacement for Chinese porcelain in the West. Shah Abbas also increased the city's weaving capacity, boosting textile and carpet production. Persia's silk trade was also centred in his new capital. Much of this trade was handled by Armenians, who were settled across the Zayandeh river in the suburb of New Julfa.

The centrepiece of Shah Abbas's city was the *maidan*, the Naksh-i-Jahan (literally 'the Image of the World'). Surrounded by bazaars, caravanserais and workshops, enclosed by a two-storey arcade which is broken by the facades of his palace and mosques, this grand square was the setting for parades and public gatherings, for the annual sacrifice of a camel and for the nomad game of polo, when teams kicked up the dust between twin pairs of domed marble pillars that served as goalposts and which are still in place. (Polo playing is now discouraged in the *maidan*, although riding horse-drawn carriages is still allowed.)

Some of the wonder of Isfahan's Safavid buildings, as with Shah Abbas's contemporary Suleiman the Magnificent's beautiful creations in Istanbul, lies in the way they harnessed the raw power of the steppes and combined it with local sensibilities. As had happened before – often and in many different ways – the best outcomes were achieved through a balanced union of the nomadic and the settled.

Isfahan is an oasis that sits – is caught – between the forbidding purple peaks of the Zagros Mountains and the vast wilderness of the Dasht-e Kavir desert. Much of the other land, the mountains, plains and coastal strip, is best suited to herding. So whatever Shah Abbas and his Safavid descendants wished to create as they redeveloped Isfahan to better express their ambitions, they could never escape the fact that their new Persian Empire, which lasted into the eighteenth century, was always and mostly a confederation of nomadic people.

Neo-Mongols

'In the month of Ramadan in the year 899 (June 1494), in the province of Fergana, in my twelfth year I became king.'[5] So wrote a young prince called Babur, one of Timur's great-great-grandsons who also claimed descent from Genghis Khan through his mother's line, which is to say that he was proud to acknowledge his nomadic blood.

The great Fergana Valley is wedged between the Pamir and Tien Shan mountains, cut through by the Syr Darya river and currently divided between Uzbekistan, Tajikistan and Kyrgyzstan. Then as now, it was one of the most fertile areas of Central Asia and supported both settled people and nomads. Between them, they raised some of Asia's finest horses, including the so-called 'heavenly' breed. These were the horses that lured the ancient Chinese into travelling west, believing that the creatures were divine and sweated blood, and knowing that they made ideal war horses. Fergana horses were also important to Babur because although, in accordance with the Persian influence on his life, he loved creating gardens as much as drinking wine and smoking opium, he was a prince of the house of Timur, which meant that he was destined to spend his life in the saddle and in conflict.

Babur kept a journal for much of his life and in it he recorded 'exactly what happened . . . to write the truth of every matter and to set down no more than the reality of every event . . . every good and evil I have seen of father and brother and set down the actuality of every fault and virtue of relative and stranger'.[6] It will be clear from this that Babur's memoir is as candid and revealing as any to have come to us from the past. It quickly reveals that the old Indo-European nomadic ways were still alive.

He needs to secure the throne and win recognition of his status.

He longs to be remembered for his deeds.

He believes in freedom of conscience.

And he was convinced that women had an equal role to play both in life and in the fight for power. 'For tactics and strategy', Babur admitted, 'there were few women like my grandmother, Esän Dawlat Begim. She was intelligent and a good planner. Most affairs were settled with her counsel.'[7]

Over the next twenty years, Babur won and lost a succession of kingdoms as his relations undermined him, in the process allowing the neighbouring Uzbeks to grow more powerful. Babur was at first ruler of Fergana, but when he moved against Samarkand he lost control of his home base. Then he lost Samarkand. In 1503, aged twenty, he set himself up as ruler of Kabul, which remained his power base, but by his late twenties he had taken control of the old Timurid heartlands of Central Asia, including Samarkand. Then in 1526, the year in which Suleiman the Magnificent defeated the Hungarians and marched the Ottoman army into Budapest, Babur, now in his early forties, turned his army southwards towards India to fulfil his destiny. 'Give me but fame,' he wrote, echoing the Sanskrit *Vedas*, 'and if I die I am contented.'[8] Fame was won, gloriously, at a place called Panipat, where Babur's 20,000-strong army overcame the Lodi emperor's 100,000 men. The victory opened the way to Delhi and Agra and the fulfilment of Babur's ambition to take control of Hind, India.

Babur celebrated his victory by visiting the Delhi fortress, some tombs and gardens. 'After the tour I returned to the camp, got on a boat, and drank spirits.'[9] But while Babur's nomadic spirit kept him restless, the dynasty he created, the Mughals – derived from the word Mongol – settled down and from Lahore, Fatehpur Sikri, most famously Agra, and finally Delhi, they ruled India until 1858, when the British exiled the last emperor to Burma. In all of those places they built with beautiful extravagance, often channelling water to create cool areas, arranging gardens reflecting the natural world and constructing their iconic pavilions, which look like tents in stone.

This theme of water, pleasure and the natural world informs a Mughal miniature of great beauty,[10] painted in the seventeenth century, which shows a man cross-legged on a raised golden throne, leaning against an orange cushion, a river behind him and green hills beyond. The throne is placed on a floral brown and blue carpet – another garden design – on which four men are seated. All four wear turbans, three of them sport daggers and one is conspicuous with jewels. The man on the throne is Timur, the four seated are Babur and the emperors who succeeded him, his son Humayun, grandson Akbar and great-grandson Jehangir. The painting was commissioned by Jehangir's son and heir, Shah Jehan, during whose reign the splendour of the Mughal court reached its peak, so eloquently expressed in the beauty of monuments such as the Taj Mahal. The painting suggests it is from the Mongol barbarian Timur and from the simple grandeur of his nomadic lands that the emperors were descended. Yet the painting also suggests that much had changed since Timur's time. The qualities that had won the Mongol his empire would no longer be enough to enable his descendants or nomads anywhere else to make their mark in the world.

Dominion

The Ottoman, Safavid and Mughal empires resonate in the West in a way that others – the Bornu in Nigeria, for instance, the Zhungars in Central Asia, even the Lakota in North America – do not, perhaps because of their strategic positions and because of subsequent colonial history. These three empires, now evolved into Turkey, Iran and India, stretched from the Bay of Bengal to the Austrian border and from the Near East westwards across North Africa. Straddling the central section of the Silk Roads, they separated Europe from the Far East and they grew wealthy off east–west trade – around the year 1700, the Mughals controlled almost a quarter of global trade. Each of these empires still had a significant nomadic core and all maintained some relationship with the seasonal cycles, not least because the lives and holy days of their Muslim rulers were regulated by the lunar calendar.

The power of these empires encouraged some Europeans to explore the viability of other trade routes and to direct their colonising ambitions elsewhere. There were many reasons why Europe would shift its gaze westwards, not least the lingering memory of the horror of the Black Death, the adventurous spirit of enquiry that animated the European Renaissance, new commercial imperatives and improvements in ship design and navigation. Christopher Columbus's crossing of the Atlantic and Vasco da Gama's transit of the Cape of Good Hope in the fifteenth century encouraged European explorers, traders, soldiers and missionaries to sail west and south across the Atlantic, into the Americas and down into Africa, in search of new markets and new routes to old markets in India and China. Wherever they went, they carried the old fear of having to face nomad power. But that fear was mitigated by the ascendance of Europe's maritime powers. It would soon be outweighed by the commercial possibilities of the voyages of discovery. And it was overcome by new ways of seeing and thinking that were spreading across Europe. These new ways, and the creations they inspired, would lead to the total eclipse of the remaining nomad power.

Some of what was being said and written in seventeenth-century Europe seems familiar today, but it was revolutionary at the time. One of the leaders of this intellectual revolution was the Englishman Francis Bacon. Bacon had been precociously talented as a youth, so much so that he was allowed to study at Trinity College, Cambridge before he was a teenager and was elected a Member of Parliament before his twentieth birthday. He would become a statesman, an Attorney General, the Lord Chancellor of England, and a legal adviser – the original Queen's Counsel – to Queen Elizabeth I, for which he was elevated to Viscount St Alban, my Lord Verulam. But unlike many other revolutionaries, Bacon became more radical as he aged and it was not until his sixtieth year, 1620, that he published the first volume of his great philosophical work, *Novum Organum or True Suggestions for the Interpretation of Nature*.

The following year, 1621, Bacon's enemies triumphed and forced him to confess to twenty-three charges of corruption while in high office. At that time, he described himself as 'a broken reed', but if that was true, the reed had already played its revolutionary tune. *Novum Organum* calls for 'a total reconstruction of sciences, arts, and all human knowledge, raised upon the proper foundations', which Bacon thought necessary, essential even, because Europe's intellectual progress had come to a standstill. A necessary development for Europe, perhaps, but it would have extreme consequences for the nomadic world.

To show his readers where the inspiration for this new information and understanding could be found, the title page of Bacon's book was decorated with two ships passing between two classical pillars. It was a metaphor, but also an expression of a new maritime era that would eclipse land-based nomads. The crux of Bacon's argument was that the old Mediterranean world had outgrown its intellectual bounds just as it was outgrowing its physical ones. It was time, he insisted, to leave behind Aristotle and the Greek philosophers and find new ways of thinking, ways that would better suit the new world coming into being, one that is recognisably *our* world. Among the stimuli for this new thinking, Bacon mentions 'the force, effect, and consequences of inventions' that had come to Europe from the nomad empires of the East. 'We should notice', he argues in his preface, 'those three which were unknown to the ancients; namely, printing, gunpowder, and the compass.' All three had been invented in China, adopted by Arabs, Mongols or other nomads, and then adapted – usually scaled up – by Europeans with world-changing consequences. 'These three have changed the appearance and state of the whole world,' Bacon wrote, 'first in literature, then in warfare, and lastly in navigation; and innumerable changes have been thence derived.' The changes would be double-edged, helpful in some ways and to some people, and harmful to many others.

Bacon was not the only one to recognise that he was living on the cusp of a new age. This was the time when Galileo was studying the movement of planets and challenging the Church-approved view that the earth was the centre point around which the universe revolved.

Soon after, the French philosopher Blaise Pascal would write that 'our nature consists in movement. Absolute stillness is death.'[11] Pascal's two short sentences appear to champion a nomadic, wandering life and for that reason they have been treated almost as a mantra in our own time★ – keep moving or die – as they were during his lifetime.

This call for movement suited the new age of pre-industrial capitalism as it had suited the empires of Genghis, Timur and Kubilai. While Bacon, Pascal, Galileo and many others were fighting the status quo of preconceived ideas, sensing the need to push forward the boundaries of knowledge, the East India Company's mercenary army, funded by wealthy stock-holders in London, was fighting Dutch and French interests for a larger share of the Indian market. Other European endeavours, many of them financed by what we would call venture capitalists, were creating trading posts or manufactories wherever they could reach, places that would sooner or later become colonies. None of these was more significant than the one created in the year before Bacon's publication, when 102 dissenting Pilgrim Fathers crossed the Atlantic on a ship called the *Mayflower*. They were travelling with the hope of creating a new home in Plymouth, Massachusetts, but on land that had belonged to the Wampanoag, the 'people of the first light', for the past twelve thousand years.

Bacon recognised that three very different kinds of ambition were driving these new ventures – and this applies as much to our own time as it did to the seventeenth century. Some people were driven by an ambition to enlarge their own power and Bacon thought they were 'vulgar and degenerate'. There were those who sought to expand the boundaries or influence of their nations or empires. These he described as 'more dignified but not less covetous'. And then there were people like himself, who wanted to increase the sum of human understanding. 'Such ambition', he believed, resting only on the arts and sciences, 'is both more sound and more noble than the other two.'[12]

If you were a person of Bacon's ability and ambition and you looked out at the early seventeenth-century world, if you knew as

★ By Bruce Chatwin and others.

he did about the voyages of discovery and the new technology that had made them possible, if you understood the workings of the new global markets and the flow of capital that made *them* possible, if you had the 'sound and noble ambition' of expanding the frontiers of knowledge, then you would have believed – as many in the twentieth century believed – that there was nothing humankind could not do, nothing we could not know, nothing we should not know. Out of this dizzying mass of possibilities, the prime task that Bacon identified as being both important and urgent was to uncover the workings of the natural world.[13]

Bacon believed that humankind had lost control of the natural world when we were expelled from the Garden of Eden. 'Man by the Fall', he wrote, 'fell at the same time from his state of innocency and from his dominion over creation.'[14] Those last three words are worth repeating: *dominion over creation*. Over nature.

Most of Bacon's contemporaries, as most people throughout history, accepted that they were an important but equal part of the natural world and that they were governed by the same laws and forces as animals, plants and everything else under the sun. They did so because they knew that the laws of the natural world were beyond their understanding, and also that the forces animating it were beyond their control. The sun shone, winds blew, rains fell. It snowed. Sometimes there were hailstorms or rainbows or comets. Sometimes there were strange visions in the skies, beyond the reach even of birds. Because of these and other natural phenomena, humankind was resigned to periods of plenty and periods of scarcity, to drought and famine, profit and loss. Since long before the building of Göbekli Tepe, they had hoped that their offerings could propitiate nature's governing forces. Tengri and the other steppe gods, the many animist deities of the world, Pan the half-man/half-goat god of shepherds, flocks and natural urges, the ancient gods of harvest and bounty from Tammuz and Xipe Totec to the Roman Saturn and Ceres, and all the many other deities connected to the mysteries of the natural world were created to provide a focus – an ear – for petitions for protection against disaster and for thanks in times of plenty. The Old Testament

God brought a new dimension to this age-old relationship, a new dynamic between humans and the natural world. The Bible, which had appeared in English for the first time in the century before Bacon published his *Novum Organum*, said that it was His will that humankind was rewarded or punished, just as He had expelled Adam and Eve from the garden and later rewarded Abel and punished Cain. From there, it was but a small step to understanding that failed harvests or flooded towns were just ways by which God punished people for something they had done, or had not done. When things went well, God or the gods were smiling on us. Man plans, God laughs, as the saying goes.

Bacon and some of his revolutionary friends set themselves against the idea that we thrive or die because of something greater than ourselves. Instead, they believed that they could, if they applied themselves to it, understand the forces at work in the world, the forces that wrecked a ship at sea or saw it safely to harbour, that provided water and sunshine for a bountiful harvest, or hard winds, scant rain and a scorching summer to wither crops. They also knew that with understanding would come control. Or, to turn it around, they knew they could win dominion over the natural world. But to do that, humankind must experiment. We must dig into the earth, melt metals and dissect plants, peer into the sky and squint into microscopes. Through a process Bacon called an inquisition, humankind would 'recover that right over nature which belongs to it by divine bequest'.[15]

Both Bacon and Galileo urged their audiences to replace ancient ideas with arguments based on observation of the natural world. Look closely, they urged, observe long enough, and nothing will be beyond our reach. Also, although they might not have been aware of this, nothing would remain sacred.

The knowledge generated by these new techniques and approaches would challenge orthodox thinking and belief, both in the Catholic Church and in society, just as Einstein's theory of relativity, particle accelerators and synthetic viruses have challenged our own thinking. Bacon and his contemporaries saw this challenge as inevitable, something that must occur if they were to take back control. What was not known, or not said at the time, was that there would be a price to pay.

Loving Lazy, 1753

Global population: *c.*750 million

Nomadic population: unknown

To understand where dominion over nature would lead, jump forward a century and more, and cross the Atlantic to the New World, to New England, to the fast-growing city of Philadelphia and to the home of Benjamin Franklin on Market Street. The son of a candlemaker and soap boiler who had started out working as a printer and publisher, Franklin had fulfilled what we recognise as the American dream. With skill, luck and a lot of hard work, he had made enough money from his publishing enterprise to choose how he would spend his time. Being wealthy enough not to need to work again, he could have devoted more time to his favourite sport of swimming, or taken up golf, the new game in the New World. He could have settled into a rocking chair on his porch to rest, read, think, maybe write a little. But 'industry' was one of the thirteen virtues by which he had lived and he was never idle. Beyond his business interests, he had created a public library, the Philadelphia fire service, the first hospital for the poor in the American colonies, the American Philosophical Society and a college that would become the celebrated University of Pennsylvania. He had also devoted years to experimenting with electricity and had discovered the lightning rod and a battery that could store electrical charge. But by his forty-seventh year he had reached some sort of impasse as his thoughts turned to the issue of human wandering.

In the spring of that year, 1753, Franklin wrote to his friend Peter Collinson, a London trader who sold cloth and other merchandise to the American colonies and who had provided Franklin with equipment for his experiments with electricity. In this letter, Franklin laid out his thoughts on the nature of settled society, the benefits of work and the lure of a wandering life. In doing so, he captured the essence of the problem that many settled people had – and have – with nomads.

Foremost in Franklin's thoughts was a recent conversation he had had with a 'Transylvanian Tartar' who may have been one of the many thousands of nomadic Turkic people living west of the Black Sea and who had come to see what America was, and to understand what it might become. One day the visitor asked why so many people around the world 'continued a wandring careless Life, and refused to live in Cities, and to cultivate the arts they saw practiced by the civilized part of Mankind'.

Before Franklin could reply, the Tartar provided his own explanation. In broken English he reasoned that 'God make man for Paradise, he make him for to live lazy; man make God angry, God turn him out of Paradise, and bid him work; man no love work; he want to go to Paradise again, he want to live lazy; so all mankind love lazy.' Francis Bacon would have agreed with this. So too would Carl Linnaeus, the renowned botanist working across the Atlantic in Sweden, who would claim that man's misfortunes began when he left his original tropical homeland, where food was abundant and wandering hunter-gatherers could thrive.[16] But for Franklin it was a puzzle.

It also created a dilemma. On one hand, Franklin was a firm

believer in Bacon's claim that humankind, and settled people in particular, should try to take back dominion over nature. Implicit in this was an ambition to regain whatever had been lost in the Fall. But Franklin also rejected idleness and would obviously refute the idea that man was born to be idle. His own work ethic would culminate in his becoming a Founding Father of the United States and signatory of the American Declaration of Independence. Franklin believed that we were born to be busy and he reasoned that we go to work each morning to achieve financial security, as he had done – what he called the freedom 'from the necessity of care and Labour' – or because we are scared of poverty.

But the more Franklin wrote, the more his own doubts seem to emerge about the joys and benefits of settled living. By the end of his letter, he was wondering whether perhaps, just perhaps, the Tartar was right. What if we *are* lazy by nature? If that was true, would we be better off living a life of greater ease on the move, in the wilderness, as many Native Americans still preferred to do?

Franklin knew settlers in Philadelphia and elsewhere who had raised Native American children as their own and he shared with Collinson their experiences of trying to 'civilize our American Indians'. Civilising, for him, meant reclaiming them from what he saw as the savage brutality of their wandering, outdoor lives. It meant dressing them in manufactured cloth instead of animal skin, and teaching them to read and write, to do arithmetic and learn other skills that would be useful in a settled life.

The main obstacle to achieving this, Franklin realised, lay in the fact that these skills were of no use in the wild because 'almost all their Wants are supplied by the spontaneous Productions of Nature, with the addition of very little labour, if hunting and fishing may indeed be called labour when Game is so plenty'. Which is to say that, like nomads and hunter-gatherers elsewhere, Native Americans could feed themselves and their families with significantly less effort than settled people. And this explains why, although 'they visit us frequently, and see the advantages that Arts, Sciences, and compact Society procure us', the wanderers had no desire to commit to living as a settled society.

'They are not deficient in natural understanding,' he wrote to Collinson – they were not stupid – 'yet they have never shewn any Inclination to change their manner of life for ours, or to learn any of our Arts.' Why might this be? The only explanation Franklin could find was that Native Americans must be naturally attracted to 'a life of ease, of freedom from care and labour'. Then the story gets darker.

Savage, wandering 'Indians' were not the only people who turned out to be idle by nature. Franklin knew that many settlers who had been captured by Native Americans and lived with them were reluctant to return home; those who were ransomed soon slipped back out of the settlement in search of the wanderers. One man in particular had been welcomed home from his 'captivity' and given a large estate to settle on. The man worked his estate just long enough to realise the effort needed to make it a success and then signed it and all his belongings over to his younger brother, took his gun and a coat, and headed back to the wild. Women, Franklin recognises, were even more likely to return to the wandering life for they seem to have found among indigenous people the freedoms they lacked in the settlements, including the right to divorce a husband.

Franklin then shared the story of a meeting between the settler colony and the Six Nations (Iroquois) at which the English Commissioners explained about their schools 'for the instruction of Youth who were there taught various languages, Arts, and Sciences . . . if the Indians would accept of the Offer, the English would take half a dozen of their brightest lads and bring them up in the Best manner.' The Native Americans discussed this offer, but one of their elders reminded them that some of their young had already enjoyed this sort of education and that when they had returned home, they had been 'absolutely good for nothing being neither acquainted with the true methods of killing deer, catching Beaver or surprizing an enemy'.[17] So they politely declined the offer and made one of their own. 'If the English Gentlemen would send a dozen or two of their Children to Onondago,' the Iroquois elders wrote, then 'the great Council would take care of their Education, bring them up in really what was the best manner and make men of them.' This, in turn and inevitably, was declined by the settlers.

But what would have been so wrong in settler children learning how to wander in nature? The answer lies in the settlers' understanding of what constituted 'civilisation'. A century before Charles Darwin constructed his theory of evolution, North American settlers were convinced that they were part not of Ibn Khaldun's circle of existence but of the upward march of civilisation. They believed their settled life was more civilised than the 'wandring careless Life' of Native Americans. Which is to say that they thought they were better humans and that they lived richer lives. In that case, why would they want their children to learn how to track animals or discover the properties of various plants, leaves and berries?

Wrapped up in Franklin's response is the age-old prejudice of the settled towards the nomadic, of the citizen towards those who live without walls. He and his fellow settlers might well have echoed the Roman historian Ammianus Marcellinus's horror of people from the East by writing that 'no one ever ploughs a field in their country'.

But Franklin was no fool and he knew how much time settlers spent in the grip of 'infinite Artificial wants' that were hard to satisfy, just as he could see that people who wandered in nature 'have few but natural wants, and those easily supplied'.

It was an eloquent summary of the problem Ibn Khaldun had identified, of the demands of the very different lives in a settlement or on the move, of farming or herding and hunting, and of the way in which settling in a town or city could corrupt the human spirit in a way that living on the move and in nature did not.

Before he closed this letter to his friend in England, Franklin allowed his thoughts to move in another direction and he wondered why people had ever decided to live a settled life. How did they come to live in what he calls 'close society' as he himself was doing? The answer he finds is that they and *he* lived this way 'not from choice, but from necessity'.

As if there was an inevitability that we should all end up living in cities.

As if it was inevitable that nomads and others who lived a 'wandring careless Life' would eventually settle inside walls.

The Good Doctor

In 1755, two years after Benjamin Franklin wrote his letter to Collinson, *A Dictionary of the English Language* was published in London. The dictionary was unusual for its scope and for including an explanation of the origins of words, 'illustrated in their different significations by examples from the best writers to which are prefixed a History of the Language, and an English Grammar'.[18] The dictionary provides a window onto England in the middle of the eighteenth century, and through it we can see how nomads were regarded at that time.

The author, Dr Samuel Johnson, came from the Midlands town of Lichfield whose name derives from a Celtic/Anglo-Saxon word meaning 'common pasture beside the grey wood'. Even in the eighteenth century pastoralists were still driving their sheep between high and low grazing around Lichfield, so we can assume that Dr Johnson knew something about nomads, even though he chose to omit the word from his great work of scholarship.

There are two views of Dr Johnson. One is of the cash-strapped Grub Street hack who agreed to compile a dictionary to 'fix the English language' for a group of London booksellers. It took him nine years, by which time 'most of those whom I wished to please, have sunk into the grave', his beloved wife Tetty among them. The other view of Dr Johnson is of a wit who, according to his Edinburgh-born biographer James Boswell, had a great thirst for alcohol, an equal appetite for sex and a mind that 'resembled the vast amphitheatre, the Coliseum at Rome'.[19] Neither of these views explains why he thought the word *nomad* unworthy of inclusion in his dictionary. We know he never set eyes on the Sahara, nor roamed the Empty Quarter or Gobi Desert, and yet the word *desart* appears in his dictionary as 'a wilderness, solitude, waste country, an uninhabited place'.

So too does the word *barbarian*, which is explained as meaning uncivilised, savage, without pity and, quoting Shakespeare, 'a foreigner'.

Wanderer is listed as 'such merchants as are wanderers by profession, and at the same time are in all places incapable of lands or offices'.[20]

But between *nolition* ('unwillingness') and *nomancy* ('the art of divining the fates of persons by the letters that form their names'), there is neither *nomad* nor *nomadic*. Nor did he see fit to include the word *transhumance*, although it was practised around his home-town of Lichfield. Nor even *migration*.*

Boswell offers a clue to these omissions in the apparently random way Johnson made selections for his dictionary. The word *civilise* was missing from the first three editions, but, as Boswell tells it, 'I put him in mind of a meaning of the word "side", which he had omitted, viz. relationship; as father's side, mother's side. He inserted it. I asked him if "humiliating" was a good word. He said, he had seen it frequently used, but he did not know it to be legitimate English. He would not admit "civilization", but only "civility".'[21]

When Johnson did finally add 'civilise', he defined it as meaning 'to reclaim from savageness and brutality; to instruct in the arts of regular life'.[22] He does not tell us who might need to be 'reclaimed' from savageness and brutality, but it is safe to assume that nomads,

---

* When the word *nomad* does finally appear – in the 1827 edition of Johnson's masterpiece, prepared by the Queen's chaplain, H. J. Todd – it is with the negative connotation of 'Rude; savage; having no fixed abode, and shifting it for the convenience of pasturage'.

migrants and wanderers were among them. That was certainly how the word was interpreted when it was used, two years after the publication of Dr Johnson's *Dictionary*, on the other side of the world when the Chinese Qianlong emperor declared war on his nomadic neighbours. The Zunghars were a coalition of eastern Mongol tribes whose empire, like that of the Xiongnu 1,400 years earlier, stretched 2,500 miles to the west and north of the Great Wall. Writing to his generals, the Qianlong emperor commanded them to 'show no mercy at all to these rebels. Only the old and weak should be saved. Our previous military campaigns were too lenient.'[23] The justification for this order, which resulted in the death of up to 600,000 people and the destruction not just of the khanate but of an entire culture, in what would be the worst genocide of its age, will sound familiar. The emperor did not approve of war, but heaven had ordained that he must fight against barbarians who had turned their backs on civilisation. It was a definitive victory for the Qing Chinese, with Professor Timothy May of the University of North Georgia noting that 'it was not until 1757 [and what he called the Zhungar genocide] that fears of nomads fully subsided from the minds of sedentary powers.'[24]

Something Beyond Nature

What Dr Johnson called 'regular life' had been unimaginable a few centuries earlier. Regular life back then had required Europe's Christian kings to petition nomad khans to fight against Mamluks and other Muslim powers, hoping that by doing so they would both defeat their long-time enemies and distract the barbarians from attacking Europe. But by the eighteenth century the idea of Abel had been banished along with the ideals of nomads, and regular life was once again tempered by a sense of European superiority and by the restored illusion that the Mediterranean was, once again, the centre of the world. The discovery of the New World and the wealth that had flowed into Europe from it had helped foster that sense of grandeur, but the rediscovery of the ancient world also had a significant part to play in the illusion. Much of that was due to the work of excavators and scholars, none more influential than an idiosyncratic German called Johann Joachim Winckelmann.

Winckelmann moved to Rome in 1755, the year that Dr Johnson's *Dictionary* was published, to study the sculpture at the Vatican and to travel around the Italian peninsula to see the great palazzo collections and the excavations at Pompeii. His most influential work, *The History of the Art of Antiquity*, which appeared nine years after his arrival in Rome, channelled the excitement caused by the latest discoveries to describe the artistic traditions of ancient Egyptians, Etruscans, Greeks and Romans. His work was radical because, really for the first time, it suggested that art history should be studied as a line of ascent, a succession of refinements and improvements, starting in deep antiquity with primitive, barbarian work and progressing via ancient Egypt to peak with the classical Greeks. For the first time, there was also recognition that not all ancient Greek art was executed to the same standards, that it had different phases, from the stylised early Cycladic figures to the perfection of later classical period sculpture.

Winckelmann selected one statue in particular to represent the ideal of Greek art and therefore of all art, and that was the figure of the god Apollo. Known as the Apollo Belvedere, it had been excavated in the fifteenth century some miles south of Rome and was eventually installed in the Vatican, where it remains today. The unknown sculptor has presented the god in larger than human form, 2.25 metres high. Carved from white marble, his athletic body polished to smooth perfection, he stands naked but for his sandals and a robe over his shoulder and arm. The remains of what might have been a bow rests in his hand, his head turned to the left as though following an arrow he has just shot. Renaissance scholars had seen in this statue all the harmonious beauty to be found in the natural world. But Winckelmann, writing after the intellectual revolution of the previous century, saw it differently. He saw in the sculpture nature at its most beautiful, 'but also something beyond nature, namely certain ideal forms of its beauty, which . . . come from images created by the mind alone'.[25] *Beyond* nature . . . This was how far humankind had established dominion over the natural world in the past century and a half, and with what beauty and power! Francis Bacon would have approved, of this at least, even if he would have been disappointed by Winckelmann's conclusion that 'the only way for us to become great or, if this is possible, inimitable, is to imitate the ancients.'[26] Where Bacon had longed to discover a new world of ideas, Winckelmann wanted Europe to rediscover greatness by imitating the past, to stand on the shoulders of giants.

There was one thing these two men could have agreed on and that was a sense of progression. Winckelmann and his colleagues presented art history as a path picked through material culture. Looking back from the late eighteenth century, they retrospectively shaped the idea of the European Renaissance, a magical movement that emerged independently in Europe, and in the process neatly obscured the influence and input of peoples living east of Europe, nomads among them. This selective view of art and intellectual history, like the history highway, disenfranchises people who prefer not to build monuments, or prefer not to build at all, or whose remains – the beautiful and highly sophisticated jewellery of the Scythians, for example – had yet to be discovered or recognised.

Certain in his judgement, Winckelmann saw the trajectory of art history not in circular terms, but as linear. Linear development, like linear time, has progress hotwired into it and is stitched through with a line that stretches back to creation and forward to the end of days, back to when we were all savages and forward to when we will all be civilised. For now, according to Winckelmann's thinking, some people were more civilised than others and most of the civilised were Europeans.

At the same time as Winckelmann was laying out his theories, curators in London were creating the world's first national museum, the British Museum. The core of the initial collection, which would be open and free to 'all studious and curious persons', although clearly not to everyone, was the 'natural and artificial rarities' that the great botanist and collector Sir Hans Sloane had bequeathed to the nation. Sloane believed, as Bacon had believed, that the world could be understood if it was studied, although he did not always get things right: among the 80,000 objects, 40,000 books and manuscripts, 32,000 coins and medals and a 250-volume herbarium of pressed plants he collected, there were small pointed slivers of stone. These Sloane had marked as 'elf arrows' although they are clearly flints. They have been dated to between 4000 and 500 BCE and may have been used by people who were nomadic. They were definitely not used by elves. Before long there would soon be an invisible line threading through the flints and everything else. The line, which would exclude both nomads and elves, would champion the development of a very specific sort of culture that had been passed, as though by divine plan, from ancient Egypt to Greece and Rome and on to Renaissance Europe and finally, most perfectly, to imperial Britain.

The Cost of Progress

What was the cost of progress and how does one calculate it? Should it include the figurative costs? The costs to humans? The costs to the planet? In most cases and many ways, the cost of general progress in the eighteenth century remains unquantifiable. But we can know the cost of specific projects intended to progress society – the first voyage of Captain James Cook, for instance, undertaken four years after Winckelmann published his great work – just as we can know the significant role it played in the expansion of the British Empire and the decline of nomad influence.

'At 2 pm got under sail,' the forty-year-old Royal Navy officer wrote in his log as he steered his ship away from England in August 1768, 'and put to sea having on board 94 persons.' His instructions were to sail to the Pacific Ocean and locate the island of Tahiti, first seen by a European the previous year. The reason for this audacious voyage was to observe the Transit of Venus. British astrologers had realised that by observing the moment when the planet Venus passed in front of the sun, they could calculate the distance from our planet to Venus, and from that they could, for the first time, calculate the size of the solar system and take another step towards understanding the natural world. The biggest challenge posed by the Venus transit was not the difficulties of observation or calculation, large as they were, but the fact that it only occurred once every 105 years, which is why the British Admiralty were involved.

The master of the royal dockyards at Deptford on the River Thames was commanded to find and equip a suitable vessel. He chose a three-masted, east-coast collier, a slow, solid, flat-bottomed cargo ship for which he paid £2,840, the equivalent of £500,000 today, and renamed it *Endeavour*. He then spent twice that amount stripping it down, sheathing and caulking it, adding a third deck and fitting it out. These were real, quantifiable, financial costs.

He then armed the ship with ten cannon and a range of advanced weapons, and loaded it with cutting-edge scientific instruments as well as pigs, chickens, a milk goat and other supplies essential for a long ocean voyage. James Cook had command of the ship, but in scientific matters he would defer to the most eminent of his passengers, the English polymath and botanist Joseph Banks.

Four years earlier, Banks had inherited a fortune that had made him one of the wealthiest people in Britain. Many young men in his position celebrated their independence and their fortune by spending seasons or years around the Mediterranean, returning home with a veneer of sophistication, with stories to tell, some art and antiquities to decorate their mansions and perhaps also a dose of syphilis. 'Every blockhead does that,' Banks replied, when asked why he would not be indulging. 'My Grand Tour shall be one round the whole globe.'[27] To make this happen, he paid for himself and seven assistants to travel with Cook 'for heaven alone knows how long, perhaps for Ever'.[28] As his great passion was botany, their voyage was also to be a global hunt for plants and other natural history exotica. They would return to Britain with the richest haul from any Grand Tour: more than 30,000 plants, some 1,400 of them previously unknown in the West, as well as 1,000 creatures plucked from the air, sea and land.

They reached Tahiti in April 1769, after eight months at sea, and were welcomed by the islanders. An observatory was built, the planetary transit was charted and then they left to discover what lay in the South Pacific. The following April, 1770, they arrived at what Cook would eventually call Botany Bay in what is now Sydney, Australia.

They reached land on an autumn Sunday with the wind blowing from the south and the skies clear. The *Endeavour* rolled gently at anchor. Visibility was good enough for Cook to make out huts on both the north and southern points of the bay, and women and children in front of the huts, with smoke rising from their fires. Cook and Banks had boats lowered and the crew rowed them towards shore.

There were no cannon pointing at them, no city walls or gates barred against their arrival. Perhaps because of this, and the fact that they had been so well received on Tahiti, the Englishmen assumed they would be welcome on shore. 'We were in this however mistaken,' Banks recorded.[29] The Aborigines watching the landing craft were clearly unhappy and 'as we approached', Cook wrote, 'they all made off except two Men who seem'd resolved to oppose our landing'. The expedition artist would later draw these men as muscular and mostly naked, decorated with plugs in their lips, ears and noses and armed with swords, spears and shields. They were Dharawal Aborigines, some of whom were nomadic, and this had always been their land.

'I orderd the boats to lay upon their oars in order to speake to them,' Cook remembered, 'but neither us nor Tupaia could understand one word they said.' Tupaia was the ship's guide and translator, but as he came from a small island 4,000 miles across the Pacific Ocean, there was no reason why he should have been able to speak Dharawal. Banks describes how 'they calld to us very loud in a harsh sounding Language'.

As they approached the shore, Tupaia, who was a holy man as well as a guide, will have understood the sacred nature of the Dharawal land. Captain Cook ordered his men to throw bags of nails and beads onto the golden sand. This gesture of goodwill was intended to smooth their way, but the Dharawal shook their lances, adamant that the foreigners should not land because, although they could not explain it to the intruders, this was sacred space. Cook then 'fired a musket between the two [men], which had no other effect than to make them retire back where bundles of their darts lay and one of them took up a stone and threw it at us'.[30]

Cook's second shot seems to have hit the older of the two men, although it may not have hurt him. Instead, he went to fetch a shield and, as the Europeans landed, the Dharawal threw spears. Although they missed their target, they provoked further shots from the British, which forced the Aboriginal men to retreat. When the intruders landed, they walked up the beach to the huts, where they found four or five children hidden behind a shield. There were also some canoes, which Cook described as 'the worst I think I ever saw'. Collecting all the lances they could find, although Banks thought these had been used for fishing not for defence, they left gifts of beads and cloth and returned to their boats.

Had they been able to write, the Dharawal men would have given a very different account of the landing. Dr Shayne T. Williams, whose grandmothers were Dharawal, has this to say about the exchange:

> If . . . you look at this same encounter from our perspective you would understand that two Gweagal [sic] men were assiduously carrying out their spiritual duty to Country by protecting Country from the presence of persons not authorised to be there. In our cultures it is not permissible to enter another culture's Country without due consent. Consent was always negotiated. Negotiation was not necessarily a matter of immediate dialogue, it often involved spiritual communication through ceremony.[31]

This last sentence is important, for it suggests another aspect to the cost of the voyage and of progress.

Cook was an officer in the Royal Navy. Banks was a wealthy scientist who had devoted his fortune to globalising knowledge, with the intention of improving the lot of people around the world, but especially in his own country. Both men were learned, culturally sophisticated and experienced, but neither suspected that the people they were shooting at *could not* let them land. Their inability to grasp the spiritual aspect to the encounter was a direct consequence of Francis Bacon's drive for dominion over nature. Centuries earlier, when most people in Europe believed in the spirit of places and objects, they would have understood that the beach, like land everywhere, had its own anima. They would have known that ancestor spirits needed to be appeased if foreigners were to land. Instead, enabled by the three inventions Bacon had identified, by compasses that guided them, books that informed them and guns and gunpowder, they had shot their way onto the beach. Imagine the chaos this would have inspired in the minds and spirits of the Dharawal.

They returned the following day and again defiled the sacred space. This time the people had disappeared. The Englishmen found their 'gifts' lying untouched where they had been thrown.

Banks, who was himself fully committed to the mastery of the natural world, came away from this encounter in Botany Bay with no apparent understanding of the insult he and his companions had delivered or the hurt they had caused. Instead, his description of their short visit mentions a vast and empty land, empty even though at night he had seen the coastline glitter with a galaxy of small fires that were tended by people whose success lay in their ability to tread lightly, to live on the move and whose extensive knowledge lay not in libraries but in the ancestor stories they passed on through their dreamings. To Banks, Australia was perhaps empty of civilised people.

Curiously it was Cook, the rough naval careerman, who had the more sensitive and thoughtful response to this brief encounter. Banks would soon recommend that the British government settle this land as a colony, a settlement that would be another victory for the sons of Cain. Cook's response is found in the journal entry he wrote as they sailed into the Coral Sea. 'In reality', he noted of the Dharawal hunter-gatherers, echoing Benjamin Franklin on native Americans, 'they are far more happier than we Europeans; being wholly unacquainted not only with the superfluous but the necessary convienecies [*sic*] so much sought after in Europe, they are happy in not knowing the use of them. They live in a Tranquillity which is not disturb'd by the Inequality of Condition.'[32] It was another call for living light, on the move, in balance with the natural world. It was another instinctive nod towards nomads.

Cook's words about these people who 'covet not Magnificent Houses, Houshold-stuff &C.' is an unexpected reminder of something that Felipe Fernández-Armesto recognised when he discussed history as a path picked through ruins. If your chief aim is to ensure the survival of your civilisation, the historian explained, 'the best thing to do is not to embark on the civilizing'. Seen like this, Fernández-Armesto suggested, Banks's colonising recommendation was not in the best interests of Britain. The societies that have been most successful – because they have survived – are nomadic, hunter-gatherer societies like the Aborigines. The reason for their success is no secret: they have survived because they 'have lived with nature and within nature and haven't tried to change it, haven't tried to crush it, to rebuild it'.[33]

The Real Agricultural Revolution, or Why We Get Nostalgic About Nomads

In 1671, fifty years after the publication of Francis Bacon's *Novum Organum*, the Anglo-Irish philosopher and chemist Robert Boyle asked, 'When we see that Timber is sawd by Wind-mills and Files cut by slight Instruments; and even Silk-stockings woven by an Engine . . . we may be tempted to ask, what handy work it is, that Mechanicall contrivances may not enable men to performe by

Engines?'³⁴ Bacon had believed that technology would give human-kind dominion over nature and history was proving him right.

Spinning was still a cottage industry when Boyle wrote those words, by which I mean that it was performed in a cottage or tent, at home, by people who might also have carded wool and spun thread. These people would have had access to a smallholding – enough land to grow vegetables and raise chickens along with a few other animals – or else they would have roamed with herds and done their spinning, weaving and rug-making on the move, as the Bakhtiari were doing in the Zagros Mountains. Which is to say they would have lived as the heirs to Cain and Abel had lived for millennia, until the real Agricultural Revolution.

'From the moment it appeared advantageous to any one man to have enough provisions for two,' the Swiss philosopher and walker Jean-Jacques Rousseau explained as he distilled into a single sentence humankind's long fall out of grace and into the problems of agri-culture, 'equality disappeared, property was introduced, work became indispensable, and vast forests became smiling fields, which man had to water with the sweat of his brow.' Rousseau was in no doubt of the immense price that we have had to pay and will continue to pay for our reliance on agriculture: 'Slavery and misery . . . germin-ate and grow up with the crops.' Money ruled the European world and, as inevitably as industriousness led to industrialisation, so new capitalism led to the invention of new machines that could do the work of many people and do it faster.

One of those machines was invented by an Englishman who had gone up to Oxford University, dropped out to master the pipe organ and then changed his mind and studied law. As soon as he had his law qualification, Jethro Tull married and took his newly-wed wife on a Grand Tour of Europe. On their return to England, instead of going to London to practise law, Tull embraced the spirit of his age by settling on his family's land and applying himself to the improve-ment of farming practices. Making farming more efficient meant making it faster and less laborious. Of the many devices he created, his great success was with a horse-drawn seed press. Ever since wheat had been domesticated more than eleven thousand years earlier, seed had been sown by hand, either scattered at random or with each seed placed in its individual hole. Tull's mechanical planter did away with all that and meant that fields could be sown faster and with less labour.

The seed planter's ingenuity and efficiency was more than matched by other inventions, none more transformational than the one created by James Hargreaves, a cotton weaver in north-west England. Hargreaves's business relied on a steady supply of spun cotton, but spinning was another of those labour-intensive cottage industries. To speed up the process and ensure a regular supply of spun cotton, in 1765 Hargreaves designed the 'Spinning Jenny', a machine capable of spinning several wheels at the same time. Along with Tull's mechanical planter and a range of inventions that mechanised other labour-intensive processes, the Spinning Jenny allowed British manufacturers to produce more textiles and at lower cost than their rivals in Europe. Success breeds success and these creative processes inspired a sequence of mechanisations and then digitisation that has culminated, in our time, in virtual offices and meetings, cloud storage and the ability to see and speak to people on the other side of the world via a thin screen held in the palm of a hand. But some threads in this long line of development were more problematic than textile weaving.

The 'mechanicall contrivances' that Robert Boyle mentioned did more than transform productivity and output; they provoked a social revolution. Take the Spinning Jenny, for instance. Because the machine was too large for most cottages, where thread had previously been spun, investors wanting to buy into the spinning business needed to construct special 'jenny buildings' and employ spinners. Most of the new buildings were not in the countryside, where yarn had traditionally been spun, but in towns and cities, which were closer both to labour and to transport links. As a result, people who had always worked at home and usually in the countryside, now found themselves having to travel to spinning rooms that were initially called manufactories, later shortened to factories. Eventually they would have to move to the city or find other work. This shift in work patterns transformed the country and prospects for everyone.

The transformation led to a huge jump in the number of people on the planet: in the century between 1750 and 1850, the human population increased roughly 60 per cent from around 750 million to 1.2 billion.[35] In the same period in England and Wales, where the

originally a nomadic language. It was also the age of the Albion Flour Mill.

For many people in London in 1786, the Albion mill represented modernity in the way that the Empire State Building would do in the mid-twentieth century and as a self-drive electric car, a biofuel plane or a 3D-printed object does today. At the time of its opening, the seven-storey mill on the Thames beside London's Blackfriars Bridge was the world's most sophisticated industrial building. In the course of a generation London's population had grown by a third, to well over a million people, many of them lured off the land and into the city by the promise of work in the new markets and factories. The Albion was more than just another industrial opportunity. It was the fulfilment of the promise of the future. Until this time, London's corn and wheat had been ground by wind- or watermills. Behind its elegant neoclassical facade that towered over the Thames, the Albion's power was generated by massive new steam engines. Its millstones could grind over 250 kilograms of corn or wheat each hour, every hour of the day and night, every day of the week. Barges could only approach the mill's basement at high tide, but carts could load and unload at any time. Even the shifting of raw grain and shipping of flour was mechanised, as it should be in a mill that represented the triumph of machine over man. It was, in the words of one of its engineers, 'a national object'[38] and nothing in the industrialised world could compare to it for scale, efficiency and wonder.

For all the symbolism, the mill, like any innovation of this sort and at that time, was driven by capital in search of profit. Everyone ate their daily bread so there were huge profits to be made, which explains why one of the mill's partners was told that however charming the lords and ladies who came calling might be, they should not be given a tour of the building because they were not prospective customers. Everything was done to maximise returns as the Albion's workers loaded, ground, sifted, bagged and shifted flour quicker and cheaper than their outdated wind- and water-powered rivals. The mill had cost around £20,000 to build and equip, the equivalent of £3 million today, but sales that first year, when it was still operating at less than capacity, reached £100,000 (£15 million today). Of course this was a speculative venture and there was always the possibility of a fall, that money could be lost. That was what happened five years after the grand opening. One evening, a flickering orange light was seen through one of the mill's windows. It was a flame. The Albion was on fire.

The blaze was dramatic and devastating and when it finally burned out, days later, the mill's roof had fallen in and its cutting-edge engines been destroyed. The elderly diarist Horace Walpole, who may have been one of the few people in the capital who had never previously heard of the Albion, reported seeing half-burnt grain scattered across his garden, a couple of miles from the fire. As word, smoke and ash fanned across the city, people came to watch. Some of them stood in horror, but many were clearly delighted and there was singing and dancing on Blackfriars Bridge. Balladeers were out all night trying to catch the mood of the moment in words, and by the following morning their verse pamphlets were typeset, printed and for sale on the street as the blaze continued:

> *And now the folks begin to chat,*
> *How the owners they did this and that*
> *But very few did sorrow show*
> *That the Albion Mills were burnt so low.*[39]

The Bastille in Paris had burned only two years earlier and winds of revolutionary change were fanning flames across Europe, so it is not surprising that among all this rejoicing, there were rumours that the Albion fire was no accident. Perhaps, some said, the fire had been started by rival mills, or by anarchists, or people who just wanted cheaper flour – and for that there was another ballad:

> *The price of bread so dear you see,*
> *Let's hope it will much cheaper be,*
> *That people all may have their fills,*
> *It will make more work for our Mills.*[40]

But in spite of the rumours, the trouble at the mill was due to something as prosaic as a lack of grease on a moving part, which caused a spark and set the place on fire.

Reactions to the destruction of this wonder of the age reveal differing concerns. The most obvious was at the pace and scale of the Industrial Revolution. But others worried about the threats that industrialisation posed to people's lives, to their sense of well-being, to what it means to be human. These concerns were never better expressed than by the poet William Blake, who lived just a few steps from the mill.

Blake was in his early thirties at the time of the fire and he used to walk past the Albion several times each week on his way across the Thames from his house in Lambeth. Instead of seeing the mill as a monument to progress, he thought it embodied many of the problems of industrialisation. In an eloquent expression of the inhumanity inherent in the new forces and machines that were reshaping society, he wrote how: 'The living and the dead shall be ground in our rumbling Mills For bread of the Sons of Albion.'[41]

The sons of Albion were in the process of creating an empire that would circle the world and on which the sun would never set. Made possible by compass, print and gunpowder, and powered by what Blake called 'these dark Satanic Mills' and other inventions of the Industrial Revolution, the British Empire and its European rivals eclipsed the old nomadic and post-nomadic empires. Even though nomads had played a major part in shaping the world since before history, from domesticating the horse and inventing the wagon to inspiring ideas of nobility, valour and the bonds that bound a band of brothers, when imperial historians wrote the story of humankind, they either omitted nomads completely or else they did as Roman historians had done and presented them as barbarians. So when Thomas Macaulay, a British politician and historian, rose to his feet in the House of Commons thirty years after Blake composed his poem, none of the honourable Members in the chamber challenged him as he reminded them that part of Britain's imperial mission was to protect itself and its colonies from 'the assaults of barbarous invaders'.

In a long and circuitous speech that mentioned Timur, Attila and other nomad leaders, Macaulay conceded that British supremacy may not last, that 'the sceptre may pass away from us . . . [and] unforeseen accidents may derange our most profound schemes.' But he knew that 'there are triumphs which are followed by no reverses . . . [and] an empire exempt from all natural causes of decay. Those triumphs are the pacific triumphs of reason over barbarism; that empire is the imperishable empire of our arts and our morals, our literature and our laws.'[42]

Macaulay's speech is a perfect expression of the most common way nineteenth-century Europeans framed the differences between settled and mobile people. Not by contrasting their customs or living standards, not by noting as the Mesopotamians and Romans had done how nomads ate raw meat, never bathed, slept rough and were not buried in tombs. Not by considering which way of life was less damaging for the natural world and therefore better for the future of the planet on which we all depend – that reckoning would come much, much later. Instead, Macaulay presented these nomadic barbarians as people without arts, morals, literature, laws or reason. None of the honourable Members of the British Parliament appears to have taken issue with that.

Manifest Destiny, 1850

Global population: 1.2 billion

Urban population: 75 million

Nomad population: unknown

The majority of people in Persia in the nineteenth century lived on the move, herding and trading. In Turkey, where the Ottoman sultan had long ago swapped his saddle for a divan and ruled from behind the walls of his many palaces and kiosks, his diverse subjects remained significantly nomadic. Nomads roamed over Mughal India as they did across most parts of Africa, even though the great Kanem–Bornu Empire had fractured. In Arabia, a nomadic tribal amir called Muhammad Ibn Saud expanded his *asabiyya* to create a new Arab state under the guidance of a reformist religious scholar, Muhammad Ibn Abd al-Wahhab. In Australia, where as many as 90 per cent of the 750,000 indigenous people had died within ten years of the arrival of Joseph Banks's First Fleet settlers, those who remained continued to go walkabout and to dream up their country, as they have done into our own time. In a world encircled by the British Empire, tens of millions of nomads roamed, hunted and gathered. But Macaulay's conviction would prove to be true and European arts, morals, literature and law would triumph over the 'barbarous hordes', nowhere more so than in North America where, a dozen years after Macaulay's speech to Parliament, a citizen of a former British colony coined a two-word phrase that continues to resonate today. Manifest destiny.

The idea of a divinely sanctioned mission was something Genghis Khan had claimed and his nomad followers had understood. It was also claimed by an American journalist, John O'Sullivan, who wrote in 1839 that his fellow Americans were destined to push the 'great experiment of liberty' the whole way to the Pacific Ocean across what came to be called, without exaggeration, the Wild West. 'This is our high destiny,' O'Sullivan explained, as Mongol khans had claimed, 'and in nature's eternal, inevitable decree of cause and effect we must accomplish it.'[43]

The Declaration of Independence that Benjamin Franklin had signed in 1776 states the 'self-evident' truths that all men are created equal and have the same rights to life, liberty and the pursuit of happiness. Franklin was also a signatory to the American Constitution, which insisted that 'Neither slavery nor involuntary servitude . . . shall exist within the United States, or any place subject to their jurisdiction.'[44] Franklin, we now know, had kept two male slaves at his home in Pennsylvania, but he later freed them and up to his death in 1790 he devoted much time and energy to agitating for the freedom and education of all slaves and for one law for settlers, pioneers and Native Americans. But the Declaration and Constitution that he helped fashion applied only within the United States. So when the citizens of that country went west beyond their borders, they were no longer subject to their home rules and often seemed prepared to forget their home values.

The inconvenient truth for these westward pioneers was that the new world was not new and the land not virgin when the Pilgrim Fathers waded ashore. Just as Australia belonged to Aborigines before British colonisers arrived, just as much of South America belonged to its wandering peoples and Central Asia to the Mongols, Turks and other nomad tribes, so North America had long been home to both nomadic and settled tribes. These arrivals from Europe were not pioneers. To repurpose Macaulay's phrase, they were barbarous invaders.

'We are the nation of progress,' the journalist O'Sullivan had written, 'of individual freedom, of universal enfranchisement.' He might have added that they were also the nation of weapons. Under the banner of progress, European settlers pushed further and faster into territories they might otherwise have left alone, into Native American territory, and they were able to do so because they had superior weapons. As early as the mid-1700s, the long-barrelled Kentucky rifle gave shooters the sort of range and accuracy that would allow a marksman in upstate New York to kill a British general with a single shot, without ever being seen. Long-range shooting was a very different prospect to facing a man on horseback with sword or bow, and it was one step in a sequence that, over the next century, saw American inventors mechanise killing in the same way that English inventors had mechanised farming. First came a hand-cranked weapon, the Gatling gun, which could fire two hundred rounds a minute. That was soon followed by the Maxim gun, an apt name for a weapon that could fire three times as fast as the Gatling. The Kentucky rifle was replaced by the repeating Winchester. Samuel Colt's revolving-chamber pistol improved on the speed and accuracy of the old muzzle-loaded pistol. Weapons created in the United States became ever more deadly.

Native American tribes are often seen as a single, homogenous

group, but if they were united it was only against the encroach-
ment of settlers and even then there were divisions among them.
Before the arrival of Europeans, there had been regular conflict
over rights to hunting grounds – the Sioux chasing the Crow off
their buffalo grounds, for instance – or because of cultural differences, as when settled tribes battled nomadic ones. The strength
of the Sioux, Dakota, Comanche and other nomadic tribes was
their ability to move, their habit of thinking on their feet or in
the saddle, and the skilful way they adapted and used their knowledge of the landscape. But the 'progress' of American weapons
left these tribes at the same disastrous disadvantage as nomads
elsewhere in the world.

Native Americans were not the only people unhappy about the
price paid to fulfil an American sense of destiny, and among them
was Henry David Thoreau. Thoreau is best known for the two years
and two months he spent in the woods at Concord, near Boston,
Massachusetts. He was still in his twenties when he built himself a
simple log house in front of Walden Pond and committed to 'earning
my living by the labor of my hands only'. The house and the
commitment to living by his own labour were part of an experiment
to show how many of his fellow settlers had been misled in their
pursuit of wealth. He opens *Walden*, the book he wrote about his
log cabin experiment, by attacking those 'whose misfortune it is to
have inherited farms, houses, barns, cattle, and farming tools'. Then,
echoing Rousseau and inspired by Native Americans, he suggests it
would have been 'better if they had been born in the open pasture
and suckled by a wolf'.

'Men,' he goes on, 'even in this comparatively free country, through
mere ignorance and mistake, are so occupied with the factitious
cares and superfluously coarse labors of life that its finer fruits cannot
be plucked by them.'[45]

Like Pascal and Rousseau before him, Thoreau regarded time
spent indoors as a form of death. 'I cannot preserve my health
and spirits', he insisted, 'unless I spend four hours a day at least
– and it is commonly more than that – sauntering through the
woods and over the hills and fields, absolutely free from all worldly
engagements.' He did at least recognise the good fortune that

allowed him the luxury of choosing how he lived, and he thought the mechanics, shopkeepers and other neighbours who lacked the freedom to walk whenever they wanted 'deserve some credit for not having all committed suicide long ago'. But there was a point to his certainty that he and his contemporaries needed to spend more time 'in the forest, and in the meadow, and in the night in which the corn grows'. If they did not, he warned, they would lose touch with the natural world, or what he calls 'this vast, savage, hovering mother of ours'.[46] The word *savage* jumps out here.

Thoreau's experiment at Walden had its critics, who pointed out how close he was to Boston and considered his self-sufficiency was in some way compromised by his mother popping over to help out with food and the laundry. But none of that detracts from the importance of his experiment nor from the urgency of his call to live more simply. By hiring out his time, gathering whatever he could in the wild and growing some of his own food, Thoreau reckoned he needed to work little more than a day a week to support himself. If that calculation is correct then he was even more efficient at using his time than hunter-gatherers. Even if it took him twice as long as he claimed, he would still have had five days each week to go for long walks under big skies and to observe the world around him.

The love of nature, the need to move, a recognition of the real cost of things – as we are being encouraged to calculate in our own time by the likes of Extinction Rebellion – coupled with a mistrust of the trappings of 'civilised life' would seem to make Thoreau an ideal champion of native nomads and their way of life. But his response to the plight of Native Americans is contradictory. 'The white man comes, pale as dawn, with a load of thought,' he wrote before his Walden Pond experiment,

> with a slumbering intelligence as a fire raked up, knowing well what he knows, not guessing but calculating . . . building a house that endures, a framed house. He buys the Indian's moccasins and baskets, then buys his hunting grounds, and at length forgets where he is buried, and plows up his bones. And here town records, old, tattered,

time-worn, weather-stained chronicles, contain the Indian sachem's mark, perchance, an arrow or a beaver, and the few fatal words by which he deeded his hunting grounds away.[47]

There is pathos here, but also pragmatism, as Thoreau recognises that this is the way it will be. In his *Indian Notebooks*, he presents the settler/Indian conflict as another version of the age-old standoff between Cain and Abel, with its inevitable outcome. '"The Great Spirit" gave the white man a plough, and the red man a bow & arrow,' he writes, 'and sent them into the world by different paths, each to get his living in his own way.'[48] But the white man turned up with more than a plough: he came with a sense of destiny, with increasingly deadly weapons and with the determination to do whatever it would take to fulfil that destiny.

Of the 10 million indigenous people living in North America before the white man arrived, not all were nomads. Over the course of centuries and through a process of negotiation and oppression, the Flatheads and Nez Perce of the Northwest Plateau, the Shoshoni and Paiute of the Great Basin, Navaho and Mescalero in the south-west, Comanche, Cheyenne and Wichita on the Great Plains, Cherokee, Shawnee and Mohican in the north-east, Chickasaw and Alabama in the south-east and many other tribes had divided the land between the settled and the nomadic. As had happened elsewhere in the world, geography had played a significant role in deciding who would live where.

The Great Plains of the United States were the dominant feature between the great mountain spine in the west and the swamps in the south-east. This huge grassy ocean, a twin to the Eurasian steppeland, stretched thousands of miles from near the Arctic Circle in Canada down towards the Gulf of Mexico and the Tropic of Cancer, and westwards from the Great Lakes to the Rockies. The central fact of the plains, for Native Americans at least, were the immense herds of bison. These huge, shaggy, short-horn, grass-eating beasts roamed hundreds of miles each year in search of grazing and to avoid the worst of the heat and cold. Wherever they went, humans followed on foot, hunting them for their meat and hides. There was a delicate balance in the way Native Americans interacted with these creatures and with the ecosphere on which all depended. That balance changed with the arrival of Europeans on the continent in the sixteenth century.

When Spanish conquistadors shipped their horses across the Atlantic in their conquest of Mexico, it was a happy return for creatures that had roamed North America ten thousand years earlier, before being hunted to extinction. It was a successful return as well because some of the Spanish horses escaped and bred in the wild. The herds they sired grew so large they were soon competing with bison for grass, but there was to be a more dramatic consequence for the bison. As Indo-Europeans had done on the Eurasian steppes thousands of years before, Native Americans learned to ride horses and, as in Eurasia, riding made wide-ranging nomadism possible on the Great Plains. Native Americans became as deadly with horse and bow as Mongols had been and for a while they were the lords of the plains. Then came the settlers.

There may have been 50 million bison[49] on the plains before the arrival of Europeans; there may have been twice that number. At the beginning of the nineteenth century when President Thomas Jefferson sent out a mission to scout the country from the Mississippi to the Pacific coast, his trailblazers Lewis and Clark described how a 'moving multitude' of the beasts 'darkened the whole plains'. The plains and bison were a key feature in most Native American narratives and in ceremonies in which the huge beasts were regarded as sacred. While they were hunted and their flesh eaten, they were also respected, their spirits pacified by chanting in the hope and belief that by doing so the spirits of the dead would be calmed and the balance in nature maintained. Pioneers and settlers unsettled the balance by massively increasing the demand for buffalo hide, as they had for beaver skin and other furs up in the Rockies and the Northwest in the seventeenth and eighteenth centuries. The 'moving multitude' was endangered.

Perhaps if it had been left to destiny, none of this would have happened, but settlers improved their chances by arriving with ploughs, weapons and dollars, among them the $15 million President Thomas Jefferson paid the French government for their 'holdings in North America'. The 1803 Louisiana Purchase gave the United States control of the Mississippi river basin, some of the most fertile land on the planet. But there was a problem with this purchase because the land did not belong to the French. It was still home to native tribes, including the Lakota Sioux, one of the most powerful groups on the continent.

Thirty years after the purchase, the seventh president, Andrew Jackson, signed into law the Indian Removal Act, which gave the government and settlers the right to clear Native Americans from their ancestral homes on the basis that the lands now 'belonged' to the United States under the terms of the Purchase. In return for their homelands, Native Americans were offered territory in what the US government had classified as the 'unorganised' west. This move was opposed by most Native Americans. Some of them even argued the case in law, taking their case to the US Supreme Court, which ruled that President Jackson's law could not apply because native nations were sovereign and were therefore not subject to United States legislation. The president acknowledged that he was obliged to follow the court ruling, but he made it clear that he would not be enforcing it. Many others followed the president's lead, as a result of which neither sovereignty nor legitimate legal claims could protect the native nations from being enticed, cajoled, bullied and ultimately forced off their ancestral lands and moved ever further westwards and with complete disregard for their lives or livelihood. In 1839, for instance, tens of thousands of Cherokee were forced to travel west of the Mississippi, in the depths of winter, on a journey that took the lives of four thousand people and that is now remembered as the 'Trail of Tears'.[50] Much blood and more tears followed at Little Big Horn, Wounded Knee and the roughly 1,600[51] skirmishes, battles and wars that the US Army fought to 'pacify' the great Indian nations and 'remove' them from land that was, in many cases, theirs not just by right, but in American law.

Both nomadic and settled Native Americans were at such great disadvantage that the outcome of this struggle was never in doubt. It was not long before one American author was able to write that the continent 'has already been nearly depopulated of its aborigines by the introduction of the blessings of civilisation'.[52]

The Dark Side of Nature

Six years after the Cherokee walked their trail of tears, Thoreau built his cabin beside Walden Pond. By that year, 1845, settlers had established 'union' over more than half the continent, building cities, laying thousands of miles of railway between the Atlantic and the Missouri river, and clearing vast tracts of forest for agriculture. Florida was created the 27th state in the Union, Texas began the year as an independent republic but Congress soon voted for annexation, Oregon in the north-west was still partly occupied by the British and the rest of the west was claimed by Mexico. But the year ended with US President Polk calling for aggressive expansion to the west and with the journalist John O'Sullivan writing in the *United States Magazine and Democratic Review* of 'our manifest destiny to overspread the continent allotted by Providence for the free development of our yearly multiplying millions'.

Manifest destiny and a hunger for land and resources to satisfy an exploding population drew settlers ever further west. In the year that Thoreau built his cabin in the woods, a New York entrepreneur called on the US Senate to fund a railway the whole way to the Pacific. It took time because there were serious objections to the idea, but the

Pacific Railroad Act was passed in 1862, the year Thoreau died. But even ten years earlier there was a sense of inevitability about the railway being pushed through and opening up the west, cutting the 3,000-mile journey coast to coast from several months to less than a week. It was inevitable because this was about more than efficiency. It was about the dominion of industrialised power over the natural world and wilderness, of a restless nation of settlers over settled nations of nomads, and the railway served as both outrider and symbol.

'The fact is,' Thoreau wrote in his *Indian Notebooks*, 'the history of the white man is a history of improvement, that of the red man a history of fixed habits of stagnation.'[53] Ibn Khaldun would have put it no better.

Native culture might have seemed stagnant to Thoreau, but unlike most in the United States he was still drawn to find out 'what manner of men they were'.[54] The eleven notebooks he filled with lore, stories, songs and observations of his own, alongside passages copied from books and pamphlets already in print, are the largest depository of nineteenth-century knowledge about Native Americans. Whatever the reason for his writing them – was it research for an 'Indian book' to preserve for posterity whatever knowledge he could glean, or just because he was curious? – his notebooks show that the 'red man' had a very different way of looking at the world. The Native American, Thoreau recorded, 'measures his life by winters, not summers. His year is not measured by the sun, but consists of a certain number of moons, and his moons are measured not by days, but by nights. He has taken hold of the dark side of nature.' What Thoreau does not mention, because he did not know, was that there had been a time when all humankind measured their lives by the moon not the sun. We are all children of the dark side.

However great his fascination with Native Americans, Thoreau thought it was inevitable that their way of life would disappear and, like many others around the world and since that time, he felt nostalgia for the imminent loss of something he had not fully experienced. The urge of the 'white man' to 'improve' would eventually allow them to overrun the continent. But although Thoreau omits Native Americans from his essay *Walking*, in which he enthuses about the idea of the westward movement of progress, the west was still wild, still needed to be 'won', the power of the native tribes was still significant, and the plains and the mountains beyond them, as one European philosopher put it, was 'not the night of European memory, but the morning of the world and of humanity'.[55] These hunters and nomads in that 'morning of the world' were living, as Thoreau had instinctively recognised, and as Ibn Khaldun had seen, in the first state of man. Settlers who farmed were in the second, more elevated state of man. 'A race of hunters', Thoreau recorded in his notebook, words he might have been copying from Ibn Khaldun, 'can never withstand the inroads of a race of husbandmen.'[56] Especially not this race of husbandmen for they carried guns alongside their shovels and ploughshares and they arrived on the railway, as if in fulfilment of Francis Bacon's vision that dominion would be driven by technology.

The railway was to Thoreau what hi-tech is to us, a measure of progress. Just as computers and phones have changed every aspect of our lives, from preparing food and heating homes to assessing us when we are sick and guiding us when we are lost – for as long as our batteries last – so the railway transformed everyday life in mid-nineteenth-century America. The first American rails were laid when Thoreau was a teenager and by the time he was in his late twenties and in his cabin they were a commonplace. So much so that a line laid by a thousand Irish labourers ran just a hundred 'rods', 500 metres, from Walden Pond and the engine's high-pitched whistle punctuated his days, ripping through woods and fields to warn walkers such as himself that the iron horse was bringing traders, bankers and lovers to town. Yet Thoreau remained unimpressed.

This lack of enthusiasm was partly due to his belief that the railway offered a bad deal. He calculated that he could walk to Fitchburg, thirty miles down the track, before the day's end. Of course his friend who took the train would be there before him, but it cost Thoreau nothing but shoe leather to walk, whereas his friend needed to buy a ticket, which cost him ninety cents, or a day's labour. That working day and the train journey was longer than Thoreau's walk. We could go around the world like that, Thoreau assured his friend, and the walker would always be ahead. 'We do not ride on the railroad,' he warned, 'it rides upon us.'

His calculation might make you think that he was missing the point. But this was about more than time and money. Thoreau worried about the effect of the railway. The industry it represented and the restless world it carried were reshaping the lives of the people who rode it and those, like himself, who lived on the land it passed through. In this as in so much else he was ahead of his time. It turns out he was right to be concerned.

The American Empire

Who could weigh the cost – to the natural world, to nomads who depended on it, to us, and to others in the future – of Americans striving to fulfil their manifest destiny? And who would want to do so? The debate continues to this day and not just about what has happened in North America in the past century and a half. The great achievements that were enabled by that American fulfilment of manifest destiny are now being weighed against the cost to the natural world and to indigenous peoples. The calculations are difficult, in some ways impossible, but there are some quantifiable costs. For instance, the United States has recently recognised 574 native tribes. Recognising these people implies acknowledging, if not accepting, their claims to land or reparation. In this vein, in June 2019, Gavin Newsom, the governor of California, formally apologised for the way Native Americans had been treated in his state. 'It's called a genocide,' the governor said as he referred to the words and actions of the state's first governor, who had said in 1850 that 'a war of extermination will continue to be waged between the two races until the Indian race becomes extinct.'[57] But the Indian race has endured, however much reduced, and here was a twenty-first-century governor, surrounded by native leaders, standing under an old oak beside the Sacramento river, saying, 'That's what it was: a genocide. No other way to describe it. And that's the way it needs to be described in the history books.'

But as history books are rewritten, they present the variety of possibilities, some saying that the troubles started in the 1830s with the Indian Removal Act, others pointing to 1803 and the Louisiana Purchase. I would push it back at least to the 1750s when Benjamin Franklin and his friends failed to understand the appeal and therefore the value of a 'wandring careless Life', or to the early 1600s and Francis Bacon calling for dominion over nature.

One of the stories the Swiss philosopher Jean-Jacques Rousseau liked to tell involved a Native American chief who travelled to London to protest against the way English settlers were encroaching on their lands and interfering with their lives. Rousseau does not specify a date and there were several visits at that time because *pow wow* still seemed to offer the hope of saving native rights to live and roam as they pleased, as they had long done. But it is likely to have been the visit of seven Cherokee chiefs in midsummer of 1730. The Cherokee were not fully nomadic, like the plains Indians, but many of them did move between summer and winter homes.

After some days in London, the chiefs were invited to visit the king at Windsor Castle and according to the London press they arrived in their best ceremonial robes. The senior among them was wearing a scarlet jacket, while the others dressed in loincloths with a horsetail hanging behind, red, blue and green paint on their faces and shoulders, and painted feathers fixed in their hair. They carried bows and arrows. German-born King George II and his courtiers received them in wigs, ermines and jewels and it is hard to know who would have been more surprised by the clash of clothing. At the end of the audience, King George vowed that friendship between the two peoples would last as long as the mountains stood, the rivers flowed, the sun rose . . . The Cherokee then presented the king with gifts they had chosen from their homeland: four enemy scalps to signify prowess, some eagle tail-feathers for glory and a cap of possum skins. As Rousseau tells it, King George had trouble knowing how to reciprocate. He may also have had trouble summoning enthusiasm for the gifts he had received. In return, he would have liked to give them a thousand guineas, but money was not enough. Nor was a bolt of red cloth, which had also been selected as a gift. 'A thousand things were put before his [the chief's] eyes in the search for a present that would please him. But the swords seemed heavy, the shoes tight, the clothes ridiculous. Then the chief spotted a wool blanket . . .' The chief wrapped the blanket around his shoulders and found it 'almost as good as an animal skin'. Rousseau thought the chief 'would not have said even that if he had worn them both under the rain'[58] and he believed the British king had the better deal. In this he was right because the possum-skin cap acknowledged King George as a Cherokee chief. It conferred status and rights that His Majesty's subjects would exploit long before the rivers had run dry and the sun stopped rising. In doing so they would continue the long process of incursion on native nomadic rights that would result in an epochal battle between those whose mobile lives depended on the balance of the natural world and those who believed that science and religion gave them mastery over all.

In June 1876, an alliance of Lakota/Sioux/Plains Indians fought the US 7th Cavalry beside a Montana river, at a site they knew as Greasy Grass. There were many reasons for Indians to have fought that summer day, not least their determination to protect the South Dakota Black Hills from pioneer settlers. This area had long been recognised as part of the Great Sioux Reservation and the land was sacred to the tribes, but gold had been struck in the hills in 1874 and the US government had sent the army to move the natives out. Two years later there was a showdown.

The Sioux were one of the last of the great native nations to have preserved their rights to roam, graze and hunt on ranges where they knew the season and property of each plant and the habit of every animal, land on which settlers intended to raise cattle and crops and mine for gold. But the coming fight would be about more than grass and open land, more than mere legal ownership, however important that might be.

Settlers believed the land was theirs by manifest destiny and by right of laws recently passed in a white man's chamber, far away. The Lakota chief Sitting Bull believed the land belonged to his people. He also believed that he and his people belonged to the land, which they held as sacred and which, as with the Aborigines Captain Cook and Joseph Banks had disturbed in Botany Bay, they had a duty to protect. Before the battle, Sitting Bull prayed, sang and smoked, and then he planted buckskin pouches filled with tobacco and willow bark to honour the spirits of the place. Crazy Horse, one of the most famous Lakota warriors, dusted himself with the dry earth of the valley, wove its long grass into his hair and burned some of the material from his medicine bag on a bison-dung fire so that the smoke would reach the gods, so that his prayers would be heard and the sanctity of the land be preserved. The battle, for these braves as for the cavalrymen riding towards them, was about belonging.

Lieutenant Colonel George Armstrong Custer led the 7th Cavalry into the Little Bighorn valley to punish these First Americans for not moving into reservations, as they had been ordered to do by the US government. Custer knew he would be outnumbered but he underestimated the size of opposition – his 197 men would eventually face up to 2,000 warriors – just as he underestimated the ability and determination, and perhaps above all the desperation, of these warriors, many of whom were now convinced it would be better to fight and die than to allow themselves to be corralled any further. Custer may also have underestimated their arsenal. He had rejected the idea of transporting Gatling guns and had even instructed his troopers to leave their sabres behind, which left his cavalry attacking with standard army-issue single-shot Colt pistols. Some of the braves they faced were armed with their traditional weapons, tomahawks and bows and arrows, from which they shot as many as ten thousand arrows. But some among the tribes had adopted the new technology and they were armed with Winchester repeating rifles.

Custer had planned to cross the Little Bighorn river to attack the Indian village, but he quickly found himself under heavy fire and was forced to retreat to a nearby hilltop. It was there that he, his cavalry force and many troopers who had come to their rescue were killed. It was the worst defeat of US troops in a century of conflict and it could not have happened at a more dramatic moment: news of the slaughter reached Washington DC on 3 July 1876, the eve of celebrations to mark a centenary of independence from Britain.

Public reaction was fierce – the slaughter confirmed what was believed to be the savagery of these native people – and the military response was definitive. Many Indians died in the reprisals. Those who survived were forced onto reservations where their tragedy was multiplied: along with the blessings of progress, pioneers and settlers brought measles, chickenpox and other diseases against which Native Americans had no natural defence. The California governor had not exaggerated when he spoke of 'a war of extermination' that would be waged 'until the Indian race becomes extinct'. There were 200,000 Native Americans in California at the start of the nineteenth century, but only 15,000 by the century's end.

Native Americans, nomadic and otherwise, were not the only casualties in the fulfilment of manifest destiny. The world they had known and nurtured, and the animals and spirits they had worshipped would all disappear. The most dramatic disappearance was that of the vast bison herds that had roamed the American prairies – remember there had been at least 50 million of them before the arrival of Europeans, perhaps even twice that number. By 1886, ten years after the Battle of the Little Big Horn, the herds were so depleted that the Smithsonian Museum's chief taxidermist William Hornaday went west to find a satisfactory specimen for the museum while it was still possible to do so. Hornaday followed the railway west and yet, over the course of several months' hunting, only found a score of the animals. The situation was even worse the following year when the naturalist Daniel Giraud Elliot, one of the founders of the American Museum of Natural History, decided to hunt a bison for the museum's collection. After three months on the move, he returned to New York without even seeing one of the creatures. Both the bison and the many nomadic tribes who depended on them were facing extinction.

Jump forward to a few years ago and to a man called T. T. Karma Chopel, who visited the big open spaces of Green River in Utah. Chopel was a member of Tibet's parliament-in-exile. He was also someone who knew about life on the vast Eurasian uplands, about nomad life. As he looked out across the river and the vast empty landscape of red rocks and red desert – hopeless for farming, but possible for herds – it seemed obvious to him to ask, 'Where are your nomads?'

Two Sides, Same Coin

Much had changed since the days when nomad khans dominated Eurasian trade and trade routes, and when Kubilai Khan could instruct the imperial treasury to distribute the state's accumulated wealth on the grounds that capital should be kept constantly moving. The nineteenth century was the beginning of the age of accelerated settlement in towns and cities. In this new age, the destruction of the Native American empires and alliances, the conquest of nomads on the southern Russian border, on the western side of the Great Wall in China, and in Africa where European powers expanded their colonies, was regarded as progress. Nomads were wanderers, drifters, migrants, vagrants, people of no fixed abode, pastoralists, herders, hunters, gatherers, noble savages . . . all of them undesirables whose days should be numbered. All this because cultures and civilisations were valued according to their monetary wealth and physical power, not on whether they had survived, or had respect for the natural world. They were valued because they had left their testament in grandiose monuments, not in stories or memories to be shared whenever friends, family or tribes gathered.

'At some future period, not very far distant as measured by centuries,' Charles Darwin wrote in his *Descent of Man*, 'the civilised races of man will almost certainly exterminate and replace throughout the world the savage races.' Darwin was certainly not condoning the extermination, but he was not alone in his certainty that he belonged to a civilised and civilising race, nor in his prediction that he and his type would prevail.

In a paper entitled 'The Extinction of Races', a fellow of the Anthropological Society of London noted in 1864 that

Hawaiians have been reduced as much as eighty-five per cent during the last hundred years. The natives of Tasmania are almost, if not quite, extinct. The Maories are passing away at the rate of about twenty-five per cent every fourteen years, and in Australia, as in America, whole tribes have disappeared before the advance of the white man.[59]

Another member of the society predicted that black Africans would all die because 'the weak must be devoured by the strong'.[60]

When Charles Darwin read his colleague and rival evolutionist Alfred Russel Wallace's book *The Origin of Human Races*, he underlined one particularly salient passage. It is where Wallace claims that the strong must devour the weak if human society is to advance, a form of blood sacrifice, if you like, by which the human stock is strengthened and perfected. This idea was echoed thirty years later in a speech given by Lord Salisbury, the British prime minister, in which he stated that 'one can roughly divide the nations of the world into the living and the dying'.[61] Nomads were among the dying.

The conquest of nomads went hand in hand with dominion over nature. By the beginning of the twentieth century, as Francis Bacon had intended when he had laid out his project four hundred years earlier, the outcome was made inevitable by a series of world-changing scientific discoveries, not least being the combustion engine, whose power was drawn from burning fossil fuel. By the 1920s, the horse, which had served for thousands of years as mankind's most efficient means of transport, was consigned to the racetrack and leisure outings, and the motor car became the preferred means of transport, at least in cities. The march of progress was as inexorable

Chicago, Tokyo, Berlin and Paris all had more than 2 million inhabitants and New York's population had just topped 6 million, which would soon make it the largest in the world. What was happening in cities was also occurring in thousands of regional towns. So where most people in Britain worked in agriculture at the beginning of the nineteenth century, by the 1870s more than half of them had moved to urban centres to find a better life. With this change, something unexpected happened, unexpected because in the industrialised world, technology was supposed to provide in every way: the more people moved to the city and severed their connection with the natural world, the more they dreamed about the wild, as though it was the place not only where they had come from but where they belonged, where they could be fully human.

Where writers in ancient Athens and Rome had fantasised about Arcadia and the other, easier, pastoral life that could be lived there, modern poets, novelists and essayists were just as happy to let their thoughts wander across remote places. 'Let Nature be your teacher,' the English Romantic poet William Wordsworth urged and many were happy to be taught. When the twentieth-century composer Olivier Messiaen was asked to explain why his music was based not on the regular metre of classical music but on what he called 'natural resonance', on patterns that he found in movement in nature, he said, 'I give bird songs to those who dwell in cities and have never heard them.'[62]

Implicit in all this is a nagging sense that something is missing or lacking in urban living. The problem had been perfectly expressed by the very first cities, for they were defined by their walls – literally so in the case of Uruk, where the great king Gilgamesh had urged his visitor to 'Climb Uruk's wall. Walk back and forth! Survey its foundations, examine its brickwork! Were its bricks not fired in an oven? Did the Seven Sages not lay its foundations?' No doubt the wall and what it contained was magnificent. So too was Homer's hundred-gated Thebes, and high-gated Troy before it was burned by the Greeks, and Jericho before the Israelites blew their horns, and so many other cities before and after. But gates and walls performed the same function wherever they were and in whatever age: they fixed people inside them, in that one place, and by the same act also separated them from everything that was outside. Nomads, whose movements were another of those 'natural resonances' that Messiaen had mentioned, by definition belong outside the walls, at large and in motion across the natural world. Even when populations increased and cities grew beyond their walls, relying on natural features or lines on maps for their municipal boundaries, they continued to function as though they were still bound by walls, separating all that lived within from whatever lay beyond. This was something the central European writer Joseph Roth captured so brilliantly.

Roth was the most successful journalist in Weimar Berlin in the 1920s. In spite of the harsh conditions imposed on Germany as a result of its defeat in the First World War, the population of the capital, Berlin, had increased by 50 per cent over twenty-five years, and at the time Roth was writing it was home to some 4 million people. In an article for the *Berliner Börsen-Courier*, Roth described the day he went in search of nature, walking through the city, where he saw 'a horse, harnessed to a cab, staring with lowered head into its nose bag, not knowing that horses originally came into the world without cabs'.[63]

Roth describes cafes and shops, a war cripple with a nail file, a dog running after a ball and then 'at the edge of the city, where I have been told nature is to be found', he becomes annoyed by a woman out for a walk in nature because, as far as he was concerned, 'it isn't nature at all' that she is looking at, 'but a sort of picture-book nature'. Roth was clear-eyed about what had happened:

Nature . . . no longer exists for its own sake. It exists to satisfy a function. In summer it provides woods where we can picnic and doze, lakes where we can row, meadows where we can bask, sunsets to send us into raptures, mountains for walking tours, and beauty spots as destinations for our excursions and day-trips.

As we know, nature's task is not merely to amuse us. By reducing it to entertainment, we have engaged in a process that has destroyed the essential balance on which the natural world depended, on which we depended. We have undermined the foundations of our biosphere. Anxiety about the destruction of nature, and nostalgia for an older, gentler way of life, go some way towards explaining why, a few years after Roth's tirade appeared in the German press, two American war veterans and a very British novelist set out for Persia.

The Secrets of Our Past

Ernest B. Schoedsack and Merian C. Cooper were on assignment in Europe for the *New York Times* when they felt it was time to move in a new direction. Both men were in their twenties and had emerged from the First World War intact, although Cooper had suffered as a Soviet prisoner. Swept up by post-war optimism, they formed Cooper-Schoedsack Productions and announced that they would make what they called 'natural drama' moving pictures. The production company's motto was 'distant, difficult, and dangerous', which is how they intended their films would look.[64]

A decade later the two friends would be celebrated for making one of the most successful movies of all time, *King Kong*, but their first film told the story of nomads on migration. Schoedsack, a tall man from Iowa affectionately called 'Shorty', remembered how 'we thought it was going to be about Kurdistan'. They had attracted $10,000 in funding and acquired 10,000 feet of film. They had also been joined by another war-veteran-turned-journalist, Marguerite Harrison, who had spent the past few years in Russia and China spying for the US government and had ended spending ten months in Moscow's notorious Lubyanka Prison. Schoedsack was unhappy to have Harrison travelling with them. Although he would later describe her as a 'fine, courageous, adventurous woman', he thought she was only with them to gather material for stories to 'thrill the ladies at her woman's club lectures . . . She just didn't belong in this kind of a show.'[65] What he did not know was that she had provided half of their funding and that without her money there would have been no show. Together the three of them headed to Istanbul.

The silent film's first title card announces, in words that would have had Francis Bacon on the edge of his seat, 'The sages have told us how our forefathers, the Aryans of old, rose remote in Asia and began conquest of the earth, moving ever in the path of the sun.' Its American audience was then reminded of their manifest destiny: 'We are part of that great migration. We are the travelers who still face to the westward.'

So why go east? Why leave Istanbul and travel through Anatolia, Syria and across Iraq? The intertitles explain that in the east they were hoping to recover 'the secrets of our own past' and find 'our brothers still living in the cradle of the race – a long since Forgotten People'.

They had intended to film a migration of Kurdish herders, but 'for months we travelled . . . turning the pages backwards – on and on further back into the centuries'.[66] It was not until they reached Persia that 'we reached the first Chapter, arrived at the very beginning'. The beginning, as they understood it, were Bakhtiari nomads, who were still living 'the ancient life of tent and tribe and herd, the life of three thousand years ago'.[67]

The Bakhtiari migration was a film-maker's dream. Fifty thousand men, women and children were preparing to herd 500,000 animals over 150 miles of challenging terrain between their winter pastures on the edge of the Mesopotamian plain and the summer grazing high in the Zagros Mountains. Not because they wanted to, although many of them might have done: they were going because they had to go. 'There is no green thing,' the titles explain while the tribe is still on the plain, 'and the flocks will die, and after them the women, the children and then men.' This age-old drama came with stunning visuals and with the highest stakes, as the nomads faced the harshness of the landscape, the speed of the river they had to ford, the height of the mountain and the depths of snow on its upper slopes. The epic quest for pasture did not disappoint. Led by a good-looking, charismatic tribal leader by the name of Haider Khan, the Bakhtiari looked every bit the people of the First Chapter, rough, resilient and determined. Women walked with babies tied in cradles on their backs and the elderly rode horses or mules. The Karun river, a stream that was said to have flowed out of the Garden of Eden, was now a torrent in full flood and as there was no bridge the Bakhtiari had to cross on makeshift rafts or on floats improvised out of inflated goatskins. The animals were pushed into the fast-flowing river in the hope that their survival instincts would get them to the other side. Some drowned, but most made it.

Eventually the horde came to the Zard Kuh, the 4,000-metre-high Yellow Mountain where they had to climb 'two thousand feet of ice and snow, straight up' to a pass, beyond which lay 'the Promised Land – the land of "Milk and Honey" – the Land of Grass'. In these uplands, the snow had already melted and the valleys were carpeted with flowers, as I had found them. It would soon be summertime, and the living was going to be easier.

After forty-eight days on the 'Bakhtiari Road', the leader of the Bakhtiari, Morteza Quli Khan, welcomed the Americans to the Shalamzar Palace, his large country house in a poplar-shaded valley off the Isfahan road. The khan was a veteran of the migration, but after several years serving as prime minister of Persia, he was no longer a man of mountains, tents and herds. Some days later, at the end of June 1924, Cooper, Schoedsack and Harrison were in Tehran. Together with Haider Khan and a prince of the Bakhtiari called Amir Jang, they went to call on Major Robert Imbrie, the American consul, in whose presence the nomads signed a document to confirm that the Americans were the first foreigners to have made the migration and to cross the Zard Kuh. This is how the film ends.

Grass premiered at New York's Explorers' Club the following January, 1925. Seduced by the exotic nature of its subject and encouraged by the huge success of a recent film about Inuit in Alaska,*

* *Nanook of the North.*

Paramount Pictures acquired the rights to *Grass* and released it in cinemas two months later. The response was rapturous.

It might seem odd – nomads catching the imagination of cinema-going Americans? – but this was the middle of the roaring twenties, a decade of boom and bust in which American wealth doubled. *Grass* was released while new wealth was changing the nature of life in the United States. Already by 1900, four out of every ten Americans lived in urban centres and particularly in the larger cities, where consumerism was rampant. This was also the beginning of the golden age of the motor car: three years before the film opened in New York the city's fire department had retired its last horse-drawn fire truck. But even in the vast countryside, where horses were replaced more slowly by machines, people were already beginning to weigh the intangible costs of the new technology. Against this background of dramatic social, economic and technological change, the story of Bakhtiari nomads and their struggle up the mountain against the elements was a balm for Americans, as it would be the following year for one of Britain's most talented writers.

Geographical Romanticism

The year after *Grass* premiered in New York, the Shah of Persia drove through Tehran in a glass coach pulled by six horses. This was a new shah and he was on his way to his coronation, wearing a cloak heavy with pearls and a new crown with a fistful of glitter at its centre, the *Darya-e Nur*, the Sea of Light, the world's largest pink diamond. The city's streets were crowded with onlookers, carpets had been hung from the flat roofs of shops and houses in honour of the man who had seized power and overthrown 150 years of Qajar rule. He emerged from the coronation as Reza Shah, the first of the new Pahlavi dynasty.

Among the guests at the coronation was British diplomat Harold Nicolson and his wife, the writer Vita Sackville-West. She had just arrived on a visit. Also present was a crowd of 'wild and picturesque figures', as Sackville-West described them. 'Hung with shields and stuck with weapons, mounted on rough ponies, they sauntered down the Lalézar with a lofty disregard of the attention they attracted.' These were the Bakhtiari khans. 'What with the tribes and the carpets,' she continued in the first of two books she wrote about her journey, 'Teheran was losing its shoddy would-be European appearance and putting on, at last, a character more reminiscent of the pen of Marco Polo.'[68]

That summer, as the shah secured his grip on power, Sackville-West, her husband and a few friends travelled into the Zagros Mountains. They went in cars with three servants, three guards, a wooden figurine of Saint Barbara and the intention of satisfying what the writer calls her 'geographical romanticism'.[69] Snow had given way to upland pasture and the Bakhtiari were on the move.

Sackville-West had wanted to migrate with them, but the mountains were austere and demanding, the slopes more vertiginous than she had imagined and the nights icy and uncomfortable. Blisters and bruises soon forced her onto a mule and after a few days out of the city Nicolson admitted that he hated mountains, to which his wife added that she hated tents. Then they met some nomads moving their herds.

'To us, who come from Europe,' she writes, 'there is something poetic in a Persian shepherd calling to his goats and sheep; but the Persian shepherd himself sees nothing except the everyday business of getting a lot of tiresome animals along.'[70] What appears romantic in one place, she understands, is the gritty realism of everyday life in another place, or at another time.

> There are thousands of them [goats and sheep], jostling, leaping, hustling each other among the boulders. Some of them are very lame, but what of that? That is reality, not romance; lame or not lame, they must go forward. There are two hundred miles to cover before the sun gets too hot and the already scant pasture shrivels up. So the shepherds come after them with their sticks. 'Oh', say the shepherds – a flat, English 'Oh' that sounds curiously out of place on the Persian hills . . . Oh. And the sea of backs surges round the legs of our mules. The smell of fleeces comes up to us, acrid. The men follow, in their blue linen coats and high black felt hats, and their sticks fall with a thud on the woolly backs. Oh. The sun is hot and high. The jade-green river flickers in the sun down in the ravine. The snow-mountains stretch like a spine in the distance. An old woman passes up on foot, carrying across her shoulders a limp baby donkey . . . A child passes, beating up his flock of lambs and kids – youth put in charge of youth. Oh. And then a fresh shower of sheep and goats, animated boulders. How stony the road is! How slow our progression! Come along, come along. Oh.[71]

What struck her more than the hardships of the migration or the beauty of the place was the simplicity of their pared-down lives. No motors, no wheeled carts – what use would they be on the vertiginous slopes? – everything dictated by the need to find pasture and the great difficulty of the grand landscape. Everyone rising, as they do now, at first light and working until dusk. Everyone knowing where to find the springs with clear water, loading pack animals to carry what little you own, knowing each one of the herd, knowing also which animal would be slaughtered next for food, the daily round of lighting fires, raising tents and then sleeping.

She found something irresistibly attractive about the pared-down simplicity of this nomad life. Evenings in particular satisfied her geographical romanticism, that moment when the tents were up, her little statue of Saint Barbara was unpacked beside her sleeping bag, fires lit, meat grilling, the men smoking . . . Water bubbled down the valley, stars glittered overhead, the moon rose over the spine of mountains and there was romance and beauty in this moment of peace after the extreme efforts of the day. It was in one of these intense, reflective pauses that this elegant, privileged and talented woman imagined what it would be like to stay up there in the mountains. I don't just mean stopping for a night or two because she had already done that. She wondered what it would be like to stay for years, to live there. She mentioned thirty years, time enough to know the cycle of each plant from seed to blossom, to know each twist in the path, each rock in the mountain, each member of the tribes that would pass twice a year on their way up and down in search of grass. She thought that would be long enough to free herself from the chains of civilised life, from 'movement, news, emotions, conflict, and doubt'[72] and to confront the essence of herself. And then what?

The travellers continued along the Bakhtiari Road and then headed back to Tehran. Nicolson and the others went about their business, but Sackville-West had been touched in an unexpected way by the experience. 'Not only had we gone far away in distance,' she acknowledged, 'we had also gone far back in time. We had returned, in fact, to antiquity . . .'

Eighteenth- and nineteenth-century European travellers had expressed similar sentiments, as had Arab scholars in the Abbasid age of setting down, and ancient Roman and Greek writers setting out for Arcadia and elsewhere, and I have expressed something similar. 'We learnt what the past had been like,' she continued, 'and what the world had been like when it was still empty. Time was held up and values altered.'[73] In this point, her response was similar to the makers of Grass, for both saw nomads as 'forgotten people' living 'the ancient life'.

In the century that separates me from Grass and the writing of Sackville-West, many fundamental things have changed in how nomads are described, but perhaps nothing more significant than the direction we are looking in when we settled people look at nomads. Sackville-West saw nomads as guides to the deep past. She looked backwards. We look backwards, but we must also look to the future.

The Balance of Things

Now

Global population: 7.8 billion

Urban population: 5.6 billion

Nomad population: 40 million[74]

Three years almost to the day after I first saw Bakhtiari at the end of their migration, I stepped into another Iranian spring. The equinox had passed and with it Nowruz, the New Year festival. 'Awaken,' the thirteenth-century Persian poet Saadi had written of this moment, 'the morning Nowruz breeze is showering the garden with flowers', and so it was. Plane trees spread fresh canopies over the streets of central Tehran, gardens bowed with buds, and the cherry, apple and almond trees were in blossom. But on that clear day, the peaks above the city roofline were still white. Spring had come late to the Zagros Mountains, and the floor of the Kouhrang Valley, where I had slept on a bed of iris and dwarf tulips on my last visit, was still hidden beneath metres of snow. This might have had serious consequences in settled communities, but among nomads it would mean an awkward but not calamitous delay to the migration into the mountains.

As the tribe would be setting out later than planned, I needed to change my proposed route. I thought the ministry that watches over foreign visitors might object because the Bakhtiari winter grazing, on the Mesopotamian scrubland at the foot of oak-scattered mountains, was near the border with Iraq. But permission was given.

On the lowest slopes of the Zagros, where some nomads had planted wheat at the beginning of winter, the time for harvest had still not come. I saw bags of acorns and was reminded of the Bakhtiari 'Song of the Acorn':

> *May my oak tree bear fruit and my she-goat bring forth young!*
> *When my ground acorns and buttermilk*
> *come together, thanks are due to God.*
> *Ripe acorn, o acorn! Dried acorns ground down:*
> *He who has and eats not, may his house perish!*[75]

The song reaches back across millennia to long before wheat was domesticated, when we all lived on the move and when people in the temperate zones of Europe, Asia and North America gathered oak-nuts, which they learned to soak and then grind into flour.

These places catered both to the settled and nomadic and they vibrated with the pent-up nomadic energy of the delayed migration. But departure was now imminent and Bakhtiari were out gathering things they would need on their journey into the mountains, men shouldering sacks of flour, one with an axe, another with a coil of rope and others sporting new black felt hats and wide studded leather belts, part of the Bakhtiari uniform. One man had even come to town on his horse. In this, as in so much else, Fereydun was an exception.

He was a short, stocky, middle-aged man with greying stubble and a persuasive twinkle in his eye. He was talking to some other men about a wedding they would all attend that evening. As I passed, he asked where I was from and then: 'Would you like to join the wedding?'

Obviously I would but . . . 'I have never even met the happy couple.'

'That's no problem,' he said and explained that hospitality here was a joy not an obligation. 'You would honour them with your presence.'

There is a Farsi phrase *ghorboonet beram*, which is as common in conversation in Iran as 'to be honest' or 'I mean' are in English. It is more emphatic than 'thank you' and literally translated it means 'I would sacrifice myself for you'. The fact that this phrase peppers everyday conversation says much about the Iranian character. But Fereydun then used an expression that went even further than self-sacrifice: he told me I could put my feet in his eyes.

This turned out to be a way of stressing how much my presence at the wedding would mean to the bride and groom, and also how welcome I would be afterwards at Fereydun's house. Only then did he ask why I had come to the Bakhtiari lands.

When I said I was writing about nomads, he asked the question that had been most frequently put wherever I had gone in search of nomads: *Don't you have them in England?*

Then he asked which nomads I was writing about and I replied, as I have done frequently, that what I am writing applies to *all of them*.

Not literally, of course. But much of what I have written about the Xiongnu and the Mongols, the Lakota and the Aborigine also broadly applies to Tuareg and Inuit, to Beja and Bedouin, the Guaraní in Brazil and all the other nomadic peoples. It can also apply, in our own time, to some digital nomads, to travellers, wanderers, vagrants, the houseless and migrants, and it certainly applies to the Bakhtiari for they, like many others through the ages, have had to learn how to reconcile their mobile ways with the demands of the settled others, how to engage with towns and cities while living with and within the natural world.

When Fereydun heard I was looking for the Bakhtiari I had met three years earlier, he checked his pockets and the petrol gauge in his car and suggested that we drive into the hills, right then and there.

'Will we find them?' I asked.

He said it was unlikely, but we would certainly find Bakhtiari preparing to migrate. 'I am Bakhtiari myself and am longing to get back into the mountains. Come on – let's go and at least we can visit some of my family.'

'What about the wedding?' I reminded him and he shrugged.

'I have been to weddings, many of them.'

From the moment I met him, Fereydun reminded me of so much that I had seen or thought or read in my years of research. Perhaps most important, he reminded me that, in the words of the American biologist Rachel Carson, 'it is not half so important to know as to feel'.[76] This sentiment seems to me to push back against Francis Bacon's hope that science would dominate nature and it suited Fereydun because he found wonder and pleasure in the natural world as he did in movement: he was twitching with excitement at the thought of leaving for the mountains.

He looked now to the sky, to the sun. In the French village where I have been writing some of these pages, the church clock chimes each quarter of an hour. During the working day, that same clock chimes a second time two or three minutes later to be sure that we have all noted the passage of time. Our lives have become regulated by machines. Fereydun comes from a place where people do not need a clock and where lives are still measured in other ways, by the cycle of the moon and seasons, of sun and wind, of long and short days, youth and age.

The narrow road worked its way around the contours of a valley and up through layers of brown and green and gold into the mountains. As we rose, I looked down on freshly sickled wheat, on fields studded with Persian oaks and on a cemetery where a row of life-size stone lions, *bardsheer*, marked the graves of the bravest of men. They had swords carved onto their flanks, in case they needed to fight their way into heaven.

There had been sheep in the valley, but as we climbed, goats grazed the fringes of radiant fields. Spring had been late here too, but there were signs of it everywhere, not least among the animals. Shaggy bitches pushed their pups against rocks to protect them from our passing and a newborn donkey grazed under an oak. Higher up, we were stopped by a mob of horses who blocked the road, the dams staring us down while two foals, hours old and unsteady on their feet, staggered across the tarmac. Later, at what passed for a village, there was a supermarket.

Nomads have always needed places to trade and a variety of people to trade with, and always needed free movement to get to their trading places, just as they have always needed to be free to find grazing. For this reason, their great empires were built around the principles of free movement, free trade and often free conscience, while many of the battles fought between nomads and settled were over access to markets or the right to roam. This market was a large steel-framed tent packed with things Bakhtiari might need, from sacks of wheat seeds, spices, dried apricots and other fruit to boxes of rough-forged goat bells, coils of handwoven rope, small jars of expensive but indispensable saffron, a huge vat of raw, unfiltered honey, toy guns and dolls for the kids and cartridges for the adults. The place was run by a Bakhtiari woman in her forties whose no-nonsense attitude was in contrast to the racy pair of sea-green pumps that graced her feet. Her black headscarf was held tight by a large silver clasp set with seven glass diamonds. She was going to need the clasp now, because it had suddenly become windy and clouds of dust were gusting as a storm blew down from the mountain. I bought a jar of honey and Fereydun, cheerful as a child at Christmas, asked her to open the canvas bag where he had spotted a paste of acorn flour. 'Tonight we will eat acorn bread,' he said. The 'supermarket' madam took our money and watched without expression as we left.

We drove towards the mighty Karun, the paradise river in which many Bakhtiari had lost their animals and their lives over the centuries. Crossing it had been one of the great challenges of the migration and one of the highlights in the film *Grass*. Now there is a bridge and we sped across it. As we went, Fereydun talked about nomads and about himself. He had been born into a migrating family and his childhood had been spent in continual movement, each day taking animals to graze, each spring and autumn taking them up or down the mountain to find seasonal grazing. The migrations had been his life and had shaped the year and the people who engaged with it. 'It brought our tribe together in this great communal effort. We needed each other's help and everyone was happy to give it.' But now he was married and he wanted his children to be educated at a school, so he had settled outside one of the frontier towns and bought some land on which to grow vegetables, an orchard for fruit and shade, some geese and chickens to pick over the dirt, and a horse to remind himself of the days when Bakhtiari riders counted for something in the world, and also just in case . . .

'Do you miss it,' I asked, 'that old life . . .?'

'*Ziadeh!* Too much . . .' These were not just words, and he paused for a while to let the emotion pass.

'This was my life, the way I was brought up. Of course I miss it . . . I miss the peace. People who migrate live a gentler life. In the city, we talk about finding silence – getting away from the noise of machines, cars, other people. But the mountain silence is not silent, for it is filled with birdsong, the shrieking of birds of prey, the wind singing in the grasses and around the rocks, with water hurrying down to the plains and the sea. Of course the journey was hard and winter was often difficult. But when I was young, whatever was happening, everyone came together at sunset to share the good and the bad, and to sing the old songs. That was what I liked best, the coming together. We were always singing – a song for walking, another for leading the animals, and so on. City life is not the same. City people are not the same . . .'

I interrupted and asked whether it was true that Bakhtiari women pass on the secrets of their carpet weavings in songs, that they sing the patterns to their daughters.

'Yes, we have songs for carpets . . .' he said and then resumed his tale: 'Then we were all in bed by nine and up at five in the morning, with the first light. It was good for us and so good to all be together. And when we moved, we *felt* the mountain, we felt in touch with it. We belonged to it. We knew its character, its moods, its sounds. The mountain was like our god . . . Now' – and he stopped to choose the words he would need for what he wanted to say – 'now we have to be Muslims. Sometimes it is difficult and some of my friends have been executed for not being good Muslims. But that's how it is. We Bakhtiari, we don't believe in Muhammad and nor do we believe in the Imams. We are not Shi'a.'

The thought sat between us as heavy as the clouds above, but after some minutes he lightened the mood with the story of how the regime had ordered a mosque to be built in one of the small villages we had just passed. When the mosque was finished, an imam was appointed. Each dawn and twice more each and every day, the imam called the faithful, but there were no believers to join him in prayers. Then one day, a cow escaped its tether and walked down the road towards the mosque. When the imam found it inside the place of prayer, he shooed it away and then went to shout at the Bakhtiari: 'You must control your cow. She was in my mosque!' To this, one villager replied, 'At least she went in. If she had been a human, she would not have gone!' and at that Fereydun creased with laughter.

'But we do believe in God, just as we believe in living a good life,' and he echoed the mantra of Zarathustra, *Humata, Hukhta, Hvarshta*, good thoughts, good words, good deeds.

Then, out of nowhere: 'Do you know my name comes from our *Shahnameh?*'

Shahnameh . . . Ferdowsi's great poem of Persian and Zoroastrian history is still as fresh and relevant as when it was composed a thousand years ago. Its 50,000 couplets start at the dawn of time and end with the Arab conquest, moving from the mythical to the heroic to the historic. *Shahnameh*, the Book of Kings, was an attempt to preserve the culture of a Persian world that had been overwhelmed by Arabs, Turks and by Islam. It was an act of setting down intended to preserve the language, culture and history of nomadic Zoroastrian Persia. In the *Shahnameh*, Fereydun is the heroic king who frees Iran from a foreign power and stands as an archetype for the strong, just ruler. Siyavash is a tragic prince of such extraordinary beauty that his face blazes like a planet and whoever sees it falls in love with him. Other great heroes – none greater nor more heroic than Rostom – dance through the epic couplets as they do through the lives and imagination of Bakhtiari, who are often mourned after death with a full recitation of Ferdowsi's masterpiece. Fereydun now recited some lines from the epic, reminding me of an encounter the great linguist and archaeologist Austen Layard had had with nomads in these same mountains, 150 years ago:

Men who knew no pity and who were ready to take human life upon the smallest provocation . . . listen with the utmost eagerness to Shefi'a Khan, who, seated by the side of the chief, would recite, with a loud voice and in a kind of chant, episodes from the 'Shah-Nameh' . . . Such was probably the effect of the Homeric ballads when recited or sung of old in the camps of the Greeks.[77]

Herodotus, whose own ballads entranced people through the ages, had thought the best of all lives would be one that was lived in accordance with the best of all humanity's customs. But he knew there would be difficulties because 'each group of people, after carefully sifting through the customs of other peoples, would surely choose its own'.[78] But what was certain in Herodotus's time is no longer so in ours, as the writer Bruce Chatwin suggests.

Everyone who knew Chatwin when he was in his twenties spoke of his good looks, his innate charm and quick wit. With a public-school education and social ease, by his mid-twenties he was a favoured expert at Sotheby's auction house, had a bright, wealthy American wife and was surrounded by a wide group of well-connected friends. Then he went on a camel trek in Sudan. In some ways, he never returned.

Chatwin spent much of his remaining twenty-four years embroidering stories. There was the story that opens his first published book, *In Patagonia*, about the hide of a woolly mammoth that he remembered in his grandmother's cabinet, and another about the day he left the *Sunday Times* by sending a telegram announcing, 'Gone to Patagonia.' He even spun a story around the disease that eventually took his life too young: he was dying from AIDS, but he claimed he had caught some rare disease picked up from a Chinese bat. Perhaps it was the stories that stoked Chatwin's fascination with nomads.

In the 1970s and 1980s, when Chatwin was travelling and writing, there were still tens of millions of nomads at large in the world; it is impossible to be more precise. Hunter-gatherers such as Pygmies, San and Hadza in Africa, Aché, Inuit and Guaraní in the Americas, Andamanese, Altai and Batek in Asia, Aborigines in Australia. Pastoralists including Beja, Boron, Berber, Fulani, Maasai, Nuer, Rendile, Samburu, Tuareg and many others in Africa, Bakhtiari, Bedouin, Kuchi, Qashqai, Mongol and Rabari in Asia. He knew some of these tribes from first-hand experience and included them in his books, the most notable being his description of Aborigine dreaming in one of his last books, *The Songlines*. But most comprehensive of all was his first book, *The Nomadic Alternative*, a 268-page manuscript that will probably never be published.

The Nomadic Alternative echoes through all of Chatwin's work, but nowhere more clearly than in *The Songlines* with its refrain that we are born to move, that we must move or die. In it, he quotes the British psychoanalyst John Bowlby, whose research at the Tavistock Clinic in London looked at the attachment between mothers and their children. Bowlby and his colleagues concluded that we come into the world with a pre-programmed need for other humans. We are also born with the ability to smile and to cry, a mechanism that seems designed to attract other humans, particularly our mothers, when we need feeding or protection. The other big discovery from Bowlby's research was that babies who are not hungry will stop crying if they are picked up and especially if they are rocked while walking. The ideal position, he discovered, is to hold the baby upright and to rock it three inches from side to side. The speed of rocking is as important as the position. Thirty moves a minute achieved nothing, fifty would quiet most babies and 'at speeds of sixty cycles a minute and above every baby stops crying and, almost always, remains quiet'.[79] The baby's heart rate would also drop from up to 200 beats a minute when distressed to around 60 when being carried by a walker.

Bowlby's research showed that babies stop crying because they understand from the rocking movement that they are being walked, and that when they are being walked they are part of a group on the move, which means that all is safe and well with the world. Chatwin saw this as proof that humankind is a migratory species. 'Day in, day out, a baby cannot have enough walking. And if babies instinctively demand to be walked, the mother, on the African savannah, must have been walking too: from camp to camp on her daily foraging round, to the waterhole and on visits to the neighbours.'[80] But there is something else fundamental going on here.

Recent researches in genetics, psychology and a range of other disciplines have shown what many have already intuited, that humankind has built what has been called a 'collective brain'.[81] This common repository is filled with the shared outcomes of millennia, with our shared development, discoveries and experiences, and while it speaks of our collective migration through time, it is also testament to our great variety, our diversity. Diversity – whether of thought, ideas, intention, colour or gene – has always been the key to humankind's progress. The 'collective brain' shows that we have been at our most successful and progressive when diverse groups have come together and pooled their understanding, their history and their ways of seeing. The best things about humankind have come through cooperation, open markets and borders, free movement, freedom of thought and conscience, and nomads have always been among the best conduits and accumulators of these elements. Of course there have been many problems in the mix, flashpoints over landholding, water resources, freedom of movement and much else. But 'the bigger, fuller picture is never as stark as "nomad" versus "settled", tribes versus peoples. It never has been.'[82] The biggest, fullest picture of humankind is one that contains both nomads – *the moving settled*, as Iranians call them – and settled people, *the settled movers*. If, as we now know, only part of history is to be found along the path picked through ruins, the other part of the human story lies far from that path, on the tracks that criss-cross the natural world. The fullest picture of our history can only be seen when these two strands are woven together and it is one that shows up the benefits of diversity and interaction.

For most of our history, we humans all lived on the move, which is why most of our world, our culture, what we call civilisation, has been shaped by nomads. Our activities are all linked to journeys, from that first one out of the womb to the last one into the grave, and evolution really *did* intend us to travel. Once upon a time movement was hot-wired into all of us and some of us are still wired that way. When the French poet Arthur Rimbaud wrote that '*Je dus voyager, distraire les enchantements assemblés sur mon cerveau*'[83] ('I had to travel, to distract the enchantments gathered in my brain'), he was not striking some aesthetic pose. He was expressing a real need that could only be satisfied by abandoning Paris, his friends, poetry and everything else he valued, a need that eventually cost him a

metres below the summit and now that we approached it I could see that the ledge supported a terrace of houses.

Houses? Can nomads have houses and still be nomadic?

They are the moving settled, so of course they can.

Fereydun knew the dozen or so people who appeared along the terrace in front of the houses and the others up on the roofs. They were distant cousins and others from his wider family. There was a moment of pleasantry as he explained to two women, mother and daughter, who I was and why I had come. Most of the men were down the slope, they explained, with the herds, while the women looked after children and prepared for the migration. Even when they seemed to stop and chat, these women were constantly busy, feeding a baby, churning milk in a goatskin to make curd and cheese, and one of them was spinning wool as she walked and talked, using the same wooden spindle that people had used here in these mountains a couple of thousand years ago. The wool would soon be woven into a carpet or a tent.

These were nomads, yes, but like all nomads they were pragmatists and they spent the winter in houses because the weather at that altitude was harsh, because the snow was too thick for them to survive under goat hair and because they could. But the more I looked, the more the house I was welcomed into appeared like a tent. Cut into the flinty limestone hillside, its roof was supported by a lattice of oak branches and its heavy cross-beams propped on piled rocks. The whole space blackened by smoke from a brazier and from a cooking pot perched on a gas burner close to the pillar. The few other possessions were in bags or tin cases, while bedding had been wrapped and stored until nightfall and a carpet rolled up and put to one side. All of this would have been the same in a tent.

The only nod to settled life was a wooden cabinet, and it looked out of place. The top shelf was piled with papers and photographs, mostly photo-booth images of members of the family. The bottom shelf was a clutter of bags and cloth, while the middle shelf was filled with a television. But what could they watch up there in the mountains? When I asked the older woman, she laughed out loud – a single thin line was tattooed from her lower lip to chin – and shook a finger: not very much because when there was a signal it was very weak. And then one more question: when would they move up the mountain? 'When it is time,' she said and looked up the slope at the looming clouds. When the weather settled. Nomadism in the twenty-first century, like nomadism throughout the millennia, is hostage to the climate.

Fereydun was mostly silent on the way back down, which left me free to think and to look, to notice, for instance, that there were no fences in the foothills, and no wire or physical boundaries higher up. There was terracing but no walls. If boundaries did exist, they did so in the communal mind. And yet so much of history has been the story of walls and borders.

When we crossed back over the Karun river and as we came closer to town, the physical divisions began again, the fences, walls, roadblocks, advertising boards, street lights and pavements, a small park and children's playground.

At Fereydun's house, his wife prepared vegetable dishes and baked the acorn paste into rounds of damp, heavy flatbread, with which we scooped up the food. Then Fereydun brought out a bottle of *Mey*, his home-made red wine, which tasted surprisingly good, perhaps because I had drunk no alcohol for a while. The *Mey* blurred the boundaries of our thoughts, softened our tongues and eased our eyes as we watched the light fade. As it went, the world closed in.

We lost the mountains and retreated inside the municipal boundaries, inside the roadblock the police had set up at the entrance to the administrative district, inside the fences. Then there was only the world inside Fereydun's mud-brick wall.

'So tell me about your book,' he asked as he poured more wine. I thought he was just asking out of politeness and so I did not answer, but when he persisted I explained how I felt that much of the history I knew only told half the story of humankind and it was the story of the settled. 'Nomads are missing from it.' But since the time of Cain and Abel, since the people of Göbekli Tepe, since hunter-gatherers learned to domesticate animals and crops, since humans had had to choose between herding and cultivation, there had been two sides to the story, the settled and mobile. I explained what I had discovered, how the ancient Persians had never settled in the way Egyptians had, how ancient Egypt had been transformed by what it had learned from invading shepherd kings, how great nomad kingdoms – the Scythians and Xiongnu – separated and linked ancient Romans and Chinese. I described *asabiyya* and the nomadic origins of the Arab Empire, the rise of the Mongols and how they had provided Europe with the materials with which to fashion the Renaissance. I explained how Francis Bacon and his colleagues had sought to dominate the natural world and how from then until our own time, this age of the American Empire, the settled had continued their project, their cities ever expanding, and their countryside turned over to mechanised and ever more profitable farming. 'But you and I know that the history of humankind has been the story of both the settled and the nomadic. Each has defined itself against the other. But because nomads have mostly not written things down – and nowhere has that been more true than here in Iran,' and he nodded at that, 'what I have tried to do in my book is to let some light in on the shadow side of history, to suggest what nomads have given us, how we have been shaped by them.'

'What has come from nomads?' Fereydun asked.

It was late and the day had been long so I avoided describing the nomadic gene and did not mention the importance of diverse thinking. But I did describe the monumental architecture at Göbekli Tepe, the taming of horses and the invention of bridles and chariots on the steppes, the devastating perfection of the composite bow, the boom years of the Mongol peace. I explained how we can string together an alternative sequence of empires from the Persian, Xiongnu and Han to Mongols, Mughals, Safavids and Ottomans, a sequence that challenges the Eurocentric view of the universality of the Egypt-Greece-Rome empires. I recited the poet Shelley's words, 'Look on my Works, ye Mighty, and despair!' and explained how I thought nomads offer us something more significant than monuments, how they encouraged us to look beyond 'works' to understand our place in the natural world. Then, because I know how much Iranians loved poetry, I mentioned Constantine Cavafy.

'There was a poet who lived in Egypt a hundred years ago . . .' I began.

Cavafy is not the most obvious person to mention beneath the Zagros Mountains because most of his life was spent in cities. He knew the dangers of life within walls, just as he knew that 'You'll walk the same streets . . . You'll always end up in this city.'[84] It was in Alexandria that Cavafy watched British troops prepare to avenge the death of General Gordon in Khartoum. In September 1898, while Cavafy sat in his office a block from Alexandria's waterfront, Beja nomads faced General Horatio Herbert Kitchener's combined British–Egyptian army on the Nile outside Khartoum. The fight was as unequal as any ever fought between nomad and settled. Kitchener had done what Colonel Custer had not and had brought cannon and the new Maxim machine gun across the desert by train. These new weapons decimated the Beja. Fifty British and Egyptian soldiers died killing 12,000 nomad fighters and wounding another 13,000.

Two months after the massacre, a thousand miles north of Khartoum, Cavafy imagined people in an ancient city waiting for the arrival of barbarians, waiting and becoming increasingly anxious. The emperor sits on his throne by the gate. He is wearing his crown, his officials around him are dressed in scarlet togas and jewellery, and the tension mounts. Will the barbarians come? What will happen when they do?

Then the tension dissipates and everyone goes home, but now they are even more anxious, and confused, and upset because, as Cavafy writes so beautifully,

> night has fallen and the barbarians haven't come.
> And some of our men just in from the border say
> there are no barbarians any longer.
>
> Now what's going to happen to us without barbarians?
> Those people were a kind of solution.[85]

This was what I tried to explain to Fereydun, in that quiet night, through the haze of red wine. Across the gulf of our experiences and expectations, I thought that the chain I had fashioned of nomad stories, the nomadic example, can offer us settled people some kind of solution or at the very least some clue as to the best way forward.

Fereydun said nothing for a while. He sipped his wine, chewed a crust of acorn bread, smoothed back his hair. He looked around his compound, at the horse in its shelter, the fruit trees, the vegetable garden, the mud buildings.

Then he said, 'I never wanted to be settled. But we all have difficult decisions and I wanted my children to be educated, so they could be a part of the modern world. I miss the nomad life every day. But now that I am here, in this house beneath the mountains where my people came from, and maybe because I am older, this is what I think: perhaps the best possible world is one in which we are all nomad and all settled, we can all move and we can all stay home for some time.' That was what he thought he or his children could achieve and in some ways, there between the mountain grazing and the city walls, it did seem to be some kind of solution.

Herodotus might have approved of Fereydun's answer, for the ancient Greek had imagined a world based on 'a selection of the very best practices . . . from the sum of human custom'. It was another version of diverse thinking – nomadic thinking – and it sounded good to me.

Now it was dark. There might have been a broad mesh of stars overhead and a crescent moon on the horizon, but I wouldn't know because the brilliance of a single electric light bulb hanging near us reduced the world to nothing more than the man beside me, the table between us, the thoughts in our minds, the food, wine and words we shared and the carpet beneath our feet.

The carpet was a symbolic representation of a garden. Its borders and central flowerbed were a woven imagining of paradise conjured by one of Fereydun's cousins from yarn she had spun from the wool her husband had sheared off the animals they had raised. The couple of square metres she had woven contained a magicked world, a world at once physical, mental and spiritual. I have a similar carpet in my house in London – millions of us do – woven by women from this tribe or one of many others around the world. Nomad women.

Time passed. We wore out the night discussing movement and stasis, nomads and settled, and that most nomadic of all qualities, the ability to think in diverse and divergent ways. But there was nothing I could hold on to, nothing that would survive the morning and the coming of light. 'Perhaps,' Fereydun laughed when I told him, 'that is as it should be. Perhaps thoughts and ideas should always wander like sheep and goats, this way and that, now together, now apart.' And so I remained in the centre of the garden-carpet, in the peace of the late-night beneath the Bakhtiari mountains, listening to the *kuch neshin*, the settled nomad. Only later, with the passing of that moment, did I realise I had glimpsed something eternal, something complete.

Acknowledgements

Many thanks to the Authors' Foundation and the Society of Authors for the John Heygate Award, which helped cover some of the costs of my travels with nomads. John Heygate was previously known to me as the man who ran off with Evelyn Waugh's wife, but it turns out he was also an author, a journalist and a generous benefactor.

I have had so many conversations about nomads in general and about this book in particular, had so much help, received so many suggestions and ideas from friends, colleagues, fellow authors, people who don't write but do read, as well as people who neither read nor write books, that it would require another book to include everyone. So many thanks to you all, but especially – and in no order – to the late Gillon Aitken, who encouraged the first seeds from which this idea has sprung, to Nicholas Shakespeare who helped with the Chatwin archive, Colin Thubron, Gwendolyn Leick, Peter Lydon, Richard Sattin, Jon Cook, Nicholas Crane, Rose Baring, Barnaby Rogerson, Chili Hawes of the October Gallery, Toby Green, Mimi and Tom Siebens, to William Dalrymple who listened to the idea many years ago in Iran and Giles Milton who cheered up long days at the London Library, to Professor Dan T. A. Eisenberg at the Department of Anthropology, University of Washington, who took time to explain his genetic research, to Giles Foden, Timothy May, Professor of Central Eurasian History at the University of North Georgia, and Dr John Hemming. The staff at the London Library, which has almost become a second home, at the Bodleian Library in Oxford and the British Library have all been as welcoming and helpful as ever. Chris Knight and the Radical Anthropology Group at University College have not had any direct input in this work, but their weekly open seminar sessions in London never fail to fascinate and have provided continued inspiration as well as a reminder that we must always challenge accepted narratives.

The late Klaus Schmidt of Göbekli Tepe provided some key thought-lines at an early stage of the book's development. Thanks to Cathy Giangrande and the Global Heritage Foundation for introducing us. Thanks also to Sarah Spankie and Melinda Stevens, both wonderful editors who sent me travelling in search of nomads when they were editors on *Condé Nast Traveller*, to Tom Robbins, travel editor at the *Financial Times*, and to Rosie Blau, Samantha Weinberg and the team at *The Economist*'s *1843* magazine. Jarrod Kyte and Steppes Travel, and Sabahattin Alkan of Alkans Tour/Eastern Turkey Tour helped organise some of my travels.

Much gratitude to Robert Irwin, Lucien d'Azay and Roland Philipps who read and gave detailed comment on the work at various stages of progress, and to Professor Jerry Brotton who gave the finished manuscript a thorough going-over when it was done and still found much to question. I owe many thanks to Sebastian Sattin and Gael Camu, who read and commented on the text at a crucial stage. The remaining errors and misjudgements are all mine.

Most of my books have been written away from home and as a result of the generous hospitality of friends. This is the fifth book I have written, in parts at least, as a guest of the wonderful Brigid Keenan and Alan Waddams in their beautiful house beneath the limestone cliffs of the Larzac plateau, just off a Neolithic pathway. A couple of decades back, the novelist Ian McEwan found black dogs in that region, I have only found calm and inspiration. I have been equally fortunate to stay in the Umbrian house of Julia and Hugo Heath, revising the book above the winter mists of the Tiber Valley.

Peter Straus at Rogers, Coleridge and White is the sort of agent all authors hope to find, supportive, encouraging, inspiring and above all understanding. Huge thanks also to all the team at John Murray Press, especially to the calm and focused Caroline Westmore who has guided me and the manuscript through the various stages of production, to Sara Marafini for designing the beautiful cover, to Martin Bryant for a meticulous copy-edit, to Diana Talyanina in Production and to the brilliant Rosie Gailer for publicity. But above all, thanks to Nick Davies for taking a great leap of faith and buying the book, and to Joe Zigmond, who listened closely before I started writing, was patient during the many years of composition and who then cut, criticised and encouraged me to shape it into the book I wanted and that you now have in your hands. He is a brilliant editor and I feel lucky to have had his help with this most ambitious of projects.

My sons Johnny and Felix have lived with nomads wandering through their lives, their minds and sometimes also through their home, and I hope they know how grateful I am for their support and tolerance. And then there is Sylvie, my mate, who discussed, embellished, enlarged, edited, argued and encouraged each step and every sentence along the way and who then created the beautiful images that decorate the book. I dedicate this book to you with thanks and love.

Copyright Acknowledgements

The author and publishers would like to thank the following: Cambridge Scholars for permission to quote from David Atkinson and Steve Roud, *Street Literature of the Long Nineteenth Century*; Tom Holland for permission to quote from Herodotus, *The Histories* (Penguin, 2013); Senate House Library, University of London for permission to quote from D. L. R. Lorimer, 'The Popular Verse of the *Bakhtiāri of S. W. Persia*', *Bulletin of the School of Oriental and African Studies*; Australian National University for permission to quote from Igor de Rachewiltz, *The Secret History of the Mongols: A Mongolian Epic Chronicle of the Thirteenth Century*; University of Chicago Press for permission to quote from Houari Touati, *Islam and Travels in the Middle Ages*; the British Library for permission to quote from Dr Shayne T. Williams, '*An Indigenous Australian Perspective on Cook's Arrival*'. Extract from 'Waiting for the Barbarians' from *Collected Poems* by C. P. Cavafy. Copyright © The Estate of C. P. Cavafy. Reproduced by permission of the Estate c/o Rogers, Coleridge & White Ltd, 20 Powis Mews, London W11 1JN. *Quotations from Baghdad: The City in Verse*, translated and edited by Reuven Snir, Cambridge, Mass.: Harvard University Press, Copyright © 2013 by the President and Fellows of Harvard College. Used by permission. All rights reserved. Extracts from *Twelve Days* are reproduced with permission of Curtis Brown Group Ltd, London on behalf of The Beneficiaries of the Estate of Vita Sackville West. Copyright © Vita Sackville West 1928.

Every reasonable effort has been made to trace copyright holders, but if there are any errors or omissions, John Murray will be pleased to insert the appropriate acknowledgement in any subsequent printings or editions.

List of Illustrations

Page 249: An Iroquois creation myth tells that the earth was created on the back of a turtle. This is a turtle dreamcatcher.

Page 251: Dr Samuel Johnson.

Page 254: Eighteenth-century specimen hunters sent birds of paradise to the British Museum without their legs, so as not to damage the plumage. In London, they were seen as angelic beings which never stopped flying.

Page 259: *Gardenia taitensis*, the national flower of Tahiti.

Page 266: The Albion Flour Mill, London.

Page 274: The American Bison, reduced from some 60 million in the nineteenth century to just 541 animals in the wild by 1889. Conservation efforts have helped numbers recover and there are now some 31,000 in the wild.

Page 277: Native American symbol for harmony, the balance that should exist in the world.

Page 282: The crow, symbolising wisdom.

Page 284: The Gila Monster, revered by some tribes in the American south-west such as the Hopi and Navajo for its strength and ability to survive for long periods without food or water.

Page 287: My dog Sacha running on Winchelsea Beach, Sussex.

Page 290: The peacock motif on Bakhtiari carpets represents divine protection and immortality.

Page 294: A campfire.

Page 309: Oakleaves with acorns, beloved of some Bakhtiari nomads.

Notes

In the Zagros Mountains, Iran

1. Deleuze, p. 73.
2. *The Marriage of Martu*, https://etcsl.orinst.ox.ac.uk/section1/tr171.htm

Part I: The Balancing Act

1. www.census.gov/data/tables/time-series/demo/international-programs/historical-est-worldpop.html
2. King James Bible, 2:9.
3. *Daily Mail*, 5 March 2009, https://www.dailymail.co.uk/sciencetech/article-1157784/Do-mysterious-stones-mark-site-Garden-Eden.html
4. Fernández-Armesto, p. 547.
5. Langland, p. 3.
6. Tolkien, p. 35.
7. Northwestern University, https://www.northwestern.edu/newscenter/stories/2008/06/ariaaltribe.html
8. National Institute of Mental Health, https://www.nimh.nih.gov/health/statistics/attention-deficit-hyperactivity-disorder-adhd.shtml
9. Quoted in *Daily Telegraph*, 10 June 2008, https://www.telegraph.co.uk/news/science/science-news/3344025/ADHD-may-be-beneficial-for-some-jobs.html
10. Speaking to Jeremy Paxman on BBC *Newsnight*, 1999. https://www.youtube.com/watch?time_continue=220&v=FiK7s_otGsg&feature=emb_logo
11. *The Travels of Ibn Battuta, AD 1325–1354*, vol. 1, ed. H. A. R. Gibb (Routledge, 2017), p. 145.
12. Herodotus, 3.38.
13. Inscribed on a clay tablet in the Ashmolean Museum, Oxford.

14. George, A. R., p. 49.
15. Ibid., p. 3.
16. Ibid., p. 2.
17. Ibid., p. 5.
18. Ibid., p. 8.
19. Ibid., p. 14.
20. Ibid., p. 16.
21. Chekhov, vol. VII, p. 165.
22. *Guardian*, 5 January 2017.
23. George, C. H., p. 133.
24. *Quarterly Review*, No. 19, p. 255.
25. *Rig Veda*, Book 6, Hymn 27.
26. Calasso, *Ardor*.
27. *Outlook India*, 4 June 2018.
28. *Henry V*, Act 4, Scene 3.
29. Lucian, vol. 3, p. 56.
30. https://www.sciencemag.org/news/2020/07/invasion-ancient-egypt-may-have-actually-been-immigrant-uprising
31. Quoted in Van Seters, p. 172.
32. Homer, *Iliad*, Book IX, 178–9.
33. Lucian, vol. 2, p. 91.
34. Rawlinson, p. 1.
35. Herodotus, p. 3.
36. Redfield, p. 111.
37. Herodotus, p. 357.
38. Ibid., p. 568.
39. Ibid.
40. Kent, p. 144.
41. Diodorus, ch.70–1.
42. Lloyd Llewellyn-Jones, *In Our Time*, BBC Radio 4, 7 June 2018.
43. Chatwin, *Songlines*, p. 185.
44. Herodotus, p. 67.
45. Quoted in *History Today*, 22 May 1972.
46. Herodotus, 4.75.
47. Donald Trump on Twitter, 19 June 2018.
48. Plato, 4.704d.
49. Ibid., 4.705a.
50. Herodotus, 1.73.
51. Ibid., 4.5.

52. Ibid., 1.205.
53. Ibid.
54. Ibid., 1.212.
55. Ibid., 1.214.
56. Ibid., 4.46.
57. Ibid., 4.126.
58. Ibid., 4.127.
59. Ibid.
60. Watson, p. 60.
61. Herodotus, 4.23.
62. Hill, p. 27.
63. Ssu-ma Ch'ien, 2, p. 129.
64. Watson, p. 60.
65. Ssu-ma Ch'ien, 1, p. xii.
66. Ibid., 2, p. 155.
67. https://depts.washington.edu/silkroad/exhibit/xiongnu/essay.html
68. Khazanov and Wink, p. 237.
69. *Han Shu* 94A: 4b, quoted in Twitchett and Loewe, p. 387.
70. Ibid., 5a, quoted in ibid.
71. Watson, vol. 2, p. 168.
72. Ibid., p. 183.
73. Ibid.
74. Frankopan, p. xvi.
75. Pliny, *Natural History*, quoted in Whitfield, *Life*, p. 21.
76. Florus, quoted in Yule, p. xlii.
77. Blockley, p. 249.
78. Ibid.
79. Raven, p. 89.
80. https://depts.washington.edu/silkroad/texts/sogdlet.html
81. Lactantius, p. 48.
82. Gibbon, ch. 26, p. 5.
83. Ammianus, Book 31, p. 578.
84. Bury, Priscus, fr.8 https://faculty.georgetown.edu/jod/texts/priscus.html
85. Blockley, p. 261.
86. Ibid., p. 275.
87. Ibid., p. 281.
88. Ibid.
89. Ibid., p. 285.

90. Ibid., p. 289.
91. Herodotus, p. 659.
92. Sidonius Apollinaris, quoted in Brown, p. 129.

Part II: The Imperial Act

1. Mackintosh-Smith, *Arabs*, p. 25.
2. Toynbee in Ibn Khaldun, *An Arab Philosophy of History*, p. 14.
3. Quoted in Irwin, *Ibn Khaldun*, p. 41.
4. Ibid., p. 12.
5. Ibn Khaldun, *Muqaddimah*, vol. 1, pp. 357–8, quoted in Irwin, *Ibn Khaldun*, p. 16.
6. Ibn Khaldun, *Muqaddimah*, p. 92.
7. *Muqaddimah*, 1967, vol. 1, p. 252.
8. Al-Ahnaf, quoted in Mackintosh-Smith, *Arabs*, p. 77.
9. Ibn Khaldun, 1992, p. 94.
10. Quoted in Fromherz, p. 114.
11. Wehr, p. 615.
12. Thesiger, *Arabian Sands*, p. 94.
13. Ed West, *Spectator* Coffee House blog, 3 August 2015, https://www.spectator.co.uk/article/the-islamic-historian-who-can-explain-why-some-states-fail-and-others-succeed
14. Ibn Khaldun, *Muqaddimah*, p. 107.
15. Ibid., p. 108.
16. '*marab'in wi fyad tar'a biha l-xur*', a fragment of an oral poem from south Jordan, in Holes, p. 183.
17. Al-Tabari, vol. II, pp. 295–6.
18. Cited in Frankopan, p. 74.
19. These details from Brown, p. 189.
20. Quran, Sura 96 (The Clot), l. 5.
21. https://www.islamreligion.com/articles/401/viewall/letter-of-prophet-to-emperor-of-byzantium/
22. Ibn Khaldun, 1992, p. 444.
23. Mackintosh-Smith, *Arabs*, p. 186.
24. Hourani, p. 102.
25. Al-Tabari, vol. 12, p. 64.
26. Ibid., pp. 94–5.
27. Ibid., p. 107.

28. A's-Suyuti, p. 265.
29. Quoted in Cunliffe, p. 365.
30. Al-Muqaddasi, p. 60.
31. Quoted in Marozzi, *Baghdad*, p. 43.
32. These figures from Modelski.
33. Quoted in Mackintosh-Smith, *Arabs*, p. 271.
34. Ibn Khaldun, *Muqaddimah*, vol. 2, p. 67.
35. Ibid., p. 68.
36. Quoted in Baerlain, p. 105.
37. Ibn Khaldun, *Muqaddimah*, vol. 1, p. 344.
38. Ibid., p. 345.
39. Ibid.
40. Snir, p. 61.
41. Quoted in Touati, p. 53.
42. 'Hellas: Chorus', Percy Bysshe Shelley.
43. Herodotus, 4.127.
44. Ibn Khaldun, *Muqaddimah*, vol. 1, p. 314.
45. Rachewiltz, *Secret History*, p. 128.
46. Ibid., p. 18.
47. Ibid., p. 125.
48. Gibbon, ch. 64, p. 1.
49. Raverty, vol. 2, p. 966.
50. Rachewiltz, *Secret History*, p. 171.
51. Ibid., p. 172.
52. Buniyatov, p. 110.
53. https://silkroadresearch.blog/uzbekistan/samarkind/
54. Quoted in Spuler, pp. 29–30.
55. Rachewiltz, *Secret History*, p. 189.
56. Quoted in Buell, p. 241.
57. Conversation with Dr John Hemming, London, 20 June 2019.
58. Quoted in Frankopan, p. vii.
59. Quoted in Grunebaum, p. 61.
60. Quoted in Rachewiltz, *Papal Envoys*, p. 39.
61. Quoted in McLynn, p. 323.
62. Quoted in Marshall, p. 125.
63. Mitchell, p. 54.
64. Rachewiltz, *Papal Envoys*, p. 213.
65. Rubruck, p. 3.
66. Rachewiltz, *Papal Envoys*, p. 129.

67. Favereau, p. 54.
68. Lane, p. 172.
69. Juvaini, p. 107.
70. Quoted in Katouzian, p. 104.
71. Rashid al-Din, quoted in Marozzi, *Baghdad*, p. 135.
72. Quoted in Marozzi, *Baghdad*, p. 138.
73. Rashid al-Din, pp. 238–9.
74. Le Strange, pp. 297–8.
75. Rashid al-Din, quoted in Marozzi, *Baghdad*, p. 136.
76. Quoted in Frankopan, p. 168.
77. Snir, p. 155.
78. Quoted by Frankopan, *Evening Standard*, 27 September 2019.
79. This and other details, Dalrymple, p. 298.
80. See Morgan.
81. Quoted in Rosenwein, p. 401.
82. Weatherford, 'Silk Route', p. 34.
83. Polo, p. 153.
84. Quoted in Lopez, p. 249.
85. Ibid.
86. Weatherford, 'Silk Route', p. 36.
87. Rashid al-Din, p. 338.
88. Favereau, p. 57.
89. Ibn Khaldun, *Muqaddimah*, vol. 1, pp. 353–5.
90. Mackintosh-Smith, *Travels with a Tangerine*, p. 321.
91. Ibn Battutah, p. 120.
92. Quoted in Horrox, pp. 16–18.
93. Ibid.
94. Frankopan, p. 187.
95. Boccaccio, p. 1.
96. Watkins, p. 199.
97. Deaux, pp. 92–4.
98. Ibn Khaldun, *Muqaddimah*, vol. 1, p. 64.
99. Ibid., vol. 1, p. 65.
100. Ibid., vol. 1, p. liii.
101. Fischel, *Ibn Khaldun and Tamerlane*, p. 35.
102. Quoted in Abu-Lughod, p. 37.
103. Ibn Khaldun, *Le Voyage*, pp. 148–9.
104. Thubron, p. 280.
105. Ibn Arabshah, p. 3.

106. Marlowe, *Tamberlaine* prologue.
107. Conversation with Jerry Brotton, July 2021.
108. Gibbon, ch. 65, p. 1.
109. Byron, p. 106.
110. Roxburgh, p. 413.
111. Ibid., p. 196.
112. Ibid., p. 194.
113. Harold Lamb's phrase in his *Tamerlane*, p. 169.
114. Clavijo, p. 220.
115. Ibid., p. 225.
116. Ibid., p. 249.
117. Ibid., p. 251.
118. Ibn Arabshah, p. 136.
119. Ibid., p. 141.
120. Irwin, *Ibn Khaldun*, p. 97.
121. Fischel, *Ibn Khaldun and Tamerlane*, p. 31.
122. Ibid., p. 35.
123. Ibid., p. 38.
124. Irwin, *Ibn Khaldun*, p. 100; Fischel, 'A New Latin Source', p. 227.
125. See Ballan, 'The Scholar and the Sultan'.
126. Ibn Arabshah, p. 232.
127. 'Hellas: Chorus', Percy Bysshe Shelley.

Part III: The Act of Recovery

1. Goodwin, p. 8.
2. In Öztuncay, p. 86.
3. Ibid., p. 92.
4. Leigh Fermor, p. 33.
5. Babur, p. 35.
6. Ibid., p. 10.
7. Ibid., p. 59.
8. Erskine, vol. 2, p. 468.
9. Babur, p. 327.
10. *Timur surrounded by His Mughal Heirs*: British Library, Johnson 64, 38.
11. Pascal, p. 126.
12. Ibid., Bacon, *Novum*, p. cxxix.
13. Merchant, 'The Violence of Impediments'.

14. Quoted in Merchant, 'Environmentalism', p. 3.
15. Ibid.
16. From Alain Hervé's *Le Palmier.*
17. All Franklin quotes from letter to Collinson, 9 May 1753, https://founders.archives.gov/documents/Franklin/01-04-02-0173
18. Johnson, *Dictionary*, 1st edition (1755), title page.
19. Boswell, vol. 2, p. 86.
20. Johnson, *Dictionary*, II.
21. Boswell, vol. 2, p. 132.
22. Johnson, *Dictionary*, I.
23. Perdue, p. 283.
24. Timothy May, 'Nomadic Warfare', in *The Encyclopedia of War* (Wiley Online Library, 13 November 2011), doi.org/10.1002/9781444338232.wbeow453
25. Winckelmann, *Reflection*, p. 7.
26. Ibid., p. 5.
27. Musgrave, p. 42.
28. *Endeavour* Journal of Sir Joseph Banks, 10 September 1768.
29. https://www.sl.nsw.gov.au/joseph-banks-endeavour-journal
30. https://www.captaincooksociety.com/home/detail/28-april-1770
31. Dr Shayne T. Williams, https://www.bl.uk/the-voyages-of-captain-james-cook/articles/an-indigenous-australian-perspective-on-cooks-arrival
32. http://southseas.nla.gov.au/journals/cook_remarks/092.html
33. Speaking on *Civilisation: A Sceptic's Guide*, BBC Radio 4, 26 February 2018.
34. Boyle, vol. II, Essay IV, p. 20.
35. Stats from worldometers.info.
36. Anderson, p. 21.
37. Goldsmith, 'The Deserted Village', https://www.poetryfoundation.org/poems/44292/the-deserted-village
38. Marsden and Smith, p. 59.
39. https://songsfromtheageofsteam.uk/factories-mines/102-other-industry/97-bar004
40. Atkinson and Roud, p. 299.
41. Blake, p. 673.
42. Hansard, HC Deb, 10 July 1833, vol. 19, cc479–550.
43. O'Sullivan, pp. 426–30.
44. https://constitutionus.com/#a1s8c3, Article XIII, Amendment 13.

45. Thoreau, *Walden*, pp. 8–9.
46. Thoreau, *Walking*, p. 21.
47. Quoted in Schneider, pp. 108–9.
48. Thoreau, *Indian Notebooks*, p. 46.
49. US Fish and Wildlife Service.
50. Library of Congress, https://guides.loc.gov/indian-removal-act
51. Hämäläinen, p. 372.
52. Quoted in Lindqvist, p. 122.
53. Thoreau, *Indian Notebooks*, p. 7.
54. Ibid., p. 8.
55. Gros, p. 100.
56. Quoted in Novak, p. 44.
57. *San Francisco Chronicle*, 18 June 2019.
58. Rousseau, *A Discourse on Inequality*, p. 169.
59. Lee, pp. xcv–xcix.
60. Quoted in Olusoga, p. 398.
61. Quoted in Lindqvist, p. 140.
62. https://www.qso.com.au/news/blog/five-pieces-of-music-inspired-by-the-great-outdoors
63. Roth, pp. 23–7.
64. https://www.britannica.com/biography/Ernest-B-Schoedsack.
65. Schoedsack's 'tape letter', 1960s or 1970s, https://www.youtube.com/watch?v=jMLIn8UTQ-E
66. Ibid.
67. Commentary from the film *Grass*, 1922.
68. Sackville-West, *Passenger*, ch. 8.
69. Sackville-West, *Twelve Days*, p. 27.
70. Ibid., p. 66.
71. Ibid., pp. 67–8.
72. Ibid., p. 80.
73. Ibid., p. 90.
74. https://newint.org/features/1995/04/05/facts/
75. Lorimer, 1955, p. 110.
76. Carson, p. 77.
77. Layard, vol. 1, pp. 487–9.
78. Herodotus, 3.38.
79. Bowlby, p. 293.
80. Chatwin, *Songlines*, p. 227.
81. The term appears in Matthew Syed's *Rebel Ideas*.

82. Mackintosh-Smith, *Arabs*, p. 518.

83. Rimbaud, *Une Saison en Enfer*, p. 145.

84. Cavafy, 'The City', in *Collected Poems*, p. 22.

85. Cavafy, 'Waiting for the Barbarians', in ibid., p. 15.

Bibliography

Abu-Lughod, Janet, *Cairo: 1001 Years of the City Victorious* (Princeton University Press, 1971)

Abulafia, David, *The Great Sea* (Penguin, 2014)

Allsen, Thomas T., *Commodity and Exchange in the Mongol Empire* (Cambridge University Press, 1997)

Ammianus Marcellinus, *Roman History*, trans. C. D. Yonge (Bohn, 1862)

Anderson, Michael, *Population Change in North-Western Europe, 1750–1850* (Palgrave, London, 1988)

Atkinson, David and Steve Roud, *Street Literature of the Long Nineteenth Century* (Cambridge Scholars, 2017)

Axworthy, Michael, *Empire of the Mind: A History of Iran* (Hurst Books, 2007)

Babur, Zahiru'd-din Mihammad, *The Babur-nama in English*, trans. Annette Susannah Beveridge (Luzac, 1921)

Bacon, Francis, *The Works of Francis Bacon* (Parry & MacMillan, 1854)

——, *Novum Organum or True Suggestions for the Interpretation of Nature* (P. F. Collier, 1902)

Baerlain, Henry, *The Singing Caravan* (John Murray, 1910)

Bakhtiari, Ali Morteza Samsam, *The Last of the Khans* (iUniverse, 2006)

Baldwin, James, 'The White Man's Guilt', *Ebony*, August 1965

Ballan, Mohamad, 'The Scholar and the Sultan: A Translation of the Historic Encounter between Ibn Khaldun and Timur', ballandalus. wordpress.com, 30 August 2014

Banks, Sir Joseph, *The Endeavour Journal*, 1768–71, http://gutenberg.net. au/ebooks05/0501141h.html

Barry, David, *Incredible Journeys* (Hodder & Stoughton, 2019)

Basilevsky, Alexander, *Early Ukraine: A Military and Social History to the Mid-19th Century* (McFarland, 2016)

Batty, Roger, *Rome and the Nomads* (Oxford University Press, 2007)

Beckwith, Christopher, *Empires of the Silk Road* (Princeton University Press, 2009)

Blake, William, *Complete Writings* (Oxford University Press, 1972)

Blockley, R. C., *The Fragmentary Classicising Historians of the Late Roman Empire*, vol. 2 (Francis Cairns, 1983)

Boccaccio, *The Decameron*, trans. Richard Hooker, sourcebooks.fordham. edu/source/decameronintro.asp

Borges, Jorge Luis, *Collected Fictions* (Allen Lane, 1998)

Boswell, James, *The Life of Samuel Johnson, LL.D.*, 4 vols (Oxford University Press, 1826)

Bowlby, John, *Attachment and Loss*, vol. 1 (Pimlico, 1997)

Boyle, Robert, *Some Considerations Touching the Usefulness of Experimental Natural Philosophy* (Oxford, 1663)

Braudel, Fernand, *The Mediterranean in the Ancient World* (Allen Lane, 2001)

Bregman, Rutger, *Humankind* (Bloomsbury, 2020)

Bronowski, Jacob, *William Blake and the Age of Revolution* (Faber, 1972)

Brotton, Jerry, *The Renaissance Bazaar* (Oxford University Press, 2002)

———, *This Orient Isle* (Allen Lane, 2016)

Brown, Peter, *The World of Late Antiquity* (Thames & Hudson, 1971)

Bruder, Jessica, *Nomadland* (W. W. Norton, 2017)

Buell, Paul, *Historical Dictionary of the Mongol World Empire* (Scarecrow Press, 2003)

Buniyatov, Z. M., *A History of the Khorezmian State Under the Anushteginids* (International Institute for Central Asian Studies, Samarkand, 2015)

Burckhardt, John Lewis, *Notes on the Bedouins and Wahabys* (Henry Colbourn, 1830)

Burdett, Richard, et al., *Cities: People, Society, Architecture* (Rizzoli, 2006)

Bury, J. B., 'Justa Grata Honoria', *Journal of Roman Studies*, Vol. 9, 1919, pp. 1–13

——— (trans.), Priscus, fr. 8 in *Fragmenta Historicorum Graecorum* (Ambrosio Firmin Didot, 1841–72)

Byron, Robert, *The Road to Oxiana* (Picador, 1994)

Calasso, Roberto, *The Celestial Hunter* (Allen Lane, 2020)

———, *Ardor* (Penguin, 2015)

Cannadine, David, *The Undivided Past* (Allen Lane, 2013)

Carson, Rachel, *The Sense of Wonder* (Harper & Row, 1965)

Cavafy, Constantine, *Collected Poems*, trans. Edmund Keeley and Philip Sherrard (Hogarth Press, 1975)

Cavalli-Sforza, Luigi Luca and Francesco, *The Great Human Diasporas* (Perseus, 1995)

Chaliand, Gerard, *Nomadic Empires* (Transaction, 2005)

Chandler, Tertius, *Four Thousand Years of Urban Growth: An Historical Census* (Edwin Mellen Press, 1987)

Chardin, Sir John, *Travels in Persia* (Argonaut, 1927)

Chatwin, Bruce, 'The Mechanics of Nomad Invasions', *History Today*, May 1972

——, *The Songlines* (Jonathan Cape, 1987)

——, *Anatomy of Restlessness* (Jonathan Cape, 1996)

Chavannes, Edouard, 'Inscriptions et pièces de chancellerie chinoises de l'époque mongole', in *T'oung Pao*, Second Series, Vol. 9, No. 3, pp. 297–428 (Brill, 1908)

Chekhov, Anton, *The Steppe*, in *The Tales of Chekhov*, trans. Constance Garnett (Macmillan, 1919)

Clavijo, Gonzalez de, *Embassy to Tamerlane*, trans. Guy le Strange (Routledge, 1928)

Cranston, Maurice, *Jean-Jacques: The Early Life and Work of Jean-Jacques Rousseau, 1712–1754* (W. W. Norton, 1983)

Crompton, Samuel, *Meet the Khan: Western Views of Kuyuk, Mongke and Kublai* (iUniverse, 2001)

Cronin, Vincent, *The Last Migration* (Rupert Hart-Davis, 1957)

Cunliffe, Barry, *By Steppe, Desert and Ocean: The Birth of Eurasia* (Oxford University Press, 2015)

Dalrymple, William, *In Xanadu* (William Collins, 1989)

Deaux, George, *The Black Death 1347* (Weybright & Talley, 1969)

Defoe, Daniel, *A Tour Through England and Wales* (Dent, 1928)

Deleuze, Gilles and Félix Guattari, *Nomadology* (Semiotext(e), 1986)

De Waal, Edmund, *Library of Exile* (British Museum, 2020)

Di Cosmo, Nicola, *Ancient China and its Enemies* (Cambridge University Press, 2002)

Diodorus Siculus, *History* (Loeb Classical Library, 1963)

Dowty, Alan, *Closed Borders* (Yale University Press, 1987)

Ellingson, Ter, *The Myth of the Noble Savage* (University of California Press, 2001)

Elliot, Jason, *Mirrors of the Unseen* (Picador, 2006)

Encyclopaedia Britannica, 14th edition 1932

Erskine, William, *A History of India*, 2 vols (Longman, Brown, Green and Longmans, 1854)

Favereau, Marie, 'The Mongol Peace and Global Medieval Eurasia' in Chris Hann, ed. *Realising Eurasia, Empire and Connectivity During Three Millennia* (Leipziger Universitätsverlag, 2019)

Fennelly, James M., 'The Persepolis Ritual', *Biblical Archaeologist*, Vol. 43, No. 3, Summer 1980, pp. 135–62

Ferdowsi, Abolqasem, *Shahnameh: The Persian Book of Kings*, trans. Dick Davis (Penguin, 2007)

Fernández-Armesto, Felipe, *Civilizations* (Macmillan, 2000)

Fischel, Walter J., *Ibn Khaldun and Tamerlane: Their Historic Meeting in Damascus, 1401 AD (803AH)* (University of California Press, 1952)

——, 'A New Latin Source on Tamerlane's Conquest of Damascus', *Oriens*, Vol. 9, No. 2, 31 December 1956, pp. 201–32

Florus, *The Epitome of Roman History* (Loeb Classical Library, 1929)

Fonseca, Isabel, *Bury Me Standing* (Chatto & Windus, 1995)

Frankopan, Peter, *The Silk Roads* (Bloomsbury, 2015)

Fromherz, Allen James, *Ibn Khaldun: Life and Times* (Edinburgh University Press, 2010)

Frye, Richard N., 'Persepolis Again', *Journal of Near Eastern Studies*, Vol. 33, No. 4, October 1974, pp. 383–6

——, *The Heritage of Persia* (Cardinal, 1976)

George, A. R., *The Epic of Gilgamesh* (Allen Lane, 1999)

George, Coulter H., *How Dead Languages Work* (Oxford University Press, 2020)

Gibbon, Edward, *The History of the Decline and Fall of the Roman Empire* (Harper & Brothers, 1845)

Golden, P. B., '"I Will Give the People unto Thee": The Činggisid Conquests and Their Aftermath in the Turkic World', *Journal of the Royal Asiatic Society*, Third Series, Vol. 10, No. 1, April 2000, pp. 21–41

Goodwin, Jason, *Lords of the Horizon* (Chatto & Windus, 1998)

Greenblatt, Stephen, *The Swerve: How the Renaissance Began* (Vintage, 2012)

Gros, Frédéric, *A Philosophy of Walking* (Verso, 2014)

Grousset, René, *The Empire of the Steppes*, trans. Naomi Walford (Rutgers University Press, 1970)

Grunebaum, Gustave E. von, *Medieval Islam: A Study in Cultural Orientation* (University of Chicago Press, 1969)

Guzman, Gregory G., 'European Captives and Craftsmen Among the Mongols, 1231–1255', *The Historian*, Vol. 72, No. 1, Spring 2010, pp. 122–50

Hall, James, *Hall's Dictionary of Subjects and Symbols in Art* (John Murray, 1986)

Halsey, R. T. H. and Charles D. Cornelius, *A Handbook of the American Wing* (Metropolitan Museum of Art, New York, 1938)

Hämäläinen, Pekka, *Lakota America* (Yale University Press, 2019)

Hammond, N. G. L., 'The Archaeological and Literary Evidence for the Burning of the Persepolis Palace', *Classical Quarterly*, 2, Vol. 42, No. 2, 1992, pp. 358–64

Herlihy, David, *The Black Death and the Transformation of the West* (Harvard University Press, 1997)

Herodotus, *The Histories*, trans. Tom Holland (Penguin, 2013)

Hill, John E., *Through the Jade Gate to Rome: A Study of the Silk Routes during the Later Han Dynasty, 1st to 2nd Centuries CE* (BookSurge, South Carolina, 2009)

Hobbes, Thomas, *Of Man, Being the First Part of Leviathan* (Harvard Classics, 1909–1914)

Holes, C. and S. S. Abu Athera, *Poetry and Politics in Contemporary Bedouin Society* (Ithaca Press, 2009)

Holland, Tom, *Persian Fire* (Abacus, 2005)

——, *In the Shadow of the Sword* (Little, Brown, 2012)

Homer, *The Iliad*, trans. Alexander Pope (London, 1760)

Horne, Charles F., ed., *The Sacred Books and Early Literature of the East, Vol. VI: Medieval Arabia* (Parke, Austin, & Lipscomb, 1917)

Horrox, R., ed., *The Black Death* (Manchester University Press, 1994)

Hourani, Albert, *A History of the Arab Peoples* (Faber, 1991)

Ibn Arabshah, Ahmad, *Tamerlane: The Life of the Great Amir*, trans. J. H. Sanders (Luzac, 1936)

Ibn Battutah, *The Travels of Ibn Battutah*, ed. Tim Mackintosh-Smith (Picador, 2002)

Ibn Khaldun, *The Muqaddimah*, trans. Franz Rosenthal (Pantheon, 1958)

——, *Le Voyage d'Occident et d'Orient* (Sinbad, Paris, 1980)

——, *An Arab Philosophy of History*, trans. Charles Issawi (American University in Cairo Press, 1992)

Ingold, Tim, *The Perception of the Environment* (Routledge, 2000)

Irwin, Robert, *Night and Horses in the Desert* (Allen Lane, 1999)

——, *Ibn Khaldun* (Princeton University Press, 2018)

Jackson, Anna and Amin Jaffer, eds., *Encounters: The Meeting of Asia and Europe, 1500–1800* (V&A Publications, 2004)

Jackson, Peter, *The Mongols and the West* (Pearson Longman, 2005)

Jardine, Lisa, *Ingenious Pursuits* (Little, Brown, 1999)

Jensen, Erik, *Barbarians in the Greek and Roman World* (Hackett, 2018)

Johnson, Samuel, *A Dictionary of the English Language* (Rivington et al., 1785)

Juvaini, Ala-ad-Din Ata-Malik, *Genghis Khan: The History of the World Conqueror* (Manchester University Press, 1958)

Katouzian, Homa, *The Persians* (Yale University Press, 2010)

Kennedy, Hugh, *The Court of the Caliphs* (Weidenfeld & Nicolson, 2004)

Kent, Roland G., *Old Persian: Grammar, Texts, Lexicon* (American Oriental Society, Connecticut, 1950)

Khazanov, Anatoly M. and André Wink, *Nomads in the Sedentary World* (Routledge, 2001)

Kim, Hyun Jin, *The Huns, Rome and the Birth of Europe* (Cambridge University Press, 2013)

Kradin, Nikolay N., et al., eds., *Nomadic Pathways in Social Evolution* (Russian Academy of Sciences, 2003)

Kriwaczek, Paul, *In Search of Zarathustra* (Phoenix, 2003)

Lactantius, *The Works of Lactantius*, trans. William Fletcher (T. & T. Clark, Edinburgh, 1871)

Lamb, Harold, *Tamerlane* (Robert M. McBride, 1930)

Lane, George, *Daily Life in the Mongol Empire* (Hackett, 2006)

Lane Fox, Robin, *Alexander the Great* (Allen Lane, 1973)

——, *The Search for Alexander* (Allen Lane, 1980)

Langland, William, *Piers Plowman* (Wordsworth, 1999)

Lawrence, T. E., *The Seven Pillars of Wisdom* (Jonathan Cape, 1935)

Layard, Sir Henry, *Early Adventures in Persia, Susiana, and Babylonia* (John Murray, 1887)

Lee, Richard, 'The Extinction of Races', *Journal of the Anthropological Society of London*, Vol. 2, 1864, pp. xcv–xcix

Leigh Fermor, Patrick, *The Broken Road* (John Murray, 2013)

Le Strange, Guy, ed., 'The Story of the Death of the Last Abbasid Caliph, from the Vatican MS. of Ibn-al-Furāt', *Journal of the Royal Asiatic Society of Great Britain and Ireland*, April 1900, pp. 293–300

Levi, Scott Cameron and Ron Sela, eds., *Islamic Central Asia: An Anthology of Historical Sources* (Indiana University Press, 2010)

Lindqvist, Sven, *Exterminate All the Brutes* (Granta, 1992)

Locke, John, *Two Treatises of Government* (A. Millar et al., 1764)

Lopez, Barry, *Arctic Dreams* (Vintage, 2014)

Lorimer, D. L. R., 'The Popular Verse of the Bakhtiāri of S. W. Persia', *Bulletin of the School of Oriental and African Studies, University of London*, Vol. 16, No. 3, 1954, pp. 542–55; Vol. 17, No. 1, 1955, pp. 92–110; Vol. 26, No. 1, 1963, pp. 55–68

Lucian, *The Works of Lucian of Samosata*, trans. H. W. Fowler and F. G. Fowler (Clarendon Press, 1905)

McCorriston, Jay, 'Pastoralism and Pilgrimage: Ibn Khaldūn's Bayt-State Model and the Rise of Arabian Kingdoms', *Current Anthropology*, Vol. 54, No. 5, October 2013, pp. 607–41

MacDonald, Brian W., *Tribal Rugs* (ACC Art Books, 2017)

Machiavelli, Niccolò, *The Discourses*, trans. Leslie J. Walker (Routledge & Kegan Paul, 1950)

Mackintosh-Smith, Tim, *Travels with a Tangerine* (John Murray, 2001)

——, *Arabs: A 3,000-Year History of Peoples, Tribes and Empires* (Yale University Press, 2019)

McLynn, Frank, *Genghis Khan* (Bodley Head, 2015)

Marozzi, Justin, *Tamerlane* (HarperCollins, 2004)

——, *Baghdad* (Allen Lane, 2014)

Marsden, Ben and Crosbie Smith, *Engineering Empires* (Palgrave Macmillan, 2005)

Marshall, Robert, *Storm from the East: From Ghengis Khan to Khubilai Khan* (BBC Books, 1993)

Maugham, H. Neville, *The Book of Italian Travel* (Grant Richards, 1903)

Merchant, Carolyn, '"The Violence of Impediments": Francis Bacon and the Origins of Experimentation', *Isis*, Vol. 99, No. 4, December 2008, pp. 731–60

——, 'Environmentalism: From the Control of Nature to Partnership', Bernard Moses Memorial Lecture, University of California, Berkeley, 4 May 2010, nature.berkeley.edu/departments/espm/env-hist/Moses.pdf_

——, 'Francis Bacon and the "Vexations of Art": Experimentation as Intervention', *British Journal for the History of Science*, December 2013, Vol. 46, No. 4, pp. 551–99

Michell, Robert and Nevill Forbes, eds., *The Chronicle of Novgorod* (Royal Historical Society, 1914)

Modelski, George, *World Cities: -3000 to 2000* (Faros2000, 2003)

Morgan, D. O., 'The "Great Yāsā of Chingiz Khān" and Mongol Law in the Īlkhānate', *Bulletin of the School of Oriental and African Studies*, Vol. 49, No. 1, In Honour of Ann K. S. Lambton, 1986, pp. 163–76

Mulder, Monique Borgerhoff and Peter Coppolillo, *Conservation: Linking Ecology, Economics and Culture* (Princeton University Press, 2005)

Mumford, Lewis, *The City in History* (Penguin, 1991)

Al-Muqaddasi, Muhammad, *Best Divisions for Knowledge of the Regions*, trans. Basil Anthony Collins (Garnet, 1994)

Musgrave, Toby, *The Multifarious Mr Banks* (Yale University Press, 2020)

Nelson, Cynthia, *The Desert and the Sown* (University of California Press, Berkeley, 1973)

Nicolson, Adam, *The Mighty Dead: Why Homer Matters* (William Collins, 2014)

Nietzsche, Friedrich, *On the Future of Our Educational Institutions: Homer and Classical Philology* (Foulis, 1909)

Norwich, John Julius, *The Middle Sea* (Chatto & Windus, 2006)

Novak, Barbara, *Voyages of the Self* (Oxford University Press, 2007)

Olusoga, David, *Black and British: A Forgotten History* (Macmillan, 2016)

O'Sullivan, John, 'The Great Nation of Futurity', *United States Democratic Review*, Vol. 6, Issue 23

Otter, Rev. William, *The Life and Remains of Rev. Edward Daniel Clarke, LL.D.* (J. F. Dove, 1824)

Öztuncay, Bahattin and Özge Ertem, eds., *Ottoman Arcadia* (Koç University Research Center for Anatolian Civilizations, 2018)

Park, Mungo, *Travels into the Interior of Africa* (Eland, 2003)

Pascal, Blaise, *Pensées and Other Writings*, trans. Honor Lei (Oxford University Press, 2008)

Perdue, Peter C., *China Marches West* (Harvard University Press, 2005)

Plato, *Laws*, trans. R. G. Bury (Harvard University Press, 1967)

Polo, Marco, *The Travels of Marco Polo*, ed. L. F. Benedetto (Routledge, 2011)

Rachewiltz, I. de, *Papal Envoys to the Great Khans* (Faber, 1971)

——, *The Secret History of the Mongols* (Australian National University, 2015)

Raphael, Kate, 'Mongol Siege Warfare on the Banks of the Euphrates and the Question of Gunpowder', *Journal of the Royal Asiatic Society*, Third Series, Vol. 19, No. 3, July 2009, pp. 355–70

Rashid al-Din, *Jami al Tawarikh* (Compendium of Histories), trans. Etienne Quatremère (Oriental Press, Amsterdam, 1968)

Raven, Susan, *Rome in Africa* (Routledge, 1993)

Raverty, H. G., ed. and trans., *Tabakat-i-Nasiri: A General History of the Muhammadan Dynasties of Asia* (Gilbert & Rivington, 1881)

Rawlinson, George, *The History of Herodotus* (Appleton and Company, New York, 1859)

Redfield, James, 'Herodotus the Tourist', *Classical Philology*, Vol. 80, No. 2, April 1985, pp. 97–118

Rice, Tamara Talbot, *The Scythians* (Thames & Hudson, 1957)

Rilke, Rainer Maria, *The Journal of My Other Self* (W. W. Norton, 1930)

Rimbaud, Arthur, *Poésies, Une saison en enfer, Illuminations* (Gallimard, 1991)

Robinson, Chase F., *Islamic Civilization in Thirty Lives* (Thames & Hudson, 2016)

Robinson, James, ed., *Readings in European History*, vol. 1 (Ginn & Co., 1904)

Rogerson, Barnaby, *A Traveller's History of North Africa* (Windrush, 1998)

——, *Heirs of the Prophet* (Abacus, 2006)

Rolle, Renata, *The World of the Scythians* (Batsford, 1989)

Rosenwein, Barbara H., ed., *Reading the Middle Ages: Sources from Europe, Byzantium, and the Islamic World* (University of Toronto Press, 2018)

Roth, Joseph, *What I Saw* (Granta, 2003)

Rousseau, Jean-Jacques, *The Social Contract and Discourses* (Dent, 1923)

——, *The First and Second Discourses* (St Martin's Press, 1964)

——, *Papal Envoys to the Great Khans* (Faber, 1971)

——, *A Discourse on Inequality* (Penguin, 1984)

——, *The Reveries of the Solitary Walker* (University Press of New England, 2000)

Roxburgh, David J., ed., *Turks: A Journey of a Thousand Years, 600–1600* (Royal Academy of Arts, 2005)

Rubruck, William of, *The Journey of William of Rubruck to the Eastern Parts of the World, 1253–1255*, trans. W. W. Rockhill (Hakluyt, 1990)

Sackville-West, Vita, *Passenger to Teheran* (Hogarth Press, 1926)

——, *Twelve Days* (Hogarth Press, 1928)

Sattin, Anthony, *The Gates of Africa* (HarperCollins, 2003)

Schama, Simon, *Landscape and Memory* (Harper Perennial, 2004)

Schneider, Richard J., *Civilizing Thoreau* (Boydell & Brewer, 2016)

Scott, James C., *Against the Grain* (Yale University Press, 2017)

Scott, Michael, *Ancient Worlds* (Windmill, 2016)

Sherratt, Andrew, 'Climatic Cycles and Behavioural Revolutions: The Emergence of Modern Humans and the Beginning of Farming', *Antiquity*, 71, 1997, pp. 271–87

——, *Economy and Society in Prehistoric Europe* (Edinburgh, 1997)

Snir, Reuven, ed., *Baghdad: The City in Verse* (Harvard University Press, 2013)

Spuler, Bertold, *History of the Mongols* (Routledge, 1972)

Ssu-ma Ch'ien, *Records of the Grand Historian of China*, 2 vols, trans. Burton Watson (Columbia University Press, 1962)

Starr, S. Frederick, *Lost Enlightenment* (Princeton, 2013)

Stewart, Stanley, *In the Empire of Genghis Khan* (HarperCollins, 2000)

Stow, John, *A Survey of London* (Whittaker, 1842)

Strabo, *The Geography*, trans. Duane W. Roller (Cambridge University Press, 2014)

A's-Suyuti, Jalaluddin, *History of the Caliphs*, trans. H. S. Jarrett (Asiatic Society, Calcutta, 1881)

Syed, Matthew, *Rebel Ideas* (John Murray, 2020)

Al-Tabari, *The History*, trans. Yohanan Friedmann (State University of New York Press, 1992)

Thackston, Wheeler M., trans., *The Baburnama: Memoirs of Babur, Prince and Emperor* (Oxford, 1996)

Thesiger, Wilfred, *Arabian Sands* (Longmans, 1959)

——, *Desert, Marsh and Mountain* (Collins, 1979)

Thoreau, Henry David, *Walden* (Signet, 1960)

——, *Walking* (CreateSpace, 2018)

——, *The Indian Notebooks*, ed. Richard F. Fleck (Walden Woods Project, 2007)

Thubron, Colin, *Shadow of the Silk Road* (Chatto & Windus, 2006)

Tolkien, J. R. R., *The Hobbit* (HarperCollins, 2013)

Touati, Houari, *Islam and Travels in the Middle Ages* (University of Chicago Press, 2010)

Twitchett, Danis and Michael Loewe, *The Cambridge History of China: Volume 1* (Cambridge University Press, 1986)

Upham Pope, Arthur, 'Persepolis as a Ritual City', *Archaeology*, Vol. 10, No. 2, June 1957, pp. 123–30

——, *Introducing Persian Architecture* (Soroush Press, Tehran, 1976)

Van den Bent, Josephine, 'None of the Kings on Earth is Their Equal in "aṣabiyya": The Mongols in Ibn Khaldūn's Works', *Al-Masāq*, Vol. 28, Issue 2, 2016, pp. 171–86

Van Seters, John, *The Hyksos: A New Investigation* (Wipf and Stock, 2010)

Wallace-Murphy, Tim, *What Islam Did for Us* (Watkins, London, 2006)

Watkins, Renee Neu, 'Petrarch and the Black Death: From Fear to Monuments', *Studies in the Renaissance*, Vol. 19, 1972, pp. 196–223

Watson, Burton, *Ssu-ma Ch'ien, Grand Historian of China* (Columbia University Press, 1958)

Weatherford, Jack, *Genghis Khan and the Making of the Modern World* (Crown, 2004)

——, 'The Silk Route from Land to Sea', *Humanities*, Vol. 7, No. 2, 2018, pp. 32–41

Wehr, Hans, *A Dictionary of Modern Written Arabic* (Librairie du Liban, 1974)

Wheelis, M., 'Biological Warfare at the 1346 Siege of Caffa', *Emerging Infectious Diseases*, Vol. 8, No. 9, 2002, pp. 971–5

Whitfield, Susan, *Life Along the Silk Road* (John Murray, 1999)

——, ed., *Silk Roads* (Thames & Hudson, 2019)

Wilde, Robert, 'Population Growth and Movement in the Industrial Revolution', ThoughtCo.com, 28 May 2019

Willey, Peter, *Eagle's Nest: Ismaili Castles in Iran and Syria* (I B Tauris, 2005)

Winckelmann, Johann Joachim, *Reflection on the Imitation of Greek Works in Painting and Sculpture* (Open Court, La Salle, IL, 1987)

———, *The History of the Art of Antiquity*, trans. Harry Francis Mallgrave (Getty, LA, 2006)

Yingshi, Yu, et al., *Trade and Expansion in Han China* (University of California Press, 1967)

Young, Thomas, 'Mithridates, or a General History of Languages', *Quarterly Review*, Vol. X, No. XIX, October 1813, p. 255

Yule, Henry, *Cathay and the Way Thither* (Hakluyt, 1866)

Zavitukhina, M. P., *Frozen Tombs* (British Museum, 1978)

Zerjal, Tatiana, 'The Genetic Legacy of the Mongols', *American Journal of Human Genetics*, 72, 2003, pp. 717–21

Ziegler, Philip, *The Black Death* (Penguin, 1997)

Index

Page numbers in italic denote illustrations